THE SHORT,
SWIFT TIME
OF GODS
ON EARTH

THE SHORT SWIFT TIME OF GODS ON EARTH

THE HOHOKAM CHRONICLES

DONALD BAHR
JUAN SMITH
WILLIAM SMITH ALLISON
JULIAN HAYDEN

UNIVERSITY OF
CALIFORNIA PRESS
BERKELEY
LOS ANGELES
LONDON

Title page photograph: Juan Smith

University of California Press
Berkeley and Los Angeles, California

University of California Press
London, England

Library of Congress Cataloging-in-Publication Data

The short, swift time of gods on earth : the Hohokam chronicles /
    Donald Bahr . . . [et al.].
        p.   cm.
    Includes bibliographical references and index.
    ISBN 0-520-08467-5   ISBN 0-520-00450-3 (pbk.)
    1. Hohokam culture.   2. Pima Indians—Legends.   3. Tohono
O'Odham Indians—Legends.   I. Bahr, Donald M.   II. Title:
Hohokam chronicles.
E99.H68S56   1994
398.2'089974—dc20
                                                    93-41131
                                                       CIP

Printed in the United States of America

    2 3 4 5 6 7 8 9

CONTENTS

ACKNOWLEDGMENTS   Bahr wishes to thank the following for their diverse help in making this book: N. Allen, H. Allison, A. Bahr, J. Bierhorst, T. Bostwick, W. Bright, D. Brumble, L. Cameron, E. Diaz, L. Evers, E. Feldman, W. Fenton, B. Fontana, S. Holwitz, T. Hutchinson, M. Jordan, J. Jorgensen, V. Joseph, D. Kozak, A. Krupat, J. Lewis, S. Lewis, J. Manwarren, D. Morris, S. Pablo, M. Schweitzer, S. Vaughn, L. Webb, and J. Wilder.

The text given in this book is a full, traditional Pima Indian creation narrative composed of thirty-six distinct stories that begin with the creation of the universe and end with the establishment of present-day villages. Versions of most of these stories have been published before, sometimes in isolation and sometimes as parts of larger texts. This text, in addition to having an interesting version of nearly every known Pima story, is the most complete natively articulated set of such stories to be written to date. They were selected, narrated, intermittently commented on, and translated by two Pimas, Juan Smith and William Allison, over several nights in spring 1935 at Snaketown, a village on the Gila River Indian Reservation in Arizona. Smith spoke in Pima, and Allison provided an English translation with comments. The white archaeologist Julian Hayden took down the English with care to preserve Allison's diction and phrasing.

Snaketown was the site of an ongoing archaeological excavation. The text was given because Hayden was interested in what the Pimas knew about the culture that he and his colleagues were investigating, a culture whose archaeological name, the Hohokam, was borrowed from Pima mythology. The word means "Finished-ones" in Pima, but it was not clear to archaeologists or to white students of modern Pima culture exactly how this old culture had ended and what its relation was to the Pimas who had lived on former Hohokam territory since they were discovered and named "Pima" by the Spaniards around 1550. It was hoped that the Smith-Allison text, taken down at a village built on a Hohokam site, would be of assistance.

In fact, the text was of no more help than others that were already known. It states maddeningly that the Pimas were both the same as and different from the Hohokam:

they were the same because they spoke the same language (there are many songs in the text that are considered to retain Hohokam language verbatim), and they were different because the text says that they conquered and "finished" the other people. The conclusion to draw from this, if both ideas are accepted, is that the Hohokam conquest was internal and fraternal, if not fratricidal, something like a civil war.

ORAL HISTORY

Unable to affirm or deny the text from the evidence of the excavations and uncertain of what to expect of a text spoken five hundred years after the events in question (it was estimated that the last Hohokam period ended in the 1400s), Hayden filed it away, awaiting the guidance of a specialist in distinguishing between history and myth. I would like to pass that cup to another, and I will do so by presenting and then applying another's ideas. The most stimulating thinker known to me on these matters is Jan Vansina, author of *Oral Tradition as History* (1985). He takes a strict, straightforward position on the history in oral texts: that which is historical is that which has been preserved intact from an original eyewitness account. Thus, the Smith-Allison text is historical if after five hundred years it preserves the content of a "report" (Vansina 1985: 29–32) uttered soon after the event.

His position is empiricist as it appeals to an original sensory observation, and it is literalist in supposing that words refer straightforwardly to things. He argues, and I agree, that tribal narrators use these standards, which amount to a kind of perfectionism. But neither the narrators nor we can be sure if the standards are met, especially relative to a text that is as long and that reaches as far back as this one and most especially when we know that contradictory versions of these events exist. Thus, the standards imply a perfectionism that is unverifiable in reality, and therefore they imply that most or all oral traditions fall short of their goals. I agree.

I think that this is the position of the Pimas. To continue with Vansina, the typical total system of a tribal people's narratives is divided into three temporal zones, or tiers, from the most recent to the most ancient: personal accounts, group accounts, and accounts of origin (23). The personal accounts differ from those of the group because they trace to known reporters. The materials of the second sort have diffused generally through the group (a group of villages, a geographic section of a tribe); and while they are considered to be historical in the empirical, literal sense, the wide dissemination of these narratives robs them of an indubitable original observational source. Years are not necessarily counted in either zone, but genealogies and natural events may time them objectively. Both zones' stories may run concurrently, and taken together the two zones commonly go back no farther than seventy-five to one hundred fifty years when they are correlated with European calendars and records.

Then, according to Vansina, comes a "floating gap" that, as he describes it, does not float as a space between discernible points of past time but is floated toward, as one travels back through the relatively confidently held zones of personal and group history. Simply, the past dwindles. "One finds either a hiatus or just a few names, given with some hesitation" (23). Beyond the gap, which is crossed instantaneously, one finds a final zone rich in tales about how the world was created and how the tribe's constituent social groups came into existence. These are what Vansina calls "tales of origin" and many others call "myth."[1]

He avoids the word "myth" for such tales because it implies deliberate invention, intentional fiction, and the making up of new pieces of the past. He believes that myths are rarely created in tribal society. All such peoples at all times have a body of ancient origin accounts that they accept as unverifiable, imperfect, but possibly true. The people are loath to stray from them. Improbable as they are and detached from the present, these stories have a kind of inertia. Thus, people are the most reluctant to change their least verifiable stories. For all that we know, their origin stories may stay constant for centuries. Now, from the archaeological perspective, the Hohokam would have had such stories, because archaeologists believe that the Hohokam civilization lasted a thousand years. However, to the Pimas, at least to Smith and Allison, the Hohokam came to an end as a people with no ancient memories: they were a young tribe at the time of their destruction. I agree with the archaeologists that the Hohokam must have had their own origin accounts, but as is explained in the next chapter, I do not think we can know them.

I neither relish nor object to using the word "myth" in reference to these good faith, fallible, histories. Now, there are four additional points to be made relative to Vansina's ideas and the Smith-Allison account. First, the conquest comes at the end of the long, multitale text, which is appropriate as this event gives the origin of the present Pima and Papago, or Tohono O'odham,[2] territorial groups. Immediately after the conquest the groups fanned out to their present locations. Thus, the conquest falls near Vansina's floating gap. He would place it on the "origins" side, and I agree. Neither Smith-Allison nor any other known narrator is clear on exactly what became of all of the Hohokam. If they were mostly exterminated, how was this done, and where are the signs? If they were mostly absorbed, which of today's groups accepted them? As I understand Vansina's idea of the second zone, matters as important as these would surely be told if people had confident knowledge of them. Therefore, I conclude that the conquest, while vividly told, is not confidently known in the sense of lending itself to probing questioning.

Second, I am content to say without reviewing the evidence here that the two zones of the Pima and Papago recent past reach back only about one hundred years. In other words, that past stops four hundred years short of the time when, according to the archaeologists, the conquest would have occurred. Thus, the gap is an ocean from our perspective, and the ocean includes the entire long period in which Europe worked its early effects on this people. Because of their remoteness from the centers of Spanish and Mexican power, the period of early effects, that is, the period in which Europe failed to reduce the Pima-Papago to its rule, lasted from the late seventeenth to the mid-nineteenth century. (The Pima-Papago had an exceptionally long period of weak European influence.)

Third and related to the first point, the stories of the conquest and all the myths that lead up to it are about individual heroes. Although Vansina does not stress this point, I note that such stories are not what most historians and prehistorians seek. Those scholars accept individuals, but they want generalizations. Thus, archaeologists are not satisfied with one Hohokam pot, they want a representative sample. Furthermore, and again something that Vansina does not stress, I suspect that the "group accounts" zone of oral traditions contains more generalizations than the zone of origins. The far side of Vansina's gap has unique individuals and unprecedented events. The near side has regularized, much more typified and quantified life. This is why I have said that the conquest account falls on the far rather than the near side of the gap. If the account were on the near side, those generalizing questions on the fate of the Hohokam would have been addressed. For their part, the individual characters on the far side are brilliantly, if not fully, drawn, sometimes down to the words they spoke. As is explained later, these words are given in song, that being the form that in Pima opinion is the most resistant to errors in reproduction. It is as if the heroes rose into song when they wanted their words to endure. Now, what Vansina desires of history is observations of events, situations, and tendencies. I take it that the last two pertain to generalization, and I conclude that the zone of myth gives primarily the first, in a highly individualizing and exquisitely limited selectivity: libretti.

A final comment on the floating gap. Because we believe that the Hohokam lived very long ago, we are surprised that the Smith-Allison text ends with their conquest. Actually, the text has a brief section on the immediate aftermath of the conquest, and then it hastens to the present. I believe this is a phenomenon of the gap. A Pima could do as Smith-Allison and start with the beginning, then proceed up to the gap, and then make a final dash to the present. Or one could start from the present and work back to the gap. The two accounts would have almost no events in common. Presumably, the second narrator would say on reaching the end of zone two that sometime before that, he or she does not know how long, there was the Hohokam conquest. Neither narrator would be disturbed, because neither is aware of anything that happened in four hundred unnarrated years.

That remarkable unawareness serves as the background for the remainder of this introduction. Immediately below I consider in somewhat greater detail how well archaeology and the Pimas agree on the Hohokam era. Following that is a discussion of the particulars of the telling and recording of the text in 1935 and a discussion of overt and possible covert Christian influence on the text and the possibility that a text such as this one could stand as the scriptural base of a Bible-acknowledging native Pima church. Finally, there are discussions of the text as literature in the Vansinian sense of remembered narrative and of technical matters of editing.

THE TWO HOHOKAMS

Archaeology and the Pimas agree that at the end of their era the Hohokam enclosed some parts of their settlements with clay walls and that some of the walled areas contained multistory clay buildings. The first Spanish explorers found these structures in ruins. They called them "great houses" (*casas grandes*), a term that archaeologists retain. Since the nineteenth century and perhaps since the conquest, the Pimas have called these buildings *wa:paki*, an etymologically untransparent word that I translate as "great-house."

The Smith-Allison text on the Hohokam conquest is a story of battles at successive great-houses. Since the narrated battle places correspond to archaeologically known great-houses (I will use the hyphenated spelling for both the archaeologists' and the Pimas' usages), one may think that the narrative is an accurate memory.

There is reason to doubt this, and doubt is all that I recommend. When we come to the conquest portion of the Smith-Allison text, we will review all the known versions of this war. We will see that there are only two accounts of a long, drawn-out march through archaeological places, that of Smith-Allison and that of another Pima, Thin Leather, whose mythology was well recorded shortly after the turn of the twentieth century.[3] There are, however, several accounts that present a specific earthly conflict with cosmic overtones, rather than a grand territorial sweep. These other versions seem no less plausible as origin stories than the grand territorial ones. The cosmic overtones are present in both sorts of texts. One can equally believe that the grand territorial, archaeologically interesting texts are latter-day enlargements in a spirit of militarism or that the others are forgetful.

The balance tips toward the latter-day enlargement theory when a pair of older Pima texts is considered, one from 1694 and the other from 1775. Here there is a single greathouse, as if there were just one, and there is no conquest whatever. These texts are discussed in a prelude to the Smith-Allison text.

Briefly, to understand the differences between the older and both sorts of the more recent mythologies, one must leave aside the archaeologically detectable great-houses and take up the chiefly persons who the Pimas say lived in them; and one must ask why and by whom those chiefs were or were not attacked. The key is the absence in the older texts of the idea, present in all the later texts, that the Hohokam were conquered because they had killed the god who made them. The god returned to life, journeyed to the underworld, and summoned the Pima-Papago, or a portion of them, to avenge his death.

Those matters will be explored as we proceed story by story through the Smith-Allison mythology, annotating it and supplementing it with other stories from the Pima-Papago. The exploration will not preclude the possibility of an actual past place-by-place conquest of Pima-Papago by Pima-Papago. But the exploration will diminish our text's standing as reliable history while letting it shine as theology and as passionate, historically conscious literature, in other words, as myth. As for my own opinion on what could have happened in Hohokam history, I repeat that all the stories or myths on this subject should be taken as good faith histories, that is, as stories that were offered by their tellers as true. Each myth might, could, and should be true as far as its teller was concerned; and thus I assume that no story was ever intentionally falsified, neither in tellings to Indians nor in transmission to a white recorder.[4]

Now, without going into detail, I say that all the stories

on the Hohokam cannot be true. They are a collection of alternative and more or less contradictory good faith histories. Finally, I note that the stories have events that I find difficult to believe, such as the god's resurrection and the ascent of the Pima-Papago from the underworld. Of course, my own Christian white people have stories that are equally difficult to believe. All accounts of mystical or supernatural things are of that nature.[5]

I do not suppose that the mystical parts of the stories will ever be proved. All our efforts at proof will concern nonmystical matters such as whether some or all of the Hohokam could have spoken a fifteenth-century form of Pima-Papago, whether all the Hohokam great-houses were destroyed or abandoned within a short period, and whether the Hohokam were more numerous, politically more centralized, and socially more stratified (with inherited differences in wealth) than the Pima-Papago of 1600 or 1900.

Simply, I cannot answer most of these questions, but I think that progress can be made toward that goal. Let me now propose a bit of an answer. As will be seen below, archaeologists believe that the great-houses only existed during the final period of a long, thousand-year, Hohokam history. Pima-Papago mythologies differ from accepted archaeological thought in that they do not grant a long temporal existence to the Hohokam. But mythology and archaeology might come together on one point, that the great-house time was troubled by warfare, specifically, that the walls around residential compounds and the large mud buildings such as Casa Grande (see below) were built for defense. I believe that archaeologists would agree that these structures would serve for defense, but it would be a further step for them to argue that the structures would not have been built except for defense. Relevant considerations would be whether the pre-great-house Hohokam had the ability to make such constructions but did not do so because the defense motive was lacking and whether some nondefense motive (storage, residential, religious) would justify the late architecture. I am not sure that these questions can be answered decisively, and I admit that they leave out the question of defense against whom (other great-house communities? mountain-based raiders?), but I offer them as thoughts on the nonmystical conciliation of Pima-Papago mythology and archaeology. Needless to say, they are offered because I believe the mythologies could have a base, if not their sole basis, in nonmystical local fifteenth-century fact.

Such are my proposals relative to the Hohokam problem. Let us now briefly review the history of Hohokam archaeology, up to, including, and after the Snaketown excavations. This review is in no sense a methodological or technical summary of that archaeology, which has now been augmented by thousands of dedicated workers. I simply wish to give the uninitiated reader a sketch of the field.

Snaketown was the third systematic excavation into the Hohokam. The first was in 1886–1888 under the leadership of Frank H. Cushing, famed for his study of Zuni religion. The second, in 1906–07 and 1907–08, was led by J. W. Fewkes, a veteran of Hopi studies. The first excavation produced extensive materials but no clear ideas on the origin, duration, and fate of the Hohokam. Archaeology's great dating technique, the stratigraphic removal of materials, was not employed. The second expedition did not use that technique either, and after twenty years of progress since Cushing in Southwest archaeological survey, in studying Spanish documents, and in collecting Pima mythologies, Fewkes found himself in agreement with the Pimas in their maddening, not necessarily true, picture of the end of the Hohokam. He believed that the Hohokam stopped making large, mud-walled great-houses and mud house compounds, that they abandoned the dozen-odd[6] great-house settlements in which they had lived, and that they emigrated north and south, to Mexico and northern Arizona. Some also stayed where they were. Those who stayed became the Pima-Papago (Fewkes 1912: 152, 153–54).

Both the Cushing and Fewkes excavations concentrated on great-houses, Cushing at a location called Los Muertos (The Dead) in today's Tempe, Arizona, and Fewkes at Casa Grande (Great House) near today's town of Coolidge. These were indeed impressive ruins, with walls as thick as seven feet surrounding their constituent subunits or compounds and with some individual buildings as large as forty by sixty feet at the base and as tall as three stories (25 ft.).

By the time of the Snaketown excavations and evermore after those diggings, the great-houses were understood as the final flourishes of a long-standing and much more modest mode of Hohokam village life. This mode started around A.D. 1 and went through four periods ("Pioneer," "Colonial," "Sedentary," and "Classic"), each with from one to four distinct subphases.[7] The modest life was housed in freestanding, single-room, brush-walled, dirt-roofed buildings, which were much like (not identical with) those of the historic Pimas. Lacking were the football field-sized, house-aggregating compounds, and lacking too were the multistory prominences with which the terminal Hohokam graced some but not all of their compounds. Present, however, almost from the start, were open, oval-shaped, mound-surrounded, flat-floored "ball courts" and long irrigation canals. Those public features were also present in the great-house period. Thus, Snaketown, which generally lacked Classic period remains, had ball courts and canals but lacked great-houses (Haury 1976: 351–357).

The Snaketown excavators concluded that the final period great-house constructors left suddenly, which was also Fewkes's opinion. But the Snaketown archaeologists also believed that the great-house people, or practice, had entered and commenced suddenly. They traced the practice to a core area to the north and east of the Hohokam, called the Salado. Possibly, then, the great-houses were Salado colonies. (No Pima-Papago mythology has said this.) Finally, the Snaketown excavators, like Fewkes, felt the Pimas were probably descended from the Hohokam, specifically, from the majority of the Hohokam who had lived in freestanding houses.

The principal archaeological interpreters of Snaketown were Harold Gladwin and Emil Haury. There has been considerable work on the Hohokam since 1935, including an important return excavation of Snaketown by Haury in 1964–65 (published 1976); and many other archaeologists, including Hayden, who wrote the Smith-Allison mythology, have contributed findings and interpretations on the origin, duration, and end, or historic persistence, of the Hohokam. My impression is that the sequence of periods and phases established by Gladwin and Haury is still considered valid and that their idea of a long in situ development and a short great-house intrusion is still taken as most probable.[8]

THE TEXT

We turn now to the text—let us call it mythology—that was recorded from Smith and Allison at Snaketown. Fully three-fourths of it deals with the Hohokam, either as stories of what happened to them before the conquest or stories of their extensive and merciless defeat. This is why I call the work as a whole "The Hohokam Chronicles." The narrative is in the third person, of course, but the common thread of character between these portions is the figure of Siuuhu (better but less attractively spelled *S-e'ehe* and meaning 'Elder-brother'), the above-mentioned murdered and revived god. Before these chronicles begin, there is a section on the creation of the earth and the first humans, who were not the Hohokam but perhaps were the ancestors of the Pima-Papago.[9] This era was ended by a flood that the ancestral Pima-Papago escaped by entering the underworld. The Hohokam were created after the floodwater subsided. Appended to the last section of the Hohokam chronicles is a very brief section on Apache wars. Europeans are barely mentioned. Their origin is given along with that of the Africans in a story set in Hohokam times; but characteristic of most Native American mythologies, I think, there is no narrative of white-Indian relations. It is as if the story stopped on the eve of the European coming, a moment that was very long ago, about 450 years in the case of the Pimas. Years are not counted in the mythology, and so we have no idea how long its events would take in years. My impression is that the time would be amazingly short, perhaps just a few generations or even only a few years, since a youthful or middle-aged Siuuhu is present throughout the chronicles and in much of the section leading up to them. When Siuuhu drops out, the post-

Hohokam, Apache-dominated, and, in effect, post-European past begins. Only then does the text give the impression of a fleeting but long passage of years.

Hayden sensibly let Allison supply the register, diction, and cadence of the translation. These things he did not change, and the translation is both readable and authentic.[10] A Presbyterian deacon, Allison was a language conscious and no doubt also socially conscious man. I imagine that he thought of his English as plain. In any case, I think so, because of his preference for simple expressions and what I will call an oral, singsong cadence. Concerning this latter, note the difference between the well-known cadence that Longfellow used for his Indianist poem, *The Song of Hiawatha*, and what seems to be the basic cadence of Allison's translation. Longfellow made his lines eight syllables long, with accents on the first, third, fifth, and seventh syllables ("THAT was HOW he MADE his POem"). The basic unit is the paired syllable, with the accent on the first of the pair. Allison did not recite his translation in lines, but he did, I think, opt for a paired syllable beat the opposite of Longfellow's, with the accent on the second syllable of the pair ("and SO he MADE it SOUND like THIS"). These are both singsong Englishes and, both are oral in that sense, but if I am correct, they are technically oppositely so. Neither is the better. I must add that Allison's cadence is not rigorously and exclusively as I have just sketched it. His speech is prose, not verse. Furthermore, not only might Hayden have moved it slightly in that direction in recording it (although he certainly did not do so deliberately) but I moved it so in instances while smoothing or shortening Hayden's rendition. Thus, the version given here is not authentic Allison, that is, not as authentic as a text made from a tape of his own voice. This could not be done in 1935. For an example of fine work of this nature, see Anthony Mattina and M. DeSautel's *The Golden Woman* (1985), a "red English" translation of a long Colville Indian story.

Here in a letter to me of September 1991 is Hayden's recollection of the making of the creation narrative text.

You ask for the background of my recording of the Pima Creation Myth. I'll do the best I can, based on my recollections, and am checking with Emil Haury for some further details or correction of mine, as he may recall. Herewith my present remembrance:

As part of a planned extensive study of the Hohokam remains of Southern Arizona, Gila Pueblo, a privately endowed research institution of Globe, Arizona, had commenced study and excavation of a very large prehistoric Hohokam site on the north terrace of the Gila River roughly south of Chandler, Arizona. There were a number of large rubbish mounds at the site, evidences of canals, and ball courts—and many rattlesnakes. In fact, the site, and the Pima village near it, was known as Snaketown. So, in the fall of 1934, a tent camp was set up at the site, and a crew of archaeologists was employed, with a number of Pima Indians from the neighborhood as laborers. My father and I, both experienced Hohokam fieldworkers, were part of the crew, which was directed by Emil Haury.

There was, of course, much interest among us all in the Pima stories about the prehistoric folk, and when a four-night telling of the Creation myth was planned by the villagers, some of us attended briefly the first night's telling. Juan Vavages of Salt River, I believe, was the narrator. He was a longhair (conservative), lived in a round house in the old way. His version was said to be the Maricopa version, since his wife was Maricopa. Bits of the tale were translated for our benefit, and we heard several of the songs, and we left.

Later we heard of Juan Smith who was reputed to be the last Pima with extensive knowledge of the Pima version of the Creation story. By pure chance, perhaps, I'd been interested in folklore since a small boy, brought up on the *Journal of American Folklore* in my father's library, and I was familiar with the disappearance of oral histories, legends, etc., through time. I also had the rather heretical belief that there might be a grain of truth in many origin tales. So, hoping to preserve the myth from loss upon Juan's death, I initiated an effort to record it. I suggested to my Pima friends, who were as interested as I, that Juan be persuaded to tell the tale through an interpreter while I transcribed it verbatim through as many nights as it might take to tell. William Allison Smith, foreman of the digging crew, volunteered to serve as interpreter, being also interested. He was literate, spoke good English, and was a deacon in the Presbyterian church of the Snaketown area. This latter has an effect on his translation, of course, since he turned to familiar biblical language, King James version, when faced with problems of interpretation, such as obsolete or forgotten words.

Juan agreed to save time by singing the songs once instead of the traditional four times; he hesitated on this count because diverging from the tradition might bring harm to us or to him, but he relented.

I have noted that on the first night of the telling, my father attended with me, and Barney Jackson, a young Pima of the crew, interested in the old ways, came also and helped Juan in the singing. My father also transcribed the first telling, as did I, and I have his manuscript notes, along with the date, March 8, 1935. I will enclose a Xerox copy of them for you. He did not attend further meetings, nor did anyone else, except for one night when I had to be absent, and a friend came and took notes.

It seems that perhaps after an interval of time, we resumed the tellings, especially after the digging season had ended and the other archaeologists had left, and I remained to backfill the trenches, close and dismantle the camp, etc. After that I lived in Chandler (nearest off-reservation town to Snaketown) with the job [dig] cartographer Fisher Motz, who was staying on to finish some mapping, notes, etc. I commuted then from Chandler to the house where we met for the telling. This was an old storehouse belonging to Louis Quisto, as I recall, adobe, roofed with mesquite logs and adobe, holes in walls patched with old baskets, and a large wagon wheel propped up against the wall beside Juan, where one night I photographed him by Coleman lantern light most successfully (see frontispiece). And, although this has no bearing on your interest, the long hours had their effect. I went to sleep returning to Chandler very late one night, in my Model T stripped-down pickup, ran off the road, and woke just in time to veer away from a line of heavy fence posts. At any rate, we worked very hard each night, Juan patiently waiting the interpretation, I writing furiously, taking down every word longhand, literally verbatim, since I had no shorthand. My transliteration of Pima words was purely phonetic, since I had no linguistics. The two Smiths worked together to present the correct meanings, as best could be.

I typed the manuscript as time permitted, but it was not complete in final typed form until some months had passed, probably after I had begun work at Pueblo Grande [archaeology site and museum in Phoenix] in January of 1936. I eventually took a carbon copy to Juan Smith, or left it with his representative at Bapchule [a village near Snaketown], and gave one to Wm Smith [Allison] also, keeping the original for myself. I have not seen either man since.

You asked if I edited the manuscript when I typed it. No, I did not. I typed up the script with very little change, as was my custom, being a competent recorder. I did not show it at any time to either Smith, due to circumstances beyond our control. I did not preserve the handwritten pages either, but I can vouch for the accuracy of the taking down and typing.

Allison[11] died in 1948, and Smith was lost track of by Allison's relatives (his daughter, Lenora Webb, and his brother, Harvey Allison) and others (principally, Simon Lewis, born in Snaketown and a retired Presbyterian minister) with whom I discussed the manuscript beginning in fall 1991. They recalled Smith as a man with no home of his own, who worked for other families in exchange for food and lodging. At the time of this narrative he was staying with Allison's in-laws at Snaketown. No one that I talked with remembered the last time they had seen him, meaning, it seems, that he passed inconspicuously out of the Snaketown orbit. All agree that he was very well versed in old Pima ways, but it could not be said that he was the only person with such knowledge in 1935. It seems that he knew and liked Allison and must have liked Hayden, and he was willing to apply himself to the narrating job on that basis.

Finally, on the subject of Smith, I must say in contradiction or supplement to Hayden that the biblical qualities of the text are not entirely from Allison but come also from Smith in this respect, that Smith provided the narrative of myth events and those events are sometimes quite biblical, not so much in repeating stories of the Bible but in drawing orientation from such stories and more broadly in drawing on the ideas and attitudes of the rural Protestant American West. Allison was surely inclined to preach along those same lines in his short commentaries about the mythic narrative. (Those commentaries are included in the document and are set off from the ongoing mythic narrative.) But from what Hayden says about how the text was produced, that it was translated segment by segment, I conclude that Allison had little influence over the actual myth content. Any editorial change that Allison might have wanted to make in one segment would have come back to haunt him in the next. Thus, the mythic narrative, as opposed to the commentary, must be attributed to Smith. It follows that Smith was not innocent of America. I greatly wish that we knew more about him. It is said that he had a bicycle for transportation, was nicknamed Skunk, and was more a vagabond than a holy man.

CHRISTIANITY

The historical shift between the two types of account, from the earlier versions of 1694 and 1775 with no conquest to the later post-1875 versions with a conquest, amounts to a shift toward Christianity, as if the biblical Jesus were the stimulus for the idea of a murdered and revived man-god. In fact, such figures are known from elsewhere in native North America, especially among the Yuman tribes to the west of the Pima-Papago and in the Midwest. They are not common, however, and the Pima-Papago version is unique in having the god's killers be his own creation who reach a collective decision to execute him. Among the Yumans the killing is done by a daughter in secret using sorcery, and in the Midwest it is by foreign but Indian enemies.

We cannot and should not say that the dying god motif, as this element is called, required European stimulation, nor can we guess what Pima-Papago mythology would be like today without Europe. In general, we can learn considerable about the *elements* of New World mythologies prior to Europe, for there are elements that are widely shared in the New World and, in some cases, scarce in the Old. John Bierhorst's three books (1985, 1988, 1990) on North American, Mexican and Central American, and South American mythologies and Stith Thompson's *The Folktale* (1946) are excellent sources on these matters.[12] They positively establish both native, non-European-influenced myth elements and generic myth types. Such compilations show what North Americans worked with, analogous to the palette of a painter, but not what native North American mythologists made, analogous to paintings. They made historical portraits of themselves, which, like their societies, were adjusting, changing, and particular; and in general, we only receive good clear versions of these portrait histories after some centuries of European contact.

Now, if the Pima-Papago made increasingly Bible-like historical portraits, starting at least as far back as 1775 (their instruction in Christianity began in 1694), there are three important things to say about the extent of the similarity. First, of course, the result was not the Bible. Second, the Pima-Papago did not seek personal salvation in the figure of their murdered, or executed, man-god. And third, as already mentioned, they did approximate the Bible in stopping the heart of their story with the departure of the man-god, with the result that one learns as little of European doings from them as one does from the Bible.

I will enlarge on the second point now and take up the first and third points a bit later, relative to another Americanist text. There is a class of actions that I call "sacraments," meaning "ministrations to the soul." Every religious tradition has them. Those of Christianity are largely derived from the biblical narrative of Jesus, and this is especially true of Protestant Christianity, which tended to limit its sacraments to just two (baptism and communion) of the Catholic seven. The limit was imposed partly because those two were the only ones directly attributable to

Jesus. If the Reformation was largely fought over sacraments, then Protestant Christians have a deliberately narrowed sacramental life. They permit few direct human ministrations on human souls, and they put great faith instead on prayer and faith and on righteous but not formally sacramental individual conduct.

The Pima-Papago have always had native sacraments, the most prominent of which are for the cure of sickness by sucking, blowing, and singing. (See D. Bahr et al., *Piman Shamanism* [1974], on this.) Unlike the Christian sacraments, these native ones are not derived from the narrated life of the murdered man-god. Thus, according to the Smith-Allison mythology (story 3), the man-god Siuuhu directed that such cures be done, but he did not undergo them himself. Furthermore, this god's death and resurrection are not mentioned in any Pima-Papago ritual or ceremony—with one exception. This is the purification of successful warriors, that is, of enemy killers. It is a sacrament. Among other things, the warriors have water poured over them, and the whole is clearly a ministration to their souls. Siuuhu the murdered man-god is just one of several mythic characters whose deaths and revivals, or *near*-deaths and revivals, are recalled in war ceremonies and speeches. As we will see, Siuuhu receives this treatment twice. His first war sacrament is performed by an old woman after he has killed an eagle that has menaced the otherwise flourishing Hohokam (story 10). The second is done by a man-god in the underworld after he has recovered from the Hohokams' attempt to kill him (story 13). This sacramental legacy differs from that derived from Jesus in two respects: (1) it is narrower, being limited to war and reserved for killers, and (2) these war sacraments are not traced uniquely to Siuuhu.

I close this discussion of Christianity with some thoughts on native and non-Indian American churches. By "church" I mean "organized religion," more concretely, "a body of sacred texts, a body of sacraments, and a body of believers in and users of both." Surely most churches in America are Christian, and America began as a Protestant Christian nation, a "righteous empire" as the historian Martin Marty (1970) called this concept of nation. The Smith-Allison text may harmonize better with that concept of America than any other Native American mythology yet published. Therefore, some readers may doubt the text's value to Indians. I doubted this when I first learned of the text from Hayden. As a white Indianist, I preferred my Indian materials to be non-Christian, or if Christian, at least not Protestant (my family's religion), or if Protestant, then not preacherly.

Now having matured and studied the text, I see it as an attempt, albeit limited and without the author's fully intending it, to establish a native Pima church. The church would have a scriptural base in this text. But since at least one of the authors (Allison) cherished the Bible, their native mythological scripture would function for them approximately as the Book of Mormon functions for Mormons, as a supplemental scripture, one that covers the New World in approximately the same spirit as the Bible covers the Old.

This much is true. The Book of Mormon and this text are both largely set in America. Notwithstanding that geographic overlap, however, the Book of Mormon and the Pima text have three important differences. First, the Mormon book is a supplement to and a conscious improvement on the Bible in a way that the Pima text is not. The clearest way to see this is by noting that the main burden of the Book of Mormon is to derive the American (New World) Indians from Israel. Most or all New World peoples are said or implied to descend from two brothers who sailed in a small party from a port near Israel around 400 B.C. Of these descendants, the group of greatest interest is said to have been extinguished around A.D. 600. The Book of Mormon is said to be largely a translation of writings made by these people and revealed to the young Joseph Smith in 1823.

The Smith-Allison text makes an equivalent claim, that the whites originated in today's Pima (then Hohokam) territory (story 10). But the Smith-Allison text does not provide the whites with a history, as it could not, I think, if Smith and Allison accepted the Bible. In short, the Book of Mormon, whose complexity is only touched on above, gives a massive accounting of ancient America, while the Smith-Allison text gives only a few sentences on Europe, or the Old World. Moreover, the massive Mormon accounting is constantly keyed to and relentlessly corrective of the

Introduction

Old and New testaments of the Bible. The Israelite emigrants are led by a hitherto undocumented prophet. After the resurrection, Christ visited the New World peoples. God revealed and clarified himself more frequently in the New World than in the Old. This is why, according to its adherents, the Book of Mormon demands reading. It improves on the Bible by expanding it.

Not so with the Smith-Allison text. It mentions God but keeps him in heaven, out of the Hohokam consciousness. It omits Jesus. The text has several gods (Siuuhu is one) in the sense of persons who create and destroy things (the latter being monsters) for humanity's benefit. Gods in this sense are lacking in the Bible and the Book of Mormon, while such gods' relations with humanity are at the core of the Smith-Allison text. I assume that Smith and Allison felt that one's belief in these gods would violate the First Commandment, except for two mitigations. First, in general, the gods do not try to direct human history (they willingly create and destroy for people, but they show little long-term interest in human destiny, at least not on my reading),[13] and second, they do not require worship. If one interprets the First Commandment as strictly against the worship of gods other than God, then the Smith-Allison text and all other Pima-Papago mythologies known to me meet that commandment.[14]

It may not be true that a tribal people such as the Pimas could not both accept the Bible and supply the whites with a history. I assume that tribal peoples including the Pimas considered the Bible to be a history of whites (not necessarily of Europeans but of whites, even *the* whites) and that they were unwilling to Indianize, or New World-ize, that history analogous to how the Mormons Israelized the Indians' history.[15] My reasoning on this is simple: whoever accepts a history should not change it. Indians accepted Europe's history of itself; Mormons did not accept Indians' histories of themselves.

Second is a difference that may be more apparent than real. The Book of Mormon was revealed to Joseph Smith in written form (written in "reformed hieroglyphs" on gold plates), while the Smith-Allison text is oral. Historians would agree that Israel had writing at the time the Mormons believe Israelites populated the New World. The Mormons hold that these literate immigrants were scrupulous keepers of history. Therefore, what was revealed to Joseph Smith was not mere oral history but contemporary documentation. I say that this difference is more apparent than real for two reasons. First, the Pima-Papago claim to have well-preserved eyewitness testimony in their songs. Second, Smith had to translate the hieroglyphs into English. Without taking away from the majesty of his reading (the plates were secluded once the reading was finished), I feel a similarity, or an equivalent spontaneity, between Smith's *reading* such a story for the first time from the plates and a Pima narrator's *remembering* a long story. If one disbelieves in the plates, then Smith created a gigantic work of prose myth from memory. If one believes in them, one feels the same awe as on hearing a Pima speak long prose stories from memory.

There is a third and final point to make on the Book of Mormon and the Smith-Allison text. The Book of Mormon is not the only founding document of that religion. There are two more, *Doctrine and Covenants* and *The Pearl of Great Price*. The first consists of revelations received by Smith concerning the establishment, governance, and codification of the church he was to found (Church of Jesus Christ of Latter-day Saints), and the second is a selection of Smith's writings, namely, portions of his uncompleted revised English translation of the Bible, a partial autobiography, and a brief early statement on church articles of faith (Jackson 1985: 74–79).[16] Those two works remind us that it takes more than scripture or origin accounts to make a church.

Surely not all churches, still less all religions, must be organized as explicitly as the *Doctrine and Covenants* organizes the Mormons. Noting that churches are collective and communal, however, let us say that they must have some shared sense of how they came into existence (possibly an account of world origins, possibly something more modest) and that they must have a body of sacraments. What they need not have is centralization and its correlate, officially authorized codification.

I now wish to contrast three contemporary Native

American formations on those aspects of churchness. The three are the Smith-Allison mythology as representative of native North American tribal mythologies in general; the centralized, officially codified constitutional governments now in effect among most tribes; and the Native American ("Peyote") church. In the background will be what I term "established" U.S. churches, such as the Mormons, Methodists, Presbyterians, and Catholics. The established churches share one trait uniquely with the Native American church and not with any tribal mythology or centralized tribal government. This is that the churches are incorporated as nonprofit corporations in one of the several United States.[17]

Now, the Smith-Allison text implies a church insofar as it enjoins sacraments; and this implied church thrives insofar as those sacraments are successfully ministered to present peoples' souls. In fact, the mythologically enjoined sacraments were ministered somewhat successfully to Pima-Papago souls in the 1930s (more to Papagos than Pimas), but this is much less true today. Not only is the war rite partially derived from Siuuhu now obsolete (it was virtually obsolete by the 1930s, being upheld only in mock battles against "straw" enemies; Underhill et al. 1979: 89–139) but the sacraments of the established U.S. churches along with folk versions of the same now have a strong hold on nearly everyone (Bahr 1988a). The one native sacramental tradition that remains strong is the medicine men's curing, the origin of which is given in story 3; but these cures are themselves shifting from old-fashioned subjects such as wild animals to more modern subjects such as God and the Devil (Bahr 1988b).

Every native tribe is densely served by missions and congregations of the established churches. The number of churches per thousand residents on Indian land is probably greater than the number per thousand anywhere else in America. Each of these reservation churches has some members who shun native sacraments. For this reason if for no other, no tribal government could easily establish its traditional mythology and sacraments as an official church. Another inhibition is the U.S. Bill of Rights, which forbids the establishment of one religion. Perhaps that law applies also to tribes, or at least to tribespeople. In any case, to my knowledge no tribe had the tradition of privileging one mythology and set of sacraments against all others, and none has recently acted to do so.

Tribes do increasingly officially involve themselves in religion or religiouslike matters. They pass resolutions and send delegations to bless and protect sacred sites within and outside their reservation boundaries, and they may require instruction in their past, uncentralized, churchlike traditions as a condition for employment. In these respects they function as attenuated state churches: attenuated in their ministry to souls but statist. One senses this statism when one considers why tribes do not file for corporate status under the laws of any of the fifty United States. Tribes are too sovereign to do this. Conversely, the established U.S. religions that do this (I believe that they all do) are less sovereign than tribes.

Finally, the Native American church is precisely an established U.S. church (incorporated in various states) and not a tribe. Its members are almost entirely Indian, but most of these members belong to a sovereign tribe with an uncentralized churchlike mythology and body of sacraments. The myths and sacraments of those tribe-churches are other than the myths and sacraments of the Native American church. Although decentralized, the offices and liturgy of this church are exceptionally well codified (see the Appendix in Omer Stewart's *The Peyote Religion* [1987] for an equivalent of the Mormons' *Doctrine and Covenants*, the *Church Canons* of 1948 for the Native American church). The central sacrament is the nightlong Peyote Meeting in which the cactus is eaten, analogous to the Christian communion. Interestingly, the church lacks a mythology equivalent to that of Smith-Allison. There is a generally shared origin story of the peyote sacrament itself. Briefly, a young woman grieved for the loss of her brother in warfare. She went in search of him, found him in resurrected form (such that he could not rejoin the living), and received the sacrament (peyote) from him along with instructions on its use in groups, in other words, instructions on how to form the ritual aspect of the church (Stewart 1987: 36). This is not a long, primordial set of origins as in Smith-Allison, nor is it a Bible-like history as in the Book of Mormon, except in this sense. Stewart's excellent book is based on his own eye-witness accounts and the personal testimony of hundreds of peyote leaders. It approximates what the Mormons believe they have in their accounts from the ancient Israelite migrants, the travails of a band of seekers.

I have made this brief survey to indicate what the Smith-Allison mythology is and is not. I believe it is very much a part of a religion and a church—traditional Pima-Papago religion—and this makes it more than a recollection of the Hohokam or a free play of the imagination. It is not a full religion because its sacraments have wavered and withered as its people have drifted to or were conscripted by other religions (including the Native American church, but still only slightly among Pimas) and because it honors the First Commandment: it honors and builds its house of myth within.[18]

PIMA-PAPAGO LITERATURE

This people's traditional literature is oral. Therefore, if its pieces are to be kept fixed, so they can be contemplated, they must be kept fixed in memory. I think the essence of literature is contemplation; thus, whatever cannot be fixed, cannot be a literature. Another way of saying this is that literature is thoughts formed in language and kept fixed for reflection.

Note that this concept of literature conforms with Vansina's concept of history, but it is more general. I hold that all literature implies contemplation, therefore fixity. But not all literature is history. Histories are fixed (but not unchangeable) texts that presumably stem from firsthand observations. Obviously, a people could elect to fix and preserve "made-up," nonobservational texts. My impression is that Pima-Papagos consider all their literature (their fixed texts) to be history and none of it to be fiction, and I suspect that this is true of tribal peoples generally. My impression of the Pima-Papago unanimity toward history is based on their always saying, "We think this story really happened," and never the opposite.

There are three levels of fixing, with associated text lengths, in Pima-Papago and perhaps all memory based lit erature. First, there are very short texts that are fixed at the level of each individual sound. Then come medium-length texts, fixed at the level of the phrase or short verbal "formula." Finally are long texts that are fixed at the level of the episode. These last are paraphrased each time they are told. The same episodes are told, but the exact wording of the episodes may be—probably is—different on each telling. The middle level of memorizing largely precludes the spontaneity and indeterminacy of paraphrasing, and the extreme level precludes paraphrasing completely.

Among the Pima-Papago, the texts of the three levels, from tightest to loosest, are properly called songs, chants (or orations or prayers), and prose (oral prose). The Pima-Papago names, all nouns, are *ñe'i*, 'song'; *ñiokculida* or *hambto ñiok*, 'talk-for-it' or 'rumbling [I believe] talk'; and *a:ga* or *a:gida*, 'telling'. Interestingly, the full and proper performance of a text such as the Smith-Allison, which I call a "mythology" (*ho'ok a:ga*, 'witch telling', in Pima-Papago), includes all three levels of text. The performance is primarily in prose, in which the narrator paraphrases his own or his teacher's last telling. But distributed through the prose are shorter more rigorously memorized texts, ideally both orations (actually absent from the Smith-Allison text) and songs (abundantly present).

It can now be seen why the songs and war orations of the Hohokam chronicles are considered as proof that the Hohokam spoke Pima. Such texts are believed to have been retained basically unchanged since they were first spoken by a Hohokam. No one is sure of this, but it is supposed to be true. It is the prose, which is the great bulk of the text, that is considered to be unreliable, that is, merely conscientiously paraphrased from one telling to the next.

I stress the Pima-Papago concern for accuracy in retelling, but one might think that I merely imagine this. My response is that we who write have great retelling accuracy at our fingertips, if only we can read our own writing. I agree with Vansina that Pima-Papago and the rest of the oral cultures wish for such accuracy. They have worked within these three levels of text to attain it, always trading off length of text against reliability of reproduction. It seems that only people who valued contemplation would undertake such a task, or rather, would involve themselves in maintaining a tribe's stock of texts. Interestingly, the one personal comment from Smith in the text, which comment seems illogical at first, addresses itself to exactly this point. He says in effect (this is how part 1 starts), "We contemplate faces in order to know things, which reminds me that I don't have these stories perfectly learned, therefore not ready to face you."

EDITING

Hayden's typescript, entitled "Pima Creation Myth," has no internal subdivisions. I have divided it into thirty-six stories and have provided the stories with titles. Hayden followed the precedent of Frank Russell (1908: 206–230), who published an equivalent Pima text from the narrator Thin Leather under the title "Pima Creation Myth" and without subdivisions. I made the divisions for three reasons. First, the stories are commonly told separately, and several collections have been published in this subdivided format (e g , by Fewkes [1912] and Lloyd [1911] from Thin Leather and by Densmore [1929], Wright [1929], and Saxton and Saxton [1973] from various Papago narrators). Second, the undivided format is difficult to read. One senses that stories are starting and finishing, and one wishes for printed guidance and confirmation on this. Third, the actual live Snaketown telling certainly had breaks, in fact, on two levels. There were breaks when Smith stopped speaking Pima so that Allison could translate, and there were breaks between story-telling sessions. These breaks were not marked in the typescript, and, as Hayden wrote in his letter, the notebook that may have shown them is gone.

My story divisions must fall between the small segments-for-translation, which would approximate episodes, and the large session divisions, which would approximate "parts." Of the three levels, that of the story is probably the most useful to the reader, and it is a level that narrators and listeners use ("Tell me the story about X"). Still, my divisions are arbitrary, and it is sometimes difficult to see where one story stops and the next begins. Without going into detail, I will say that it would have been possible to divide the text into somewhat fewer than these thirty-six stories but more difficult to establish a larger number of story divisions. Thus, the thirty-six represent a maximum segmentation into whole, self-standing stories.

I have also grouped the stories into larger divisions called parts, to which I have given titles. This grouping is entirely my own. It is meant to highlight the main narrative chunks of the mythology, partly as a means for comparing this mythology with others and partly as an editorial device, that is, a means to divide the text for the placement of introductory essays (at the beginnings of parts) and supplementary myth texts (at the ends).

The story and part titles are arbitrary in that other titles might have been given. Those that are used were chosen in the interest of brevity and description. Although they could all be said in Pima, I imagine that some of the titles would seem blunt to some Pimas, for example, "Destruction Through Sex." Still, that title describes an undoubted theme of the story, and I would say it is the main theme. Further, I defend the occasional bluntness on the precedent of Allison's commentaries. As a preacher, he was sensitive to moral matters, and I let that sensitivity guide the titling. Last, the titles are meant to win the reader's interest.

Concerning changes in the wording of Hayden's typescript, I made conservative changes in the prose for the sake of brevity, clarity, and sometimes for cadence; the songs were not changed. The prose was changed in the awareness, first, that oral prose is always only a paraphrase of itself (see above), and second, that Hayden had been unable to edit the English with Allison. Having some familiarity with how Pimas speak and write English and some writing tastes of my own, I tried to arbitrate between what the manuscript actually said and what I imagined Allison might have said had he polished the text for publication as plain-speaking American Indian English. This arbitration gave weight to the actual manuscript, so changes were not made simply because they seemed possible.

I wish the song renditions could have been changed, because I am sure that they are poor summaries of the original Pima-language poems. (Each Pima song is a poem; that is, each syllable is part of a word, each word part of a line, each line part of a compact, studied, and studiable poem). This

is certain because the earlier mentioned mythology published by Russell from Thin Leather contains the Pima-
language texts for a few of the songs in Smith-Allison. The
Thin Leather versions include good literal translations that,
while as short as those in the present manuscript, generally
convey the form and substance of the Pima poem better
than the translations by Allison. The latter generally tell
what the poem is about, but they lose and misplace key
words, juxtapositions, connotations, and so on. Still, the
translations are surely from Allison, and, being songs, they
stand for texts whose wording is not supposed to be al-
tered. I have usually footnoted the songs for which other
known versions exist. They are, in fact, a small portion of
the total number of songs in the Smith-Allison text, which
is to say that Smith knew an exceptional number of songs.[19]

Next, the Hayden typescript does not distinguish between the ongoing mythic narrative, which I attribute almost entirely to Smith, and Allison's commentary on the
same. That distinction, between telling a story and telling
about it, is common in Pima-Papago narratives, although
generally it is the same person, the narrator, who does
both. I found it rather easy to separate the two kinds or
uses of prose—for they are both prose—and it seems useful
and enlightening to set them off from each other. This is
done by placing Allison's commentary in the outside mar-
gin, next to Smith's mythic narrative. It will be seen that
the great bulk of the text is Smith's narrative (as translated
by Allison), but the comments are rather frequent, especially in the "Hohokam Chronicles" part of the text. The
songs are set apart from both kinds of prose by moderately
indenting and italicizing them.

Last, a brief comment on the orthography used to spell
Pima words. Hayden's manuscript is salted with words,
usually nouns, that he wrote in a rough-and-ready orthography. I have respelled these words and others as well according to the orthography now officially adopted by the
Papago or Tohono O'odham tribe. The Pimas have not yet
passed on an orthography, but at least a few Pimas use the
Papago orthography that is given here, although they normally make one change in it. To be true to Pima pronun-
ciation, they often use the letters "v" or "t" where Papago

would spell the equivalent sound with a "w." Ofelia Zepeda's book, *A Grammar of Papago* (1983), gives a good discussion of the sounds and letters of Pima-Papago. For the reader who wishes a rough idea of how to pronounce the words in this book, I say to pronounce them as if they were Spanish (with the sound values used for reading Spanish), but always put the stress on the first syllable of a word.

FORMAT

The text is given with minimum interruption. There are footnotes and backnotes to deal with linguistic and other interpretive matters, respectively. There are brief essay introductions to the text's parts, of which there are eleven, and at the end of part chapters there are supplements to the Smith-Allison version from other Pima-Papago narrators. The parts are Prelude, the Font Text (part 0, because it is background for the Smith-Allison mythology); Genesis (part 1); The Flood; New Creation and Corn; The Whore; Wine and Irrigation; Morning Green Chief and the Witch; Feather Braided Chief and the Gambler; Siuuhu's Death and Resurrection; The Conquest until Buzzard; The Conquest until Sivañ Wa'aki; and After the Conquest.

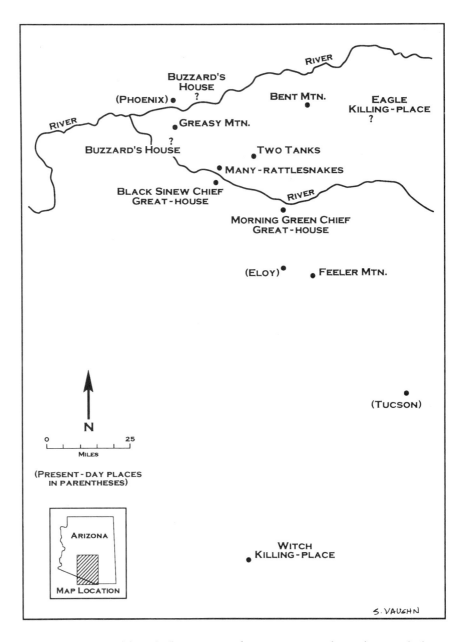

Map 1. Important places mentioned in the mythology.
(Drawn by Shearon D. Vaughn)

THIS SHORT, no doubt truncated, two-part mythology was recorded at a Pima village near to-day's Casa Grande National Monument by Pedro Font in 1775. The village name was registered as Uturituc, possibly [T]u[k] Tu:dagi, an old way to say the name of to-day's village of Cuk Ṣu:dagi, 'Black Water'. The text is important because its first part gives a nonconquest version of the end of the great-houses and the second, a non-death-and-revival biography of the figure called Siuuhu in the Smith-Allison text. Those and a fragment from 1694 are all that we have in writing from the long period between the end of the Hohokam and the mid-nineteenth century. As I will explain, the old texts illuminate much in Smith-Allison, that is, much pertaining to the imagination and symbolism of power, especially powers over wetness and heat. As I will also explain, we should be doubtful about what the texts teach on the substance of Hohokam life, which is what they wish to represent. The year 1775 is not halfway between us and the Hohokam, and 1694 is just a bit more than half. We will take the Font stories in se-quence, placing the temporally earlier fragment in between them.

The first Font story was given in explanation of Casa Grande Ruin, the great-house later excavated by Fewkes. To the Spanish, the Mexicans, and early Anglo-Americans, this place stood preeminent among the clay-walled Hoho-kam ruins of the region. It was *the* Casa Grande, which means "Great House" in Spanish. It retains that Spanish name and status in present-day Arizona, although as we saw, by Fewkes's time American archaeologists applied the English term "great-house" to all clay-walled ruins.

The late nineteenth- and early twentieth-century Pima

language on great-houses was as follows. They called most or all of the clay-walled ruins *wa:paki* in the plural or *wa'aki* in the singular. The word does not literally mean "great house" as does the Spanish *casa grande*. ("Great house" in Pima would be *ge'e ki:*). It is not clear what *wa'aki* means etymologically.[1] I translate the word simply as "great-house," that is, I equate it with the Spanish-inspired English term for these structures.

One way that the nineteenth-century Pimas named these wa:paki/great-houses was in reference to the Hohokam "chief" (*siwañ*) who they thought lived there. Thus, the great-house that Font visited was called Morning Green Chief Great-house (Si'al Cehedag Siwañ Wa'aki) by nineteenth-century Pimas. Another way that they named them was in reference to geographic features, for example, Gravel Great-house (O'odkam Wa'aki). Whichever the naming practice, the *wa:paki*/great-houses were several, and one thinks of each as having its chief, whether remembered or not, and its distinct geographic setting. Accordingly, nothing in the name "Morning Green Chief Great-house" marks this place as special. In fact, the textual record on great-house naming is spotty and puzzling. Of the two long conquest narratives, by Thin Leather and Smith-Allison, only Thin Leather uses differentiating names like "Morning Green Chief Great-house." Smith and Allison appear to be wedded to the unmodified words "Chief" and "Great-house." I do not think this is accidental. As stated in the introduction, there is a Papago text that reduces the conquest to a single battle at none other than Chief Great-house (Siwañ Wa'aki); and as was also stated earlier and we will now see, the Font text implies that the present-day status name siwañ, 'chief', was originally the personal name of one character, that is, the name of a man called "Bitter" (recorded as Siba), the chief at *the* Casa Grande, the place excavated by Fewkes. Possibly then, the Pimas of Font's time called this place "Siba Wa'aki," that is, they called it by the same term used in the single-battle conquest text. The implications are that the proliferation of specially named chiefs and great-houses was a latter-day phenomenon and that the idea of a march to all these places is also recent.

The Font text states that the great-house chief's name

was Bitter Man (Siw O'odham in present-day Pima-Papago), but the text does not give the actual Pima expression. Luckily, a 1694 journal report written by Juan Manje does give the Pima, as Siba. Manje, we should note, is generally considered to be the first European to see Casa Grande Ruin (Fewkes 1912: 33, 54–56). Accordingly, he was the first person to write Pima.[2] His spelling of the name could represent Pima words pronounced as "siba," "siwa," or "siva"; the Spanish letter "b" could cover that range of sound. Note that "siba" is about equidistant from present-day Pima-Papago *siw*, 'bitter,' and *siwañ*, 'chief.' In my view, the old Siba is ancestral to both of those words: the present-day status term *siwañ* derives from the mythic personal name Siw/Siba.[3]

Here is the text.

PRELUDE 1

THE BITTER MAN (GOVERNOR OF UTURITUC)

In a very distant time there came to that land a man who, because of his evil disposition and harsh way, was called the Bitter Man; and that this man was old and had a young daughter; that in his company there came another man who was young, who was not his relative nor anything, and that he [Bitter] gave him in marriage his daughter, who was very pretty, the young man being handsome also, and that the said old man had with him as servants the Wind and the Storm-cloud.

That the old man began to build that Casa Grande and ordered his son-in-law to fetch beams for the roof of the house [the house beams are cedar, which does not grow in the Pima desert]. That the young man went far off, and as he had no axe or anything else with which to cut the trees, he tarried for many days, and at the end he came back without bringing any beams.

That the old man was very angry and told him he was good for nothing; that he should see how he himself would bring beams. That the old man went very far off to a mountain range where there are many pines and, calling on God to help him, he cut many pines and brought many beams for the roof of the house.

That when the Bitter Man came, there were in that land neither trees nor plants, and he brought seeds of all, and he reaped very large harvests with his two servants, the Wind and the Storm-cloud, who served him.

That by reason of his evil disposition he grew angry with the two servants and turned them away and they went very far off; and as he could no longer harvest any crops through lack of the servants, he ate what he had gathered and came near dying of hunger. That he sent his son-in-law to call the two servants and bring them back and he could not find them, seek as he might. That thereupon the old man went to seek them and, having found them, he brought them once more into his service, and with their aid he had once more large crops, and thus he continued for many years in that land; and after a long time they went away and nothing more was heard of them. (Quoted in Fewkes 1912: 43)

The Bitter Man appears as a harassed small-scale chief. He fetches his own rafters when his son-in-law assistant cannot get them for him. He is chief in a farming community with resident wind and rain. Assuming that this is one community among several, although perhaps the preeminent one (this is stated in Manje), we can imagine a scene more or less as the archaeologists envisioned, of river valleys with a sprinkling of small great-houses, each with its own rain and each attended by its own chief.

What might surprise the archaeologists is that the text does not mention irrigation. In fact, the actual prehistoric Casa Grande and the other great-houses were served by irrigation canals, and the historic (post-1694) Pimas practiced irrigation from some of the same rivers (but principally the Gila). We will find a myth about the origin of Hohokam irrigation in Smith-Allison (story 8), but we will also find Smith-Allison's Hohokam history to be more fundamentally concerned with rain than with irrigation. I will be explicit on the rain side of this issue after the next Font text is given. But for now let us simply note that, like Siba, the principal characters of later Pima-Papago myth seem to care more for rain than for irrigation.

Note then the following possibilities. The actual Pimas of 1900 and 1694 appear to have been diligent irrigators. Anthropologists have observed that their opportunity and ability to tap rivers liberated them from the fickle rains of their region (Russell 1908: 86–89; Ezell 1983: 151). However, it is possible—in fact, it is evidently true—that the Pimas, like their riverless relatives the Papagos, were more fascinated by rain than by rivers. Thus, they ceremonialized rain making more than they did river tapping, the former considerably (Russell 1908: 331–334, 347–352) and the latter apparently not at all.[4] It is also evidently true that they believed the Hohokam shared this fascination with rain. Finally, it is possible, although there is no evidence for this, that the Hohokam shared this fascination. If that were true, the Hohokam may not have been as dedicated to river tapping as the archaeologists suppose; or rather, if they were dedicated in practice, they may have neglected the subject in myth.

The other possibility is that the Pimas have gotten the Hohokam wrong, that they would be surprised if they could hear what the Pimas have said about them. I will return to this. By the end of this prelude we will understand the seventeenth- through twentieth-century Pima and Papago ideas on rain, but we will not know if the Hohokam had the same ideas.

Let us resume with Font's story and note the reason that Siba abandoned his house and farm: there is none. He suffered a weather reversal, but he set it right again and then left. This may be hard to believe, but it could symbolize what some archaeologists have thought about the end of the great-houses, that as a result of the salting of the soil or changes in rainfall—rainfall on the mountain watershed, according to the archaeologists—the Hohokams' farming became too lean to support the great house life-style. Surely that may have been a real factor or at least a nagging anxiety. As it happens, however, a brief mention of the Siba myth by Juan Manje in 1694 gives another often-cited archaeological explanation, warfare. In this oldest of written documents on Pima myth, the war is not fratricidal or rebellious as in the later versions. Rather, the war is in the form of raids by the east-living, Athabascan-speaking Apaches. Such raiders were surely a factor in the lives of the Pimas of 1694. It is a moot point whether they were or would have been a factor in the actual end of the great-houses, ca. 1400.

Here is the Manje textlet.

The guides said that they [Casa Grande and several
other great-houses] were built by a people who came
from the region of the north, their chief being El
Siba, which according to their language means "the
bitter or cruel man," and that through the bloody
war which the Apache waged against them and the
20 tribes allied with them, killing many on both
sides, they laid waste to the settlements, and part of
them, discouraged, went off and returned north-
ward, whence they had started years before, and the
majority went east and south. (Quoted in Fewkes
1912: 55–56)

What matters to us in both of these texts on Siba is the absence of a Pima-to-Pima conquest. Before taking up the second of the Font myths, which has a figure equivalent to the
conquering Siuuhu of the later texts, I will connect the concern of Font's Siba with wind and rain to later texts from
Pimas and Papagos. These form a series of variants of the
same myth that Font recorded about Siba. The first in the
series (ibid., 48–49), replaces Siba with a Siwañ chief at
Casa Grande Ruin. The second carries the same myth into
the Papago desert, with no mention of a great-house or siwañ (Saxton and Saxton 1973: 317–340). Finally are texts
that replace wind and rain with corn and tobacco. All these
will be given and discussed later, for the Smith-Allison mythology has versions of the final step, on corn and tobacco
(part 3).

The series as a whole underscores the point made above
on the Pima imagination of the Hohokam. We can see how
the Siba of 1775 fits into the mythology of the later Pimas,

but we cannot know if Siba was a man who walked the Hohokam earth or if the Hohokam had a myth of a man or god like Siba. I do not regret this. If we never learn what the Hohokam thought of Siba, at least we know what we are missing. We have not lost anything, but we have gained awareness of a city that we cannot visit, the city of the Hohokams' myths.[5]

We come now to Font's second myth, which establishes a discontinuity between the eighteenth- and late nineteenth-century Pima-Papago relative to the Hohokam chiefs and the man-god who walked among them. If we were granted the opportunity to hear just one myth from the Hohokam city, I would not choose a myth on irrigation directly but on the problem of a creator god who either does or does not take vengeance on the chiefs of his people. In the discussion that follows, I will show how this god opposes the chiefs (*sisiwañ*) imagined by the nineteenth-century Pimas and also the earlier character of Siba. He is an anti-rain chief but not in a way that places him in charge of rivers. Rather, he is a sun-heat god.

The second Fond myth centers on the character cognate with Smith and Allison's Siuuhu, but it gives this character a different name. The name of the Font character is "the Drinker" (El Bebedor), a well-attested variant name—actually an alternative—for Smith-Allison's Siuuhu. The Pima language for this alternative name is I'itoi, 'Drink-it-all-up'.[6] What matters from the Font myth, given below, is that the Drinker/I'itoi never dies, is never revived, and never leads a conquest against the Hohokam. In this myth he castigates people, presumably Pima-Papago and *not* Siba's great-house people, by turning them into saguaro cacti and by causing them to be scorched by the sun. But he never conducts a vengeful war, and he exterminates no one.

PRELUDE 3

THE DRINKER (GOVERNOR OF UTURITUC)

He [the village governor] said also, that after the old man [Siba] there came to that land a man called the Drinker, and he grew very angry with the people of that place and he sent much water so that the whole country was covered with water, and he went to a very high mountain range which is to be seen from here, and which is called the Mountain of the Foam (Sierra de la Espuma), and he took with him a little dog and a coyote. . . . That the Drinker went up, and left the dog below that he might notify him when the water came too far, and when the water had touched the brow of the foam [marked today on the mountain] the dog notified the Drinker, because at that time the animals talked, and the latter [the Drinker] carried him up.

That after some days the Drinker Man sent the rose-sucker [hummingbird] to Coyote to bring him mud; they brought some to him of the mud he made men of different kinds, and some turned out good and others bad. That these men scattered over the land, upstream and downstream; after some time he sent some men of his to see if the men upstream talked; these went and returned saying that although they talked, they had not understood what they said, and that the Drinker Man was very angry because these men talked without his having given them leave. That next he sent other men downstream to see those who had gone that way and they returned saying that they had received them well, that they spoke another tongue but that they had understood them. Then the Drinker Man told them that these men downstream were good men and there were such as far as the Opa, with whom they are friendly, and there were the Apache [upstream], who are their enemies.

He [the governor] also said that at one time the Drinker Man was angry with the people and killed many and transformed them into saguaros [cacti], and on this account there are so many saguaros in that country. . . . Furthermore, he said that at another time the Drinker Man was very angry with the men and caused the sun to come down and burn them, and was making an end of them; that he [they?] now begged him much not to burn them, and therefore the Drinker Man said that he would no longer burn them and then he told the sun to go up, but not as much as before, and he told them that he had left it lower in order to burn them by means of it, if they ever made him angry again, and for this reason it is so hot in that country in summer.

He [the governor] added that he knew other stories; that he could not tell them because the time was up, and he agreed to tell them to us another day; but as we laughed a little at his tales, which he related with a good deal of seriousness, we could not get him afterward to tell us anything more, saying he did not know any more. (Quoted in Fewkes 1912: 43–44)

The striking difference between this two-myth mythology and the later, conquest mythologies is that this 1775 version separates the Drinker/Siuuhu from the great-house people. These people were earlier than the god, who came on the scene, did not like what he found (presumably, the people who remained after Siba's departure), caused a flood, and created the Pima-Papago, Apaches, and a good downstream people who lived as far as the Opas, generally considered to be a Yuman language-speaking people who extended in 1775 from around Gila Bend, Arizona, along that river toward today's town of Yuma (Spier 1933: 25).

One wonders if Font and his interpreter were truly attentive to the governor on the dissociation between the Drinker and the Hohokam. I assume that they were because, as we will see later, there were mythologies in the 1850–1940 period, and there are still some today (see n. 1 for part 8) that make a little of the great-houses and the sisi-wañ chiefs; and while war is certainly a factor in these mythologies, the relevant war is not against the Hohokam but against Apaches and Yumas, as it seems to have been also for Font's governor.[7]

Thus, the text should not be dismissed as poorly heard. In fact, in its brevity it expresses a theme that we will find in the conquest mythologies. This is the opposition between rain and sun. In the Font text, Siba is a rain god, or at least a man blessed by rain. He keeps rain as a retainer, a "servant" Font said. The Drinker, in contrast, chastises people with the sun.

The narratives of conquest say the same thing. One of the two greatest battles in the long accounts is against a man simply called "Chief" by Smith-Allison and "Black Sinew Chief" by Thin Leather. This man has an armory of water defenses—fogs, mists, and so on. Siuuhu evaporates them. The other great battle is with a solar figure, the Buzzard who the Hohokam had enlisted earlier to kill Siuuhu. Buzzard had killed him by borrowing the sun's bow or gun for a day and shooting him with it. During the revenge battle, Buzzard does not have the bow, and Siuuhu's forces outfly him with their eagles and hawks.

In both great battles the invaders prevail, thanks to solar power. Curiously, the Hohokam have both rain and sun, but the invaders have only the one. Neither Siuuhu nor his army are ever said to cause water, the implication being that the last real water magician was a Hohokam siwañ, long ago.

If we cannot say why the Font text lacks irrigation, at least we have said what it has instead. I will now take a final look at how Font's myths are reflected in Smith-Allison, for the above remarks are limited to the last part of their text, that is, their narrative of the conquest. There is no loss of Rain and Wind (or Cloud) myth in Smith-Allison, but there is an equivalent one, on the loss of Corn and Tobacco. Like the story of Siba, this myth starts with a society blessed with the things about to be lost. The blessing is special: the primordial society includes those things as human members, that is, as men (Tobacco is a woman, however, in a variant by Thin Leather). In one way or another (this is complex and not perfectly clear), the people of the society eat of, smoke of, or are wafted and watered by the things while also having them as human companions. The eventual loss that the myths speak of is not at all of the non-human aspect of the things, for example, of corn and tobacco as material products. Rather the loss is of the human aspect, that is, of Corn and Tobacco as human companions. These humans leave and stay gone, although they may be approached from a distance. Also gone are the vague but unlimited pleasures and uses that the things yielded while they were humans.

These are stories of the loss of a certain kind of paradise, unfamiliar to the West, in which a useful material thing and a human person become separated. The very commonly heard Native American stories of animals that are like people suggest the same idea, except that these stories are usually not understood to entail a loss. They do not stress that humanity lost something when the species became itself, so to speak. Perhaps the Font text on Siba is also of this type, but it was recast by or for the Spaniards. (In that story, Rain and Cloud resume their residence.)

In Smith-Allison and all the late nineteenth-century stories of the type, the persons who are lost to society always leave voluntarily, as do Font's Rain and Cloud ("Wind," in the later versions). But whereas the Font text characters leave because of unspecified dissatisfaction with their master, Siba (perhaps because of his overbearing character), the characters of the later stories all leave unmarried, and in some cases they leave because they would like to be married but cannot. And there are many hints that their provision of unlimited pleasures—Corn through his person, Tobacco through his person, and so on—is linked to their unmarried, virginal, and unsexually reproducing condition. They are presexed creators. We will consider these matters in discussing Smith-Allison's part 3.

BY THE TIME of the conquest mythology, from the mid-nineteenth century onward, nearly every Pima-Papago narrator had an account of the creation of the world out of nothing, or almost nothing. All of the dozen-odd accounts known to me begin with a god in a dark void, the same as the first sentences of Genesis. In the Smith-Allison text, this god is God, who soon creates the god with whom the rest of the Pima-Papago texts begin. At the moment of his first mention this native god is either in the process of becoming a material man or has already become one. Thus, he differs from the Christian God the Father who remains heavenly and spiritous. The Pima-Papago man-god will live on the earth, and his name is always given as Earth Doctor, Jewed Ma:kai.[a] He is in all versions a completely nice person, neither bitter like Siba nor capable of anger like the Drinker. He makes the earth, generally from crusts off his own skin, then the sun, moon, stars, Vulture, and the first humans; and he causes the sun, moon, earth, and sky (which may have preceded him) to make Siuuhu/the Drinker and Coyote.

Immediately below is the Smith-Allison version of these events, and then afterward two other versions are presented, one from the Lloyd rendition of the Pima Thin Leather (1911: 27–33) and one as rendered by the Papago Juan Dolores and edited and published by Dean Saxton and Lucille Saxton (1973: 1–10). The bulk of this text is from a turn-of-the-century Papago narrator. The last segment was rendered by Saxton and Saxton from the recent Papago nar-

---

[a]Sometimes translated as "Earth Shaman" or "Earth Medicine Man." The word *jewed*, 'earth', also means "land" or "ground" as opposed to sky or water. At its lowest level of contrast, the word also means "soil" or "dirt" as opposed to sand or rock.

rator, Joe Thomas. Finally, for comparison is Genesis, chapter 1, as given in the New English Bible (1970: 1–2).

STORY 1

FIRST CREATION

[Juan Smith says, William Smith translates,] It is a great pleasure to me to be here with you tonight. I have looked into your face, you have looked into mine, and we know each other now. I'll do my best. It seems I ought to know the story clear through because I was raised among some of the old Indians that know it clear through, but I was young at the time and was like most young people, running around and paying no attention to what I was doing. For that reason there are places in the story that I have forgotten. But this is the way the story begins.

When there was no earth, no heaven, nothing but darkness, the only person that was here was Jeoss.[b] Jeoss had no form, no flesh, no bones, and was nothing but pure spirit, like the wind. This Jeoss planned out a way that he could form an earth on which to rest his soul. This earth that he formed was really the heavens (*damkatchim,*[c] something over above).

He made a person up in damkatchim who was nothing but light.[1] The next person that Jeoss created was a man who came down and made the world where we now are.

Now here's what this Jeoss was singing:

> *Earth Doctor, Earth Doctor (*Juut makai*)*[d]
> *You make the earth now*
> *And started it going.*[2]

Now, this Earth Doctor thought he might make another person and thought to call his name Siuuhu.[e]

---

[b]*Jioș*, from Spanish *dios*, 'god'.
[c]*Da:m ka:cim*, 'on top lying', 'sky', 'heaven'.
[d]Jewed Ma:kai.
[e]S-e'ehe.

While he was thinking of making another person, he sang:

Earth Doctor was just thinking about this, while he sang.

Siuuhu doctor, Siuuhu makai[f]
You've made the mountains
And placed them around.
And you started it going.

Now the earth and heavens came closer together and connected, and in that Siuuhu came out, son of the earth (mother) and of the heavens (father).

Now this Earth Doctor and Siuuhu made another man, from whom the Pimas came. They made some clay and from that formed a man. While this clay figure lay with no life, they sat around it and were looking at what they had made. Then they formed the insides of this clay. But it still had no life. Then they breathed life into the form, and it moved around and was living.

This first one was made as a man, and the next was a woman, made in the same manner as the man. When they finished the two persons, these three, Jeoss, Earth Doctor, and Siuuhu, were living with the same spirits that they have now. At that time there was no sun. All was dark, but after everything was completed, it was good. The thing the man and woman needed was sleep.

Then later, Jeoss, Earth Doctor, and Siuuhu worked to create the dawn, and it began to dawn in the east.

---

[f]*Ma:kai*, 'doctor', 'medicine man', 'shaman'.

Morning came and the two persons woke up. When everything came out as the three wanted, they sang a song:

> I have made the morning
> I have made the morning
> I have set it in the east
> And the morning came out of the east
> And began to light the earth.

Then they worked and made the sun and made it follow the dawn, and it came out and began to shine on the earth. They placed it where the dawn came out, and it followed the dawn. Then they sang:

> I have made the sun
> I have made the sun
> I have placed it in the east
> And it is coming out and lighting the world.

By this time the two persons they had made were waking up, and now the three worked to make the food that these were to live on. They made the deer, which a person must kill and eat, and they sang:

> This gray deer that I made for you,
> Whenever the mountains in the distance look dusty,
> As if in a dust storm,
> Then the deer comes out.

Then they worked on the next animal, the jackrabbit, which people must also kill and eat for food. Another song:

This meant that the jack-rabbit was to live in desert spaces without water for many months. The jackrabbit would have the water of the mirage for its drinking water.

On singing songs, sing it once clear through, then repeat the last half; or sometimes twice clear through, and the last part twice.[3] At dances, you dance in one direction while the whole verse is sung, and when the half verse is sung, you dance in the opposite direction. At the beginning the singers go through the whole verse very softly to make sure they all know it. Then they sing it loud for the dancers to dance.

The grey jackrabbit, the grey jackrabbit,
This is for you, this is for you.
The earth looks like a mirage,
Water all over.

Then they worked and made the wind storm and clouds, and it began to rain. When the rain stopped, grass came out. Certain kinds of grass [*neantum*][g] the people used for their food. The woman went out and picked some of the grass and took it and cooked it and ate it. When through eating, the man went out with bow and arrow and killed a deer, and they had it for supper that evening. At that time, the sun went down, and darkness fell over the earth, as it had been before. This was the end of the first day.

Then they worked and made the moon, and it came out at night and lighted the earth a little bit. When it went down in the west, darkness fell over the earth, just as it was before.

At that time, the sun and moon got very close together and touched, and another person came out. They called him Coyote—not an animal but a person. The moon was his mother and the sun his father.

The creators saw that at night when the moon goes down there is nothing but darkness on the earth.

---

[g]*Ñiadam*, malva, an annual, not actually a grass, whose leaves are boiled to make liquid for pinole "in time of famine" (Russell 1908: 76). The flat round seeds are also eaten (Mathiot n.d.: 130). This word and the English plant name "malva" are absent from Saxton and Saxton's 1969 dictionary.

They decided to make smaller lights in the heavens. They sang:

> We're going to make the stars
> We're going to make the stars
> And we're going to place them in the skies.
> We're going to make everything,
> And place them in the skies
> To light the earth
> To light the earth.[4]

All these things were created with a decision of some kind. This means that people living on earth must not be like Jeoss and know what they are going to make and what they are going to do. But they [Jeoss and his godly ancient companions] make everything in a way that we might not be able to understand, and today whenever we try to do anything, we always have trouble before we succeed. Meaning: there is a rule from the beginning that man has to learn [things], that man cannot be God, cannot understand these things.

Coyote spoiled it with his breath. That's why there are dim spots in it.

After they created all three lights in the skies, they thought that that would be all, but seeing that there would not be enough light, they decided to make the Milky Way (Tomuk).[h]

They are going to make the Milky Way so that when a man goes to an unknown place, he could guide himself by the Milky Way. They sang a song before they made it:

> We are going to make the Milky Way
> We are going to make the Milky Way
> And it is made
> And it is stretching in the sky
> From one end to the other
> Grey Coyote, our cousin, was breathing in
>   the Milky Way.

After they completed the Milky Way, they threw darkness in the east. That is why night begins there. Before they threw the darkness, they sang a song:

---

[h]To:mog.

I am acting one of the great earth doctors
And I have thrown the night toward the east
Which goes over all the land
Down to the setting sun in the west.

Now the sun was setting, and the dark was beginning to fall.

After they completed these things, the earth wasn't still but was shaking. When Siuuhu saw that the earth was shaking, he had a hat with a gold hatband. He reached for his hat, took the hatband off, and broke the band into pieces. He scattered this gold and put it in the mountains so its weight would hold the earth down. He reached his [right?] hand way back in the east and held the earth down, and with his right foot he reached toward the west and put the foot on the earth and held it down. He sang two songs:

He has reached way back in the east
And felt that the land was shaking over there.

Away down in the west
Where I set my foot
I found out that the mountains were shaking
Which I have found out.

Then the land was still, and everything was all right.

At that time the earth was all level, no hills, no low places. Everything was even. The mountains, too, were all even and smooth. Now it was Earth Docauthority to Buzzard to make these things. The reason was, by the signs of these low places and peaks, there was a guide to human beings. If they should get lost and then come home, and anyone asked anything, they could tell what kind of mountains they saw and what kind of ground they traveled through, and that would be a guide to the people.

tor's turn to make something. He was sitting with streams of light coming out of his eyes, with which he sees everything. He reached and got some of this light and made a buzzard (Nui)[i] with it.

When this was made, Juut makai and Siuuhu sang two songs together:

> Buzzard bird, buzzard bird,
> You have made the land just right.

> Buzzard bird, buzzard bird,
> You have made the mountains just right.

Now they have completed everything, and everything is perfect for their people. Now he's [Jeoss?] going to talk to the two [Earth Doctor and Siuuhu?] that created human beings and tell them they must not have any separation, jealousy, or foolish talk, and they must bring up children in the same way, and they were perfect.

That is the way it was from the beginning with these two persons [first man and woman]. They were perfect in everything.

Then they sang two more songs:

> The land is still now
> And on it everything seems to be all right
> Everything is made perfect.

> The mountains were shaking
> But now they are still
> And on them everything is perfect.

This demonstrates that the woman is weak, for the left hand is weak, and the man is stronger, for the right hand is stronger. This means that the man is more understanding and ahead over [beyond] the woman.

Earth Doctor picked up his two children. He picked up the woman with his left hand and the man with his right.

---

[i]Ñu:wi.

[Comment by William Smith] Juan says he has forgotten this story. The only thing he remembers is that the woman did wrong in here, and from here on the wicked ways kept growing and spread far and far [wide], and the people got so wicked that a great flood destroyed them, and something happened again, and all the people were destroyed again, and a third time they were destroyed. Here he takes up the story—and there will be fourth destruction of the here and now, when you and me and everybody is going to be destroyed, maybe by wind.

So they lived together happily, for a certain period, in the ways Earth Doctor told them to live. Then the evil spirit got into the woman. Then Earth Doctor saw that what he had made perfect didn't come out the way he wanted, so he made a rule for women. From [after] twelve years, she must have sickness every month, and in pain she must bring out her children, and that would be all right for her. Since then this sickness was upon the female, and they multiplied from then on.

Then they [man-gods] got a stick and made a shallow hole in it and placed another stick in the shallow hole they had carved and twisted it and made fire from that wood. They also got a stone and got fire from the stone. That was the way they should get fire and cook their food with it.

SUPPLEMENT

FIRST CREATION (THIN LEATHER)

The old man, Comalk Hawk-Kih [Komalk Hok] (Thin Buckskin) began by saying that these were the stories he used to hear his father tell, they being handed down from father to son, and that when he was little he did not pay much attention, but when

The Story of Creation.

In the beginning there was no earth, no water—nothing. There was only a Person, Juh-wert-a-Mah-kai [Jewed Ma:kai] (the Doctor of the Earth).

He just floated, for there was no place for him to stand upon. There was no sun, no light, and he just he grew older he determined to learn them and asked his father to teach him, which his father did. And now he knew them all.

floated about in the darkness, which was Darkness itself.

He wandered around in the nowhere till he thought he had wandered enough. Then he rubbed on his breast and rubbed out moah-haht-tack,[1] that is, perspiration, or greasy earth. This he rubbed out on the palm of his hand and held out. It tipped over three times, but the fourth time it stood straight in the middle of the air, and there it remains now as the world.

The first bush he created was the greasewood bush. And he made ants, little tiny ants, to live on that bush, on its gum that comes out of its stem. But these ants did not do any good, so he created white ants, and these worked and enlarged the earth; and they kept on increasing it, larger and larger, until at last it was big enough for himself to rest on.

Juhwerta Mahkai's song of creation:

> *Juhwerta mahkai made the world—*
> *Come and see it and make it useful!*
> *He made it round—*
> *Come and see it and make it useful!*

Then he created a Person. He made him out of his eye, out of the shadow of his eyes, to assist him, to be like him, and to help him in creating trees and

---

[1]*Muhadag*, 'grease', 'skin oil', 'perspiration'.

human beings and everything that was to be on this earth. The name of this being was Noo-ee [Ñu:wi] (the Buzzard). Nooee was given all power, but he did not do the work he was created for. He did not care to help Juhwertamahkai but let him go by himself.

And so the Doctor of the Earth himself created the mountains and everything that has seed and is good to eat. For if he had created human beings first, they would have nothing to live on.

But after making Nooee and before making the mountains . . . , Juhwertamahkai made the sun. In order to make it he first made water, and this he placed in a hollow vessel, like an earthen dish, to harden into something like ice. And this hardened ball he placed in the sky. First he placed it in the north, but it did not work; then in the west, but it did not work; then in the south, but it did not work; then he placed it in the east, and there it worked as he wanted it to.

And the moon he made in the same way and tried in the same places with the same results. But when he made the stars he took the water in his mouth and spurted it up into the sky. . . .

Now Juhwertamahkai rubbed again on his breast, and from the substance he obtained there he made two little dolls, and these he laid on the earth. They were two human beings, man and woman.

Now for a time the people increased till they filled the earth. For the first parents were perfect, and there was no sickness and death. But when the earth was full, there was nothing to eat, so they killed and ate each other. Juhwertamahkai did not like the way the people acted . . . and so he let the sky fall to kill them. When the sky dropped, he, himself, took a staff and broke a hole thru, thru which he and Nooee emerged and escaped, leaving behind them all the people dead.

And Juhwertamahkai, being now on the top of this fallen sky, again made a man and a woman, in the same way as before. But this man and woman became grey when old, and their children became grey still younger, and their children became grey younger still, and so on till the babies were grey in their cradles. Juhwertamahkai, having made an earth and sky just as there had been before, did not like his people becoming grey in their cradles, so he let the sky fall on them again and again made a hole and escaped, with Nooee, as before.

And Juhwertamahkai, on top of this second sky, again made a new heaven and new earth, just as he had done before, and new people. These new people made a vice of smoking. Before, human beings had never smoked until they were old, but now they smoked younger, and each generation still younger, till the infants wanted to smoke in their cradles.

Juhwertamahkai did not like this, and he let the sky fall again, and created everything new in the same way, and this time he created the earth as it is now.

But at first the whole slope of the world was westward, and though there were peaks rising from this slope, there were no true valleys, and all the water that fell ran away, and there was no water for the people to drink. So Juhwertamahkai sent Nooee to fly among the mountains and over the earth, to cut valleys with his wings, so that the water could be caught and distributed, and there might be enough for the people to drink.

Now, the sun was male and the moon was female, and they met once a month. The moon became a mother and went to a mountain that is called Tahs-my-et-tahn Toe-ahkᵏ (Sun Striking Mountain), and there was born her baby. But she had duties to attend to, to turn around and give light, so she made a place for the child by tramping down the weedy bushes and there left it. And the child, having no milk, was nourished on the earth.

This child was a coyote, and as he grew, he went out to walk and in his walk came to the house of Juhwertamahkai and Nooee. . . . When he came there, Juhwertamahkai knew him and called him

---

ᵏTaṣ Mai'ihit-an [perhaps] Duag, 'Sun Hit-on Mountain', not a mountain that I have ever heard of or seen. Perhaps the place is not considered to be within Pima-Papago territory.

Toe-hahvs,[1] because he was laid on the weedy bushes of that name.

Now out of the north came another powerful personage, who has two names, See-ur-huh and Ee-ee-toy.[m] Seeurhuh means older brother, and when this personage came to Juhwertamahkai, Nooee, and Toehahvs he called them his younger brother.[5] But they claimed to have been here first and to be older than he, and there was a discussion between them. Finally, because he insisted so strongly and just to please him, they let him be called older brother.

SUPPLEMENT

CREATION
(DOLORES)

Long ago, they say, when the world was not yet finished, darkness lay upon the water and they rubbed each other. The sound they made was like the sound at the edges of a pond.

There, on the water, in the darkness, in the noise, and in a very strong wind, a child was born. The baby lay upon the water and did as a child does when it is being made to stop crying. (Like when its mother sings and tosses it up and down and walks

[1]*Tohawes*, 'brittlebush' (*Encelia farinosa*).
[m]S-e'ehe and I'itoi, 'Elder-brother' and 'Drink-it-all-up'.

back and forth with it.) The wind always blew and carried the child everywhere. Whatever made the child took care of him, fed him, and raised him.

One day he got up and found something stuck to him. It was algae. So he took some of the algae and from it made termites. Then he sent them out to get more algae to be put in one place so he could sit down and think about things to do. And the little termites did that for the firstborn one.

The termites gathered a lot of algae and First Born tried to decide how to make a seat so the wind could not blow it anywhere. This is the song he sang:

> *Earth Medicine Man finished the earth.*
> *Come near and see it and do something to it.*
> *He made it round.*
> *Come near and see it and do something to it.*

In this way, First Born finished the earth. Then he made all the animal and plant life. There was no sun or moon then, and it was always dark. The living things didn't like the darkness, so they got together and told First Born to make something so the earth would have light. Then the people would be able to see each other and would live contentedly with each other.

So the First Born said, "Alright, you name what will come up in the sky to give you light." They discussed it thoroughly and finally agreed that it would be named "sun." But about then Coyote came running and said, "It rose! It rose! It will be named 'light.' " But nobody agreed.[6]

The sun rose and went over to one side, but it didn't light up the whole earth. Then it went down, and again it was dark. So the firstborn one sang like this:

Didn't we make the sun and talk with it? Hihih.
Didn't we make the sun and talk with it? Hihih.[7]

Then it began to get light again, and First Born said, "The sun will rise and come overhead." It did as he said, but it came very low and so was hot. First Born sang again and pointed to another place, saying that this sun would come up there. This is the way he did so it would always come up there.

Next he made the moon and stars and the paths that they always follow. Now the living things could see themselves. Some were large and some very small, some were very fast and some very slow. Many of them were dissatisfied with themselves. Those that were small wanted to be large, and those that were slow wanted to be fast.

Along came the Black Beetle and said, "Soon the living things will multiply and crush me with their feet because I'm not a fast runner and have no possible way to save myself. I think that when someone has lived a long time he should die and go away and never come back here again. That way the earth will never get overpopulated and no one will crush me."

At that time Rattlesnake's bite was harmless. The children would play catch with him and take out his teeth. He could never sleep and always cried, so he went to First Born and said, "The children are making life miserable for me. You must make me different so I can live contentedly somewhere."

First Born changed many of the animals. When he finished them, he took Rattlesnake, pulled out his teeth, and threw them far away. They landed and grew into what we now call "Rattlesnake's Teeth."[8]

As the sun was about to rise, its rays beamed over the horizon. First Born got them and threw them in the water. Then he took them out and made teeth . . . and said, "Now that I have done this for you, when anything comes near you, you must bite it and kill it. From now on the people will be afraid of you. You will not have a friend and will always crawl modestly along alone."

Then the sun rose in the place it is now, and First Born looked at it and sang:

> *First Born[9] made the earth.*
> *First Born made the earth.*
> *Go along, go along, go along.*
> *It's going along. Now all will remain as it is.*

When he finished his song, he told them where they would be living. Some would live in the forests, some in the mountains, and some would live in the valleys. He also said this, "I have finished all things and they will always be as they are now."

In the east, as you know, the singing and dancing had begun for those who will die here. They will go to the singing and dancing ground. The land around the dancing ground will be beautiful. There will be plenty of prickly pears, and the people will always be happy.

That's the way First Born prepared the earth for us.

[Here begins the segment added by Joe Thomas]

The sky came down and met the earth, and the first one to come forth was I'itoi, our Elder Brother. The sky met the earth again, and Coyote came forth. The sky met the earth again, and Buzzard came forth. (Saxton and Saxton 1973: 1–10)

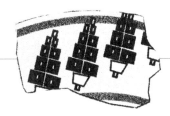

SUPPLEMENT

GENESIS, CHAPTER 1 (NEW ENGLISH BIBLE)

In the beginning of creation, when God made heaven and earth, the earth was without form and void, with darkness over the face of the abyss, and a mighty wind that swept over the surface of the waters. God said, "Let there be light," and there was light; and God saw that the light was good, and he separated light from darkness. He called the light day, and the darkness night. So evening came, and morning came, the first day.

God said, "Let there be a vault between the waters, to separate water from water." So God made the vault, and separated the water under the vault from the water above it, and so it was; and God called the vault heaven. Evening came, and morning came, a second day.

God said, "Let the waters under heaven be gathered into one place, so that dry land may appear"; and so it was. God called the dry land earth, and the gathering of the waters he called seas; and God saw that it was good. The God said, "Let the earth produce fresh growth, let there be on earth plants bearing seed, fruit trees bearing fruit each with seed according to its kind." So it was; the earth yielded fresh growth, plants bearing seed, plants bearing fruit according to their kind and trees bearing fruit each with seed according to its kind; and God saw that it was good. Evening came, and morning came, a third day.

God said, "Let there be lights in the vault of heaven to separate day from night, and let them serve as signs both for festivals and for seasons and years. Let them also shine in the vault of heaven to give light on earth." So it was; God made the two great lights, the greater to govern the day and the lesser to govern the night; and with them he made the stars. God put these lights in the vault of heaven to give light on earth, to govern day and night, and to separate light from darkness; and God saw that it was good. Evening came, and morning came, a fourth day.

God said, "Let the waters teem with countless living creatures, and let birds fly above the earth across the vault of heaven." God then created the great sea-monsters and all living creatures that move and swarm in the waters, according to their kind, and every kind of bird; and God saw that it was good. So he blessed them and said, "Be fruitful and increase, fill the waters of the seas; and let the birds increase on land." Evening came, and morning came, a fifth day.

God said, "Let earth bring forth living creatures. . . ." Then God said, "Let us make man in our image and likeness to rule the fish in the sea, the birds of heaven, the cattle, all wild animals on earth, and all reptiles that crawl upon the earth." So God created man in his own image; in the image of God he created him; male and female he created them. God blessed them and said to them, "Be fruitful and increase, fill the earth and subdue it, rule over the fish of the sea, the birds of heaven, and every living thing that moves upon the earth." God also said, "I give you all plants that bear seed everywhere on earth, and every tree bearing fruit which yields seed:

they shall be yours for food. All the green plants I give for food to the wild animals, to all the birds of heaven, and to all reptiles on earth, every living creature." So it was; and God saw all that he had made, and it was very good. Evening came, and morning came, a sixth day.

T HE FLOOD in this story is caused by an abnormality in sexual relations. This cause is an extension of the causes of the world destructions in Thin Leather's creation text. There we understood that worlds or creations were ended because of eating one's own kind, that is, cannibalism, and because of two seemingly more minor abnormalities in aging: the progressively earlier onset of greyness and tobacco smoking. Here the abnormality is the ever shorter length of pregnancies, that is, of the time period between making love and giving birth. The flood comes after the shortening reaches zero, and a baby is born from a man's penis.[1]

The flood is caused by nothing explicit in the Smith-Allison text, but in most other versions it is caused by and even consists entirely of the tears of the baby born from the penis. (Those stories will be treated in backnotes.) Therefore, the flood is salty. There is at least a hint of the father's "crime" in this baby's action. The baby's tears first wet the cheeks, then the surrounding ground, then the whole world, recalling the geographic extent, if not the actual seminal fluid, of the philanderer's wanderings.

The gods Siuuhu, Earth Doctor, and Coyote all survive the flood, and they do so by means that clearly recall the philanderer's crime. Siuuhu saves himself by entering a gum jar that he had made, a man-made womb, while Earth Doctor and Coyote use penislike life preservers. Earth Doctor entered a "cane" that he always carried (it is not clear whether this was a solid wood staff or a hollow cane of bamboo), and Coyote entered a bamboo flute. Thus, the gods divide and vote two-to-one in favor of recapitulating the baby.

After the flood, each god emerges from the container; in

other words, each is reborn. There is always a discussion about who emerged first. In Smith-Allison, the discussion concerns the depth of the water into which each god claims to have stepped on leaving his container. Other texts give other discussions, for example, on the distances traveled on earth after emergence. In all versions the situation is slightly comical, since the three gods come to ground out of sight of each other and cannot be sure if their measures are true and coordinated. Siuuhu always pronounces himself first but without real proof. The other gods, although probably miffed, do not contradict him. It is sometimes said that he acquired the name "Elder-brother" (S-e'ehe) at this moment. The pegging of the name to this episode affirms that the flood vessels are seen as means for rebirth.

Thus, the theme of abnormal procreation runs through the whole story. As such the text is a proper sequel to the Pima "Genesis." In that text we have Earth Doctor making the whole of creation by various combinations of extrusion (his skin scales), molding, and spurting (the stars), in contrast to the Bible where God creates primarily by speaking, "Let there be. . . ." One can say that the Pima mythology is more physical, which reminds us of something simple and disconcerting. If there is nothing but one god in the universe, and if he has to act rather than command or to do rather than say, then he really has nothing to act on but himself.[2]

The flood story continues with this line of reasoning, only now to the point of disaster and, in effect, perversion. Whereas Earth Doctor had no choice but to make people from an earth that had begun as his own body grease, the philandering young man was an anomaly in a world of normally reproducing people, in other words, a perverse extension of Earth Doctor. Surely, then, the abnormality at the beginning of the story is not just that women take less time to have babies but that a man would have one himself. A disaster follows, and following that there is this curious leveling of the surviving three gods, after which Siuuhu becomes the disputable but undisputed senior.

The Flood

When the evil ways of the people were at their height and Earth Doctor and Siuuhu saw that the people were so wicked, they planned to punish the world. They made a man like the Indians used to have, with long hair and beautiful earrings.[3] He was a good-looking man. They gave him a bow and quiver, and they told this man to go among the people, where their houses were, and find a girl who had just reached maturity. He would sleep with the girl and bring out a child the same night.

That's the way he went on. Every night he brought out children, the same night. There was a young girl living someplace, and she was afraid when she heard this man was coming. She cried all the time. The father of this girl was a powerful medicine man, and he knew why Earth Doctor and Siuuhu were making this trouble. He was wise, and he worked to make this man have a baby himself. He wanted the trouble to happen quickly, to punish the world, to make it worse, and to make happen what Earth Doctor and Siuuhu did that for. He was even going to make this man have a baby!

When the sun set, this man came and lay down with the girl. When the morning came, the baby came out. It was crying. The father of the girl came and called the

The Pimas call the grand-
child of a daughter by a different term from the child
of a son, *bamat* [daughter's
child] and *wosmat*
[son's child].[4]

baby "grandchild" (*bamat*).[a] The girl spoke up and said, "You mustn't call the baby that." It [the baby] wasn't from his daughter but from this man.

That was the greatest sin that was committed, because the man brought out a baby. When he brought out this baby, he picked it up and held it in his arms and took it to Earth Doctor and Siuuhu. Earth Doctor and Siuuhu knew that this was going to happen, because they were the creators and knew everything.

When the man with the baby got close to Earth Doctor and Siuuhu, he got ashamed and laid the baby down and went on home. When he came to their place, Earth Doctor asked what he'd done with the baby, "For I know you've had a baby and what you've done with it. Bring it and we will look at it, for this is the custom when a baby is born."

All this time Earth Doctor, Siuuhu, and Coyote had been living together. Siuuhu was working to make a home to go into when trouble comes, and Earth Doctor had picked up a cane and held it. Coyote didn't know what was going to happen or that the world was going to be punished. He didn't stay much at home but was always running around among the people. Well, he had been doing so, as usual, and was going back home, but water was coming out of the earth, and everywhere this Coy-

---

[a] *Ba'amaḍ, Wosmaḍ.*

ote made a track, water came out. When he came to Earth Doctor and Siuuhu, he told them, "I am really a true medicine man, better than anyone else, because when I came over, in my tracks I saw water coming out!"

Siuuhu said to Coyote, "Do you think it's for the good of the people that this happened? It's for a trouble to these people, and that's why I made this house to go into when trouble comes." Earth Doctor told him, "You think it's something great you've done for these people, but it's trouble." When Coyote learned what was going to happen, he got afraid and walked back and forth feeling sad because he didn't know what to do, and sometimes he cried. Siuuhu said to him, "If you had known what was going to happen, you wouldn't have run around."

Coyote had a flute made of a reed hollowed out inside. Siuuhu got this flute and stopped up the holes. He blew some air in it to make it bigger, put Coyote in it, and stopped the holes in the ends.

The man that had the baby went after his baby, but by that time the water began to rise, and the man never returned. Siuuhu got into the house he had built[5] and shut himself in there while Earth Doctor sat down with his cane in his hand. Earth Doctor sang a song:

> *I'm sitting here*
> *Rocking back and forth*
> *With my cane in my hand.*

When the water was under Earth Doctor, he raised himself, stood, and sang a song:

Kukulickim [is] an old word [in this song that] means as when one is seated for a long time and stands, feeling weak in the knees, and staggers.

I'm standing now
I'm standing now
Swaying and staggering around
With the cane in my hand.

Now the water was up to Earth Doctor's waist. He stuck his cane in the ground and lifted himself (like a pole vaulter), went straight into the air, across the heavens, and came to his father's (Jeoss's) place.[6]

The water rose for twenty days. It destroyed all the people and all creatures of the land and air. Well, two birds saved themselves from the flood: woodpecker (Hikovik) and Veekh koskum (Juan didn't know what the second bird was, only its name).[b] Today the signs that you see on the woodpecker's tail show that it was saved from the flood. The water rose to a certain height, almost to where the woodpecker was hanging [e.g., from the sky], and it touched his tail making signs on it.

At that time, the people thought that Superstition Mountain[7] was the highest mountain on earth, so they fled to that mountain. When the water was rising to the top, there was a powerful medicine man

---

[b]*Hikivig* and *vi:g koṣkam*. The latter means 'down-feather nested'. No one seems to know whether these latter birds still exist, or precisely what they looked like. They are famous because of the mythology, and one often hears of them in songs. The woodpeckers are well known and frequently seen birds.

who thought he could make the mountain go higher. He sang a song:

At that time it was lower than it is now. It did rise a little.

Superstition Mountain
With a song is going to grow higher
On which I am standing.

The water kept rising and overpowered this medicine man. He owned a dog which he took on top of that mountain. The dog looked to see how far the water had risen. When he came back, for [because of] the wickedness of these people, the dog spoke like them and told them, "This water has reached us," and that's all he said. Then they all perished. All people were destroyed.[8]

There is a word that Juan doesn't understand. This house was going to land in a certain direction, with a name, but Juan doesn't know which way it means: *Vakilif.*[c]

The water took twenty days to rise and twenty to fall. At the end of these days, when the water was falling, the two [Siuuhu's and Coyote's] houses came back with the water. Siuuhu's house moved in a circle, four times.

This was the third punishment made to the world. In it there was to be a new law or rule that will tell us of the next destruction of the world.

When the water was low, it made rivers and oceans, which means that the water that destroyed the earth gathers itself into certain parts of the earth. The

As this house moved around in a circle four times, the water became calm, you might call it, became quiet, and it made the mark [little petrified foam] that we now see on Superstition Mountain. That is the sign that the flood really happened. Also, as the house made its circle, it splashed water which made

---

Vakilif, 'south', 'trash' (the direction in which flood-borne trash piles up). Generally speaking, considering the lay of the land in the southwestern quarter of Arizona, the downhill direction is southerly; or at least this directional term implies that it is.

water that turned into ocean contains dead animals, birds, and human beings.

a rainbow. When that showed, Jeoss appeared in the heavens and told the earth, or world, that the rainbow meant that the world would never again be destroyed by flood. Whenever it rains, the rainbow will appear as a reminder that the world will not be destroyed like that again.

A name was given for the Siuuhu house: "Chokwee-cum," which Juan doesn't understand.[9] The house that Coyote went into isn't a flute literally, but the word means a whole pile of the reeds of which a flute is made. The Pima word *vap-kwuchk* means a pile of those materials.[10]

When the water lowered, the house that Siuuhu went into came onto a certain place, and Siuuhu came out with the water just up to his waist. The next thing to come back to earth was the flute that Coyote went into. He came out and saw that Siuuhu was the oldest and he was the youngest.

NEW CREATION AND CORN

HERE BEGIN the Hohokam chronicles with the creation of that people by the now-senior Si-uuhu. After a brief discussion of different versions of what became of the original creation, we will move to the real matter of this part, the Corn and Tobacco stories that were mentioned in connection with the Font text.

First, what happened to the old creation. According to Smith-Allison, these people all died. They spoke Pima-Papago, the Hohokam will speak Pima-Papago, and the people who will conquer the Hohokam, who will emerge from the underworld, spoke it, too. Smith-Allison hold that these last people were created by Earth Doctor after he sank to the underworld. Other narrators hold that the conquerors were the first-created people. Thus, Thin Leather, the Papagos consulted in the 1930s by Underhill (1946: 8–12), the Papagos I now know around Santa Rosa Village, and possibly Dolores[1] all hold that Earth Doctor used his cane (solid or hollow) to open a subterranean escape passage for a portion of the original people. Thus they entered the underworld, a kind of master womb analogous to Si-uuhu's earth gum jar of the flood myth. Symbolically, they, too, were leveled with the gods, but their rebirth will come much later, in Smith-Allison's story 14.

Such are the conquest mythologies' answers to the question of what became of the first creation. I should mention that practically all Pima-Papago mythologies of record have a flood and new creation, and all but Font's (the oldest one) have a Hohokam conquest. There are about a dozen such mythologies. I have discussed the few, possibly misrecorded exceptions to the trinity of flood, re-creation, and conquest in a paper (1971).

Once Siuuhu creates people, he makes various plants for them: corn, cotton, pumpkins (or squash), various beans, nettle leaf goosefoot, and tobacco. Recall that the earlier creation was provided by Earth Doctor with the wild plant malva, deer, and rabbits, which, since they still exist, must have survived the flood. We can now note that the new plants place agriculture in the province of Siuuhu, not Earth Doctor. Of these new plants, only corn and tobacco receive further mythological attention. Smith and Allison dedicate much of the second creation story and the remaining two myths of this part to them, making the part more concerned with the new peoples' relation with the plants than with Siuuhu's concern with the people.

Really, the first problem of Hohokam existence is to establish a stable relation with the plants. The relation is a loss or, better stated, a double separation. From an initial state (delivered by Siuuhu) of union between the plant and a human, in which the plant-person lives with the Hohokam, (1) the plant-person becomes separate from the plant-object (i.e., the botanical plant), and (2) the plant-object remains in human hands while the plant-person goes to live somewhere else, far from humanity.

As stated in discussing the Font text, there are Pima-Papago versions of this story with Rain and Wind in the place of Smith-Allison's Corn and Tobacco. Two of these myths are placed in the supplement to this part, as is Thin Leather's single text version of what Smith-Allison treat as two myths ("Corn and Tobacco Leave" and "Corn Returns").

Also stated earlier was the fact that most of the preseparation persons do not marry, but they seem to wish to do so, and perhaps they could not do so while retaining their paradisiacal relation with humanity. Here is the testimony, including two more versions of Rain and Wind that are not given in this supplement. Smith-Allison's Corn leaves without sexual or marital desires, but he returns to marry a human woman. The couple have a child who is nurtured in the woman's womb but was engendered by the woman's eating a worm that she picked from Corn's hair. The child is killed: Siuuhu causes the mother to drop it while walking. Corn-man leaves, but corn-object stays. Smith-Allison's Tobacco leaves without sexual or marital desires, and he stays away. He sends seeds back to the people.

Thin Leather's Corn does the same as Smith-Allison's, but this time the child turns into a saguaro from which the Hohokam will gather fruits to make wine for rain ceremonies. Thin Leather's Tobacco, a woman, leaves because no man likes her. She stays away but supplies seeds to humans. In the Thin Leather version of Wind and Rain (included in the supplement), Wind and Rain are expelled because, following a bet, Wind exposes the crotch of a virgin for Rain's viewing. Humanity wants the two back. They will only return periodically, not as men but as fickle wind and rain. The two additional versions tell essentially the same story (Wright 1929: 55–61; Saxton and Saxton 1973: 317–340).

This entire collection of failed and un-marriages is significant in light of where the Smith-Allison stories fit in those authors' larger mythology. The stories—stories of this type—come immediately after "Destruction Through Sex" and immediately before "The Whore." The latter treats a succession of too-short marriages (and without children) between a flighty human woman and various birdlike or bird-man husbands. Thus Smith-Allison place their Corn and Tobacco text in a series on marriage. Before it is the story of a man who has too many women and ultimately reproduces through his own penis; and *he* indirectly makes a salty flood, an oozing superabundance of water that even in moderation is not good for earthly life. No irrigation god (relative to the discussion of Font's text), he is an ejaculation god. After the Corn and Tobacco text comes the story of a woman who is not a god or a goddess but a threat to mundane Hohokam family values.

In conclusion, from the details of Smith-Allison's crop myths and from the myths' position in the larger mythology, it is evident that to Smith-Allison the origin of crops is continuous with the origin of marriage. In fact, one can say that they are more interested in the latter than the former.

The three would have to work very hard. That is why man is more powerful than anything on earth, and more valuable.

Earth Doctor came down and came to the two persons, Siuuhu and Coyote. The three made plans on how they would make more people. They decided that the first thing they should make is ants who would only work in the summer and would show how they are powerful, good workers. They could not decide for a while how they would make man again. Finally they decided to make them the same way as before, in their own likeness.

This is a sign that when the water was gone [the flood ended], it was spring [and new mesquite leaves had come out].

The next thing they made was just two quails (*cokaycho*).[a] Then they made a roadrunner (*tata*),[b] only one. Then they got pieces of mesquite leaf and placed them on top of the quails' heads.

This showed that if they wanted to find the right place, they must work hard. To this day human beings must work hard to find the things they want to know.

They sent the quails to the west to find how far the water had gone to the west, and they sent the roadrunner to the east to find how far the water had gone that way. Coming back, they would find the middle of the earth. When the quails and roadrunner came back, they met right at the center.

The three persons sat down in the middle of the earth. They got some water and made clay and formed persons. While forming them, they did not

---

[a] *Kakaicu.*
[b] *Taḍai.*

work together. One person making his man was facing the east, one was to the north, and one was to the west. When Siuuhu found how Coyote was making his people, he didn't like them, because they were no good, he said. So Siuuhu picked up the people that Coyote had made and threw them into the ocean. Those were the fishes and ducks, and he told Coyote that they were just food for people.

You can still see the marks of his hands in the heavens today. It is called *matk*, like spread fingers.[c]

Earth Doctor felt sorry about what had happened between Siuuhu and Coyote, so he got up, got his cane, and pointed it to the heavens, meaning that he was to drop the heavens and smash the earth. Jeoss spoke up [from the sky] and told him it was not right to do that. Then Siuuhu worked and placed his hand against the heavens.

This was a sign of the way people should come to their death.

While Siuuhu held this above him, Earth Doctor was going down in the earth. He went down to his neck. When Siuuhu saw this, he reached to grab him. Earth Doctor just spit all kinds of sickness in Siuuhu's hand.

That's why people die of sickness everywhere.

When Siuuhu saw that he held something nasty in his hand, he waved the hand all over the earth, and sprinkled sickness all over.

Sickness is more powerful than medicine men because sickness was made first and medicine men afterward.

Siuuhu said he didn't intend to give the world such painful diseases, and he worked and gave men power to overcome sicknesses. This is the power of

[c]*Matk*, 'palm of hand', 'hand and fingers'. The constellation Pleiades, as Hayden was told by the Papago Juan Havier.

medicine men who sometimes will heal sickness and sometimes won't do it.

While Earth Doctor was going down into the earth, he made four kinds of liquid in the earth (oil), which would take fire quickly. When he got to the other side of the earth, he made some more people.

These songs were a sign that some day we would find out that the earth is turning around all the time.

Siuuhu stayed up on this earth, and he changed everything that he had decided to do. He made his people, and he had them talk many different languages. He sang two songs:

> *The earth is spinning around*
> *The earth is spinning around*
> *And my people are spinning around with the earth*
>
> *The earth is spinning faster*
> *The earth is spinning faster*
> *And my people are spinning faster with the earth.*[2]

The first people that talked were the Apaches. When Siuuhu heard them, he got some ice and splashed it on them. This was to show them that they could stand the cold and make clothes out of deer skins. The second people that talked were the Yaquis. The third people were the Ju:kcum,[d] a kind of Indian.

Really means the first Spaniard to come here, but it is now applied to Indians. Plural, Juchkum.

The fourth that spoke were the Pimas, *Ohtum*.[e] They got cold and were crying, so Siuuhu got a cotton blanket and spread it over them. The next people

---

[d]Ju:kam, sing.; Juckam, pl.; 'Mexican'.
[e]O'odham.

who spoke were the Obniu (the Maricopas and Yumas, those who can understand each other).[3] To the people who spoke Obniu he gave tree bark, that they should make their clothing from. From this time, all those different kinds of talking people would know how to take care of themselves.

This rule was given to the Pimas, that they were the first to learn to lay out their land and plant crops in it, to farm. The farm [sing.] that the Pimas made at that time didn't have ditches. They were raising crops from the rains. So Siuuhu planted some cotton for the Pimas. Song (what the little seed was singing):

Just as today everything says something all the time, the lantern and everything,[4] so the cotton-seed was singing.

> *You have planted me now*
> *And now I am coming up with a load of earth*
> *And I have thrown the earth down*
> *And now I have got blue leaves on*
> *And now I have yellow blossoms.[5]*

The cotton kept growing. Finally it was ripe. The cotton sings another song:

> *Now you are working very nice with me*
> *You are spinning me by a stick.*

When Siuuhu saw that his children were doing pretty well with the cotton, he decided to do more for them. He put out the rule that his children should dream certain signs on how to use their cotton in more ways. Everybody was asleep, and he sang two more songs:

So up to now this same thing was happening, and sometimes dreams come true.

I just now made the world
And in that world I have gotten everybody to sleep
And the breath of man in that darkness
went out with more understanding.

I have made the mountains
And in among those mountains
I have put my people to sleep
And the understanding of those people has gone out
And dwells there.

Juan says that we [archaeologists] probably found some beads here in the ruins.

So a man slept and dreamed that he would make fine cloth. Not all of those people were going to make cloth. Another slept and dreamed that he would be a good hunter. A woman slept and dreamed she was going to make a fine straw mat (of tules, for bedding), and a fine carrying basket. This woman also dreamed that she would be a good picker of all the kinds of fruit that they used at that time for food. Then a man slept and dreamed he would be a good maker of arrowheads. And when the smaller things were made, the beads and so forth, the man and woman planned out and made them.

Everything was finished and was good for man and woman to make a living on. Next Siuuhu rubbed his breast with his hands and brought out two corn seeds and put them in the ground. Song:

This song means that when the wind blows, it is going to bring out clouds.

You look in the fields
And you will see corn coming out

The clouds will bring rain and make the pumpkin grow and get ripe.

These two seeds, corn and pumpkin, that Siuuhu put into the ground are a demonstration of how a man and woman should be tied into marriage together, to bring out children, to increase and multiply.

The leaves are swaying back and forth
Made by the wind.

Second verse:

You look in the fields
And you see the pumpkin is coming out
The leaves of the pumpkin are like clouds
And the decoration on the pumpkin is like decorated
clouds.

Siuuhu's second [corn] song:

(Literal translation of the second corn song)

Which means that, when the corn is ripe, they would use some of it and keep some seed for the next planting season, and the same with the pumpkin.

Hai lo Hya'an, a repeated line in these songs, ends the verses. It means that the proper [Pima] words have been forgotten.

Evening red
Inside is singing
Corn tassels plume
Plume have in his hand
Pointing this way and that way
And singing.

(Free translation)

The sunset is red
And the seeds are gathered together
They will go and plant the seeds again.
This corn has tassels on top
And it is swaying back and forth
And singing
And the blossoms of the pumpkin
Are swaying back and forth
And singing.

The next morning they planted this corn and pumpkin and saw it turned out to be good. The next thing that Siuuhu made was the little Indian white bean. Then he made another kind of bean that they used to call speckled beans (you don't see them anymore now). Corn song:

(Literal translation)

He e yana heo(lt) vava heo(lt)
Is singing
Farms in is singing
This little white beans and the corn are singing
Then the speckled bean and the pumpkin are singing
    together.
Vava heo(lt) *is singing*
Haich e ya.
Ya ee na.

This song sings about corn, pumpkins, little white beans, and speckled beans. Juan doesn't understand some of the words.

Another song:

Hay ee yana heo(lt)
Water breeze come out far away
The breeze runs a long ways
It reaches far away
The corn tassels it breaks to pieces
Haych ee ya ya ee na.

The water clouds come out far away
It came from far away
And reached, pumpkin leaves
It breaks to pieces
Haych ee ya ya ee na.

The [earlier] two songs are called corn songs. The other two that we just sang are called "the kind that goes with rubbing a stick across a basket, basket rubbing song."[6] So that is the four things that Siuuhu made, and that is all, because four is an important number, and everything is made in four and is finished.

Juan said he had never seen what it looks like.

Then the black-eyed peas were made but didn't have any song. The next thing made was some kind of food, called *koff*,[f] that is raised on a farm.

And there were no lies at that time, there was no pride at that time, there was no murder at that time. All the people were loving each other and were doing their work together and helping each other.

All these things were made to be used for food. So one [man] was given this corn and was called the corn man. The next thing made was tobacco (coyote tobacco) that is called in Pima "green tobacco," and it was only for the old people. So it [receiver? plant?] is called the tobacco man. The people learned to use this corn and pumpkin, and they smoked the tobacco. So everything was completed. There was no cruelty for men.

STORY 4

CORN AND TOBACCO LEAVE

It was not their wish to play this game. It was the people's idea.

At a certain time the corn and tobacco met together, and the people decided the corn man and tobacco man should play a game of *gins*.[7] Corn and tobacco believed what the people said, so they started the game.

---

[f]*Kof*, or *ko:f*, nettle leaf goosefoot plant (*Chenopodium murale*), an annual weed actually introduced from Europe (if *murale*; *C. desiccatum* is native—Parker 1972: 104–105) whose seeds can be gathered in early summer, parched, and made into pinole (Russell 1908: 73). The plant grows on moistened, "disturbed" ground in or near fields. It is a semidomesticate. Saxton and Saxton do not list *kof*, *ko:f*, or *ko:w* in their Papago dictionaries, nor does Mathiot list it. Perhaps it is more a Pima than a Papago plant.

They cheated each other. That was the first time that madness [anger] came into the world. Corn spoke up to Tobacco. Corn said, "You are nothing, Tobacco, only the old people smoke you. For my part, men, women, and children eat me. I am raising the young people."

Tobacco said, "I think the same about you. You are nothing, but medicine men smoke me and doctor the people."

So they were talking, which was not right. They felt sorry for the mean words they said, and the people didn't help them out but just let them speak. So the tobacco left and went toward the west. He followed down the river (Gila), and when he got to a certain distance he felt sorry. He cried like this—song:

> *Black bobcat*
> *Toward the sunset*
> *is going*
> Hay ya ha'a hah *(crying)*.

This [last phrase] has no meaning. It is just the way his mind went when he was sad.[8]

He went and stopped at the west part of the Navajo country. Corn stayed here for four days, waiting for the older people to bring him soft feathers and beads, so he would not have to leave the country. The people didn't give him what he needed, so he sang this song:

> *I deep beat (deep win)*
> *Tobacco was mad*

And was talking.
The people, they will get [aɂ] soft feather
And give it to me
The people will get a bead
And give it to me.

So he went out, toward the east. He got all the corn that the people had and took it with him, and the people were hungry. The old people were also scarce in tobacco.

When Siuuhu saw this, he didn't like it. The people had learned how to get mad, and Siuuhu made a rule that every morning the old people were to talk to their young children and tell them what was right to do.

When the people wanted something to smoke really badly, they got a man to go after Tobacco and bring him back home. This man went and tried to tell him to come back, but Tobacco said he doesn't want to come back. He said, "Corn called me some mean things so I don't want to go back." The man prayed to Tobacco and said Tobacco should sympathize with him and go back home.

If anyone wants to know what a man is planting, he won't tell them. If the man tells what he is planting, the tobacco won't come up.
So this man brought the seed home, planted it, and

The tobacco didn't want to come home, but he gave the man one of his little seeds and told him to take the seed with him, prepare the ground, plant the seed, and sometimes the tobacco would come out pretty well and sometimes it won't.

kept it a secret; and it came out and was good tobacco. Today we have that tobacco which is smaller than the one that went to the west and stayed over there.

The corn that went toward the east stopped there and sang two songs:

The big corn stalks
They called me corn
I have come out here.

My stalks are stout
And are standing straight up
My fruit is [are?] stout
And are standing straight up.

So the people were hungry here.

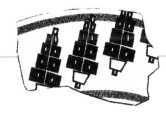

STORY 5

CORN RETURNS

East of Santa Cruz, signs of a ruin.

Just southwest of here are signs of where people used to live, at the place called *top-oiduk*,[g] or rabbit farm.

The reason why they called it top-oiduk is that there used to be a lot of rabbits there. When the people planted their crops, the rabbits would eat it all up.

From there one woman went to Superstition Mountain [40 miles eastward], gathered some [cholla] cactus fruit, and baked them in ashes, because they

---

[g]To:bi Oidag, 'Rabbit Field'.

were hungry. While the corn was standing in the east,[9] he saw what the woman was doing. The woman happened to be a young girl, very pretty, so the corn loved the girl and came toward her.

He came to a mountain, called Vatcum (means a hole)[10] at a certain place in the east, and at the base of the mountain he sang this song:

> *I have gone*
> *I am going*
> *And now I am passing by Vatcum*
> *Flat-headed (corn, me)*
> *Little bit crazy (I am).*

This refers to freak corn with a flattened end.

Then he came to another mountain called White-thin and sang:

> *I am passing by White-thin (Stoa Kom)*[11]
> *Flat-headed (corn)*
> *(I am) little bit crazy,* chupa[h] *(like a woman).*

There is a word for a little bit crazy applied to a man and another word as applied to a woman. He uses the word applied to a woman.

As he gets closer to the woman he sings this song:

> *I went and met a girl*
> *I ran and met this girl*
> *A cliff which decorated itself very pretty*
> *I'm getting closer to top-oiduk*
> Hay do way ha'an.[12]

Cliff is a symbol of the minds coming together. The girl wants a man, and corn wants a woman. It means he is going through rocky country and everything was pretty, just like when one goes to meet a woman. *Chupa* is applied to a woman who swears and smokes and goes with bad boys, a little but not much.

So this corn man went and came to the girl's home and stayed with her for one day. He told the girl that

---

[h]*Ce:pa'owi*, 'prostitute', 'whore'.

his head felt itchy, so she looked for something in the corn man's hair and took out a worm. She put it in her mouth and chewed it up. The corn man was also decorated. When his clothes peeled off the front of his chest, he appeared to have kernels of corn on himself.

When the sun was about to set, he went out of the house with one of his arrows and stuck it in some cactus fruit that had been cooked. When they took this cactus fruit out [from the pit in which it had been cooked], it appeared that it wasn't cactus fruit but pumpkin and corn. The girl got this changed food and went away. She was glad and sang two songs:

> You have made a woman out of me
> And you have made a basket for me
> Which is made of corn tassels.
>
> You have made a woman out of me
> And you have made a basket for me
> Which is made of pumpkin blossoms.

The girl went to where her parents were and gave them the pumpkin and corn, and they ate it. This happened four times. She went back to where the corn man was and got the same thing from him four times.

The fourth time the corn man talked to her and told her that when she got back to her people, she could talk to them and tell them to make a special house for him to live in. He was going to live with the people. He also told her to tell them to clean up their houses and get everything ready, such as dishes and pots, and they must turn them [face] up.

When the fourth day was up, the corn man went. As he started he sang two songs:

> *Toward the west*
> *Closer to the setting of the sun*
> *Where is much understanding*
> *To this land I come*
> *And over this land*
> *It is raining corn.*

> *Toward the west*
> *Close to the setting of the sun*
> *There lies some land*
> *Over this land*
> *The clouds are roaring*
> *And it's raining pumpkins*
> *Over this land.*

When Corn got to the land that he mentioned, just to give you an idea how he got [what he did] there, it [he] came like hail, it rained corn, it rained pumpkins in every dish, and it filled everything that they had turned up. When Corn got there, he went into the house that the people had made for him, and the girl that he had met came and lived with him.

When some people saw this thing happen, they couldn't believe that it was really corn and pumpkins. When Corn found this out, he sang two songs:

It is true that I am Corn
And you see that I have white kernels.

It is true that I am the Pumpkin
With white seeds.

When the people prepared and ate it, they were filled. They gathered it and stored it away for their food.

All this time the worm that the girl chewed had turned into a baby in the girl's womb. The girl stayed with the corn man four times four days. When the fourth fourth day was up, the baby was born. It was the child of corn man and was a girl.

When Siuuhu saw this, he didn't like it. The baby was taken care of for four days. Then the girl picked it up in her arms, to take it someplace. On the way, somehow she dropped it and the baby died. It was Siuuhu's scheme that this should happen. When the corn saw it, he got mad and went off to the east. This was the first time the people saw death.

What Siuuhu meant was that human beings were made of earth. Whenever a human dies, it goes back to earth, and the bones also turn back to earth again. The life of a dead person,

The elder people, who were called wise men, went to Siuuhu and asked where the life of the child went to. Siuuhu said that out in the desert there is a mountain which is tossed back and forth by the wind. The wise people asked what he meant by after it leaves the body, should go to the east where land was prepared for the spirit. The land was called Paradise, and everything is blooming prettily. When the spirit gets to that land, it should receive "good air" (fragrance) and should be happy with the people already over there. Life when it gets there will never be thirsty or hungry. This is only meant for Pima and Papago Indians, not any other kind of people.

that. Siuuhu told them that he explained this to them because what happened to Corn and the girl was not right.

The next question that the people asked Siuuhu was, what was going to happen to that life [after death] in the future. Siuuhu told them it is not man's purpose to know what those lives were going to do, but it is Jeoss's business to know what he wants to do with them.

The people asked what was going to happen here, on earth. Siuuhu told them that in the earth there are four kinds of water with which the world will burn up with fire. The people asked him a stronger question, how the people would know when this thing [burning] was to come to pass. The reason they asked these questions was that they wanted more understanding, or to be more powerful, than Siuuhu.

So from that time until now, when a child gets cross or mad, you give him some sweet things, and he'll be all right.

Siuuhu told them that at this time they have one song, and when the end is near there will be all sorts of people dreaming all sorts of songs about birds and animals and everything. Also, when the time is coming, young men will grow old in a short time, and a young woman will grow old in a very short time. He also made a statement about the corn. When the time is near, they will plant corn and sometimes it will fail, and with the corn will come up all kinds of weeds. At that time, man must work hard to get a good crop from that corn. He must clean the weeds and cultivate it to get a good crop. Then Siuuhu made a bitter pumpkin, and he told them that this would be a sign of what had happened, that corn's baby had died. It was right here, then, that Siuuhu made watermelons and musk melons. When he gave these melons to the people, they stopped being mad and were all right again.

Then Siuuhu made four commandments by which people should unite in marriage—not like corn did. The four commandments are that the father of the girl and mother of the girl should agree, and the mother of the boy and father of the boy should agree, which makes four commandments by which they should be married.

From then until now, when a person should die, the people should bury him in the ground. So the people were getting along nicely.

SUPPLEMENT

THE STORY OF CORN AND TOBACCO (THIN LEATHER)

There was a powerful mahkai [medicine man] who had a daughter, who, though old enough, was unmarried and who grew tired of her single life and asked her father to bury her, saying, we will see then if the men will care for me. And from her grave grew the plant tobacco, and her father took it and smoked it, and when the people who were gathered together smelled it, they wondered what it was and sent Toehahvs [Coyote] to find out.

Although the tobacco still grew, the woman came back to life and came out of her grave back to her home. One day she played gainskoot [gins, a dice game] with Corn, and Corn beat her and won all she had. But she gave some little things she didn't care for to Corn, and the rest of her debt she did not pay, and they quarreled.

She told Corn to go away, saying, "Nobody cares for you, now, but they care a great deal for me, and the doctors use me to make rain, and when they have moistened the ground is the only time you can come out." And Corn said, "You don't know how much the people like me; the old as well as the young eat me, and I don't think there is a person that does not like me." And Corn told Tobacco to go away herself.

There were people who heard them quarreling, and although Tobacco stayed on, whenever she would be in a house and hear people laughing, she would think they were laughing at her. She became very sad and one day sank down in her house and went westward and came to a house there.

A person who lived there told her where to sleep, saying, "Many people stop here and that is where they sleep." But she said, "I am traveling, and no one knows where I am, and if anyone follows me and comes here, you tell them that you saw me, that I left very early in the morning and you do not know which way I went." And she told him she did not know herself which way she would go, and at night, when she went to bed, she brought a strong wind. When she wanted to leave, she sank down and went westward, and the wind blew away all her tracks. She came to the Mojaves [Indians along the Colorado River] and lived there in a high mountain, Cheof Toe-ahk,[i] or tall mountain, which was a cliff, very hard to climb, and Tobacco stood up there.

After Tobacco had gone, Corn remained, but when corn-planting time came, none was planted because there was no rain. So it went on all summer, and people began to say, "It is so. When Tobacco was here we had plenty of rain, and now we don't have any, and she must have had wonderful power." The people scolded Corn for sending Tobacco away and told him to go away himself. Then they sent for Tobacco to come back, that they might have rain again.

Corn left, going toward the east, singing all the way, taking Pumpkin with him, who was singing too, saying they were going where there was plenty of moisture.

---

[i] Cew Duag, 'Tall [or long] Mountain'.

The next year there was no water, and a powerful doctor, Gee-hee-sop,[i] took the Doctor's Stone [divining quartz crystal] of Light and the Doctor's Square Stone [possibly a flat slate], some soft [down] feathers, some eagle tail feathers, and went to where Tobacco lived, asking her to come back, saying, "We're all suffering for water, and we know you have power to make it rain. Every seed buried in the ground is begging for water and is likely to be burned up, and every tree is suffering, and I want you to come home."

The Tobacco said, "What has become of Corn? He is still with you, and corn is what you ought to eat, and everybody likes it; but nobody cares for me, and I don't want to go back, and I'm not going." But Geeheesop said, "Corn is not here now, he has gone away, and we do not know where he is." And again he asked Tobacco to come back, but she refused. But she gave him four balls of tobacco seed and said to him, "Take these home with you, and take the dirt of the tobacco-worm, and roll it up, and put it in a cane tube and smoke it all around, and you will have rain, and then plant the seed, and in four days it will come up. When you get the leaves, smoke them, and

---

[i]Gi:supi, 'Black phoebe bird', *Sayoris nigricans* (Saxton, Saxton, and Enos 1983: 167). Saxton and Saxton (1969: 167) spell this bird name as *gi:soki*, and at that time they identified it as a large hummingbird. No doubt, the later 1983 spelling and identification are corrections. These "flycatcher"-type (at least to Americans) birds always live near water. They make their nests from leaves mixed with mud (Peterson 1961: 182).

call on the winds, and you will have clouds and plenty of rain."

So Geeheesop went home with the seed balls and tobacco-worm dirt and did as Tobacco had told him; and the smoking of the dirt brought rain, and the seeds were planted in a secret place and in four days came up and grew for a while but finally were about to die for want of rain. Then Geeheesop got some of the leaves and smoked them, and the wind blew, and rain came, and the plants revived and grew till they were ripe.

When the tobacco was ripe, Geeheesop gathered a lot of the leaves and filled with them one of the gourdlike nests which the woodpecker, *koh-daht*,[k] makes in the *har-san* [*haṣañ*], or giant cactus, and took a few of these and put them in a cane-tube pipe, or watch-kee [*uacki*], and went to where the people gathered in the evening.

The doctor who was the father of Tobacco said, "What's this I smell? There is something new here!" And one [person] said, "Perhaps it is some greens that I ate today that you smell," and he breathed toward him. But the mahkai [doctor] said, "This is not it." And the others breathed toward him, but he could not smell it. Then Geeheesop rolled a coal toward himself and lit up his pipe [not previously lit], and the doctor said, "This is what I smelled!"

---

[k]Might be *hokkaḍ*, 'cactus-wren' (*Heleodytes brunneicapillus*).

Geeheesop, after smoking a few whiffs, passed the pipe around to the others, and all smoked it. When it came back to him he stuck it in the ground.

The next night he came with a new pipe to the place of the meeting, but the father of Tobacco said, "Last night I had a smoke, but I did not feel good after it. The man who had eaten the greens kah-tee-gum[1] the day before said, "He does not mean that he didn't enjoy the smoke, but something else troubled him after it, and I think it was that when we passed the pipe around we didn't say 'My relatives,' 'brother' or 'cousin' or whatever it was but passed it quietly without using any [relationship] names."

And Tobacco's father said, "Yes, that is what I mean." . . . So Geeheesop lit his pipe again and passed it around in the way to satisfy the doctor. The people saved the seeds of that tobacco, and today it is all over the land.[13]

Corn and Pumpkin had gone east, and for many years they lived there, and the people they had left had no corn and no pumpkins. After a while, they returned of themselves, and came first to the moun-

---

[1]Sounds like what I would spell as *kadigam*. In story 6, "The Whore," Hayden spells what is undoubtedly the same word as "Cadigum." Here in this text the word is apparently taken as the name of a plant with fragrant leaves, but Hayden was told it is the name of a kind of bird unfamiliar to Smith and Allison. I have not found anyone who knows the word, so I cannot confirm either interpretation. The word does not sound particularly Pima-Papago and may be adapted from another Indian language. In any case, it seems to be obscure.

tain Tahtkum[m] and lived there a while and then crossed the [Gila] river and lived near Blackwater, at a place called Toeahk-Comalk,[n] or White Thin Mountain, and from there went to Gahkotekih[o] or, as it is now called, Superstition Mountain.

While they lived at Gahkotekih, there was a woman living near there at a place called Kawt-kee oy-ee-duck[p] who, with her younger brother, went to Gah-kotekih to gather and roast white [probably cholla] cactus, and while they were doing this, Corn saw them from the mountain and came down. The boy saw him and said, "I think that is my uncle coming," but his sister said, "It cannot be, for he is too far away. If he were here, the people would not be starving now."

But the boy was right, and it was his uncle, and Corn came to them and stayed while the cactus was baking. After a while, as he sat aside, he would shoot an arrow up into the air, and it would fall whirling where the cooking was, and he would go and pick it up. Finally he said to the woman, "Would you not better uncover the corn and see if it is cooked yet?" She said, "It's not corn, it's cactus."

Again . . . he said, "Would you not better uncover the pumpkin and see if it is cooked yet?" She replied,

---

[m]Ta:tkam, 'Feeler', a mountain east of Eloy, Ariz. See note 9.
[n]Toa Komalk, 'White Thin'.
[o]Gakoḍk, 'Bent'.
[p]Probably Kokotk Oidag, 'Seashell Field'—To:bi [Rabbit] Field in Smith-Allison.

"It's not pumpkin we are baking, it's cactus." Finally he said, "Well, uncover it anyway," and she uncovered it and there were corn and pumpkin there, . . . nicely mixed and cut. . . . Then he asked about the Tobacco woman, if she were married yet, and she said, "No, she is not married, but she is back with us again now."

Then he asked her to send the boy ahead to tell the people that Corn was coming to live with them again. First the boy was to go to the . . . father of Tobacco and see if he and his daughter wanted Corn to return. If they did, he would come, and if they did not, he would stay away. He wanted the boy to come right back and tell the answer that he got.

So the little boy went and took some corn with him to the doctor, and said, "Corn sent me, and he wants your daughter, and he wants to know if you want him. If you do, he will return, but if you do not, he will turn back again. He wants me to bring him word what you say."

The doctor said, "I have nothing to say against him. I guess he knows the people want corn. Go and tell him to come."

And Corn said, "Go back and tell the doctor to make a little house . . . and to cover it with mats instead of bushes, and let Tobacco go there . . . until I come. And tell the people to sweep their houses . . . and if anything in their house is broken, such as pots, . . .

to turn them right side up [outside]. For I am coming back openly. There will be no secret about it."

[So it was done and] before sunset the woman [who met Corn] came home with the corn and pumpkins she had cooked at the mountain, but Corn stayed out until evening. When evening came there was a black cloud where Corn stood, and soon it began to rain corn, and every little bit a big pumpkin would come down bump. It rained corn and pumpkins all night, while Corn and his bride were in their house, and in the morning the people went out and gathered the corn from the swept place around their houses.

. . . So Corn lived there with his wife, and after a while Tobacco had a baby. It was a little crooked-neck pumpkin of the sort that Pimas call dog-pumpkin. When the child had grown a little, one day its father and mother went to work in the garden, and they put the little pumpkin baby behind a mat leaning against the wall. Some children . . . found it there and began to play with it for a doll, carrying it on their backs as they do dolls. Finally they dropped it and broke its neck.

When Corn came back, he found his baby broken and was angry, and left his wife, and went east again, and stayed there a while, then bethought him of his pets the blackbirds, which he had left behind, and came back to his wife again. After a while he went again to the east, taking his pets with him, scattering grains of corn so the blackbirds would follow him. Corn made this speech while he was in the house with Tobacco:

> In the east there is the Tonedum Vahahkkee,[q] the Vahahkkee of Light where lives the great doctor, the kingfisher. And I came to Biveschool,[r] the kingfisher, and asked him for power, and he heard me asking, and flew up on his house, and looked toward the west, and breathed light four times, and flew and breathed again four times, and so on—flying four times and breathing after each flight four times, and then he sat over a place in the ground that was cut open.
>
> And in the west there was a Bluebird, and when I asked him for power he flew up on his house and breathed four times, then flew toward the east, and he and Biveschool met at the middle of the earth.
>
> And Biveschool asked the Bluebird to do some great thing to show his power, and the Bluebird took the blue grains of corn from his breast and

[q]Tondam Wa'aki, 'Shining Great-house'.
[r]Probably *he:wacud*, the "bluejay" according to Saxton, Saxton, and Enos 1983: 20. Saxton and Saxton spelled the word *"he:wasjel"* in 1969 (15) and identified it then as a "large blue bird." Kingfishers (Lloyd's identification) are large blue birds. Smith and Allison refer to this bird in their Whore story. They consider it a bluebird. Hayden spells the name as "her-va-chut."

then planted them, and they grew into beautiful tall corn, so tall that its tops reached the sky and its leaves bowed over and scratched the ground in the wind.

And Biveschool took white seeds from his breast and planted them, and they came up and were beautiful to be seen and came to bear fruit that lay one after another on the vine—these were pumpkins.

And the beautiful boys ran among these plants and learned to shout and learned to whistle, and the beautiful girls ran around these plants and learned to whistle.

And the relatives heard of these good years and the plenty to eat, and there came a relative leading her child by the hand, who said, "We will go right on, for our relatives must have plenty to eat, and we shall not always suffer with hunger." So these came, but did not eat it all, but returned. So my relatives, think of this, and we shall not suffer with hunger always.

And Corn made another speech at that time to Tobacco's father:

Doctor! Doctor! Have you seen that this earth that you made is burning? The mountains are crumbling, and all kinds of trees are burning down. And the people over the land, which you have made run around, have forgotten how to shout, and have forgotten how to walk, since the ground is so hot and burning. And the birds, which you have made, have forgotten how to fly, have forgotten how to sing.

And when you found this out you held up the long pinion feathers, mah-cheev-a-duck,⁵ toward the east, and there came the long clouds one after the other.

There in those clouds there were low thunder-ings, and they spread over the earth and watered all the plants and the roots of all the trees; and everything was different from what it had been.

Every low place and every valley was crooked, but the force of the waters straightened them out, and there was driftwood on all the shores: and after it was over every low place and every valley had foam in its mouth.

And in the mouth stood the Doctor, and [he] took the grains from his breast and planted them, and the corn grew and was beautiful. And he went on further, to another low valley,

---

⁵*Ma:cwidag*, literally "learning-thing" [for medicine men], the long wing or tail feathers primarily of eagles, perhaps also of owls, hawks, and buz-zards. The feathers, usually two, always of the same species, are mounted with their bottoms lashed together, so that they curve apart to form a "Y." Medicine men fan things with them.

and planted other seeds, and the pumpkin grew
and was beautiful.

And its vine to the west was black and zigzag
in form, and to the south was blue and zigzag
in form, and to the east was white and zigzag
in form, and to the north was yellow and zigzag in form.

So everything came up, and there was plenty
to eat, and the people gathered it up, and the
young boys and girls ate and were happy, and
the old men and the old women ate and length-
ened even their few days. So think of this, my
relatives, and know that we are not to suffer
with hunger always.

And the Dog-Pumpkin Baby lay there broken, after
Corn went away, but after a while [the baby] sank
down and went to Gahkotekih and grew up there
and became the Harsan, or Giant Cactus.

The mother and grandfather could not find the Dog-
Pumpkin Baby and called the people together, and
Toehahvs [Coyote] was asked to find it, and he
smelled around where it had been and went around
in circles.

And he came to where the Giant Cactus was and
thought it was the baby but was not sure, and so he
came back and told them he could not find it. They
wanted Nooee [Buzzard] to go, and Toehahvs said to

Nooee, "I did see something, but I was not quite sure, but I want you to examine that Giant Cactus."

So Nooee flew around and around and examined the Giant Cactus and came back, and when the people questioned him he said, "I have found it and it is already full-grown, and I tell you I think something good will happen because of it."

When the cactus had fruit the people gathered it and made tis-win [local Spanish name for cactus wine and other kinds of homebrew] and took the seeds and spread them out in the sun. And Badger stole these seeds, and when the people knew it they sent Toehahvs after the thief.

Toehahvs went and saw Badger ahead of him in the road, and he saw him go out and around and come into the road again and come toward him. When they met, Toehahvs asked him what he had in his hand, and Badger said, "I have something, but I'm not going to show you." Then Toehahvs said, "If you'll only just open your hand so I can see, I'll be satisfied." Badger opened his hand and Toehahvs hit it with a slap from below and knocked the seeds all around, and that is why the giant cactus is so scattered. (Lloyd 1911: 217–230)

SUPPLEMENT

HOW MORNING
GREEN LOST
HIS POWER
OVER THE
WINDS AND
THE RAIN
GODS (THIN
LEATHER)

Morning Green [mythic successor to Siba] is reputed to have had special magic power over two supernatural beings known as Wind-man and Rain-man. It happened at one time that many people were playing a game with canes in the main plaza of Morning Green's settlement (Casa Grande), on the south side of the compound; among these were Rain-man and Wind-man. The latter laid a wager that if he lost, his opponent should look on the charms of a certain maid. When Wind-man lost, in revenge he sent a great wind that blew aside her blanket, at which indignity she cried and complained of Wind-man to Morning Green, who was so angry that he made Rain-man blind, obliging him to be led about by his servant, the wind; and he also banished both from Casa Grande. They went to the San Bernardino Mountains in what is now California and lived at Eagle Mountain, near the present town of Wadsworth, where as a consequence it rains continuously.

After the banishment of these two the rain ceased at Casa Grande for four years, and Morning Green sent Hummingbird to the mountains where Wind-man and Rain-man resided. Hummingbird carried with him a white feather, which he held aloft to detect the presence of the wind. Three times he tried to discover Wind-man by the movement of this feather but was not successful. When at last Hummingbird came to a place where there was much green grass, he again held up the feather to see whether it showed any movement of air. It responded by indicating a slight wind, and later he came to the spot where Wind-man and Rain-man were but found them asleep.

Hummingbird dropped a little medicine on the breasts of Wind-man and Rain-man, which caused them after a time to move and later to awake. When they had risen from their sleep, Hummingbird informed them that Morning Green had sent him to ask them to return and again take up their abode with him at Casa Grande. Rain-man, who had no desire to return, answered, "Why did Morning Green send us away?" and Wind-man said, "Return to Morning Green and tell him to cut off his daughter's hair and make from it a rope. Bring the rope to me and I will tie it about my loins, that Rain-man, who is blind, can catch hold of it while I am leading him. But advise all in Casa Grande to take precaution to repair the roofs of their houses so they will not leak, for when we arrive it will rain violently." Hummingbird delivered the message to the chief of Casa Grande and later brought back the twisted rope of human hair. Wind-man and Rain-man had barely started for Casa Grande when it began to rain, and for four days the downpour was so great that every roof leaked. Morning Green vainly used all his power to stop the rain, but the magic availed him but little. (Fewkes 1912: 47–48)

THIS IS THE STORY of a footloose woman. It is largely self-explanatory. Beyond its general continuity with the marital theme of the previous part, there is a particular shared item to point out. The name given for the woman's second father-in-law (who appropriates the woman for himself on her humbled return) is Cadigum. Smith and Allison thought this was the name of a bird, but they did not know which bird. Thin Leather gave what is undoubtedly the same name either for a village companion (co-resident, not the same family) of the father of the girl Tobacco or for a fragrant leafy green that the companion had eaten. Both references are very ambiguous; Cadigum is a hazy word and thing.

No matter. The occurrence of the word links the two myths. I know of no other version of this "Whore" myth. It seems unique to Smith's mythology, which brings us to my second point. There is no doubt that as a preacher, Allison was interested in family morality, specifically, in everyday domestic wickedness. This myth shows that Smith shared that interest. Allison obviously did not create it. Neither, probably, did Smith, at least not altogether. The myth's serial position next to the corn myths, its sharing the obscure "Cadigum" name with a Thin Leather corn myth, and its subject matter of a woman's flight from farming give it good Pima credentials. To revert to our earlier discussion, this myth is two steps past the dreadful creation through the penis and one step past the farming-and-family origin tales. This step takes us to a world of accomplished farming and supposedly normal family life. Note in this regard that while the woman hero is terrible at the beginning of the story, she becomes proper at the end, *except* that her erstwhile father-in-law has improperly taken up with her. In this myth Smith and Allison give us something quite close to an American soap opera or *Confession* magazine story, which in my opinion is not a criticism. If this is a folk soap opera, born of Pimas in Pima, more power to it and the tribe.

STORY 6

THE WHORE

From then the wickedness of the Apaches became stronger, and the time came that the Pimas were fighting them. They were fighting and killing each other. As you know, the Apaches were older than the Pimas, but they were stupid. The Pimas were wiser and always succeeded in killing them.[1]

The people were getting along nicely. The Apaches went to the mountains and made their homes there, from where they came here and robbed the people.

The Apaches made bows and arrows from reeds. The Pimas also made bows and shields and tomahawks and made arrows from arrow reeds. When Siuuhu saw that these people were fighting, he saw that in the future the Pimas and Apaches would become friends. When the Pimas heard this, they didn't believe it because they felt in their hearts that they were very mad and would never stop fighting.

So these people lived here, and one time something evil happened through an old woman. She was very proud. One time when she was going after firewood with some other women, she made a lie to them. That was the first time that pride came to them and the first lie that happened.

While the women were returning home, they talked about a certain girl who lived someplace and had no husband. They talked about who was going to marry that girl. The old woman told the other women that she had a son who was in love with the girl and that he was going to marry her, which wasn't true.

When the old woman got back home, she told her son to go and meet the girl at some place where there was water, where the girl came to bathe every day. He would meet her there and talk to her. The boy went and met the girl and tried to talk to her, but she wouldn't talk. So the boy went home sorry because he couldn't make the girl talk. He didn't eat anything because he was so sorry, and he wouldn't drink any water.

The old woman was thinking about her boy all the time. She tried to plan to do something to her boy because she knew she had lied to those people. Finally this was her plan. She would go to a very respected person, who knew very much, and that person could take her son and lead him and go to the girl's house and talk with her parents about the boy marrying the girl.

That man went with the boy and talked to the girl's parents. Finally her father decided to let her marry the boy, and the mother agreed that it was all right. Here is the name for the girl, By-av-chu-luv,[a] which

---

[a] Ba'i-cuklim, 'Throat-black', the black-throated desert sparrow (*Zonotrichia querula*)—Saxton, Saxton, and Enos 1983: 5. (Saxton and Saxton [1969] define this bird name as "small black bird," 3, and "unidentified," 167). Smith does *not* seem to have the same bird in mind, and his description baffles me because I think the name literally means "throat-black."

means a certain bird, something like a quail, with a crest, dark blue with a white collar.

This By-av-chu-luv didn't like the young man, but at that time the rule was that children should obey their parents. So if her father and mother agreed, she'd have to do it. When everything was all fixed, the man laid down with the girl, but some time in the night the girl left and went away.

When the girl left her house, she came this way [toward Snaketown], west. This [departure] happened just east of the San Tan Mountains at a place the Pimas call today Two Tanks (*Gok Wapchki*).[b] The girl passed through the town there, but she didn't stop. She passed through Showing River (*Mas Akimo*)[c] and went down to the west to a place they call Mounds of Sand (*Yea Huk*).[d] There lived a man with a son whom the young girl liked. The man's name was Cadigum,[e] a bird's name. The girl married the son, that she loved.

When this happened, it was a great sin because they had broken the four commandments. We have found that if we are proud, then jealous things like that will happen. This boy had gone home and told his parents that he was married. Siuuhu put fear in all animals, such as deer and rabbits and other food animals, so that man would have to work hard. He also

Well, back at Two Tanks, when the girl's mother found her daughter was gone, she told the boy, or

---

[b]Go:k Wapcki, 'Two Tanks' (or 'Reservoirs', 'Ponds'). I have heard other narrators call a mythical place in this region 'Two Ponds' (Go:k Wo'o). They consider it to be the place where a man was turned into an eagle (Smith-Allison story 10).

[c]Ma:s Akimel, 'Showing River'.

[d]*Hia*, 'sand', and an unknown word.

[e]This might be Kuhigam, identified by Saxton and Saxton (1969: 27) as a "black bird species" and on p. 167 of the same dictionary as "unidentified." The name would seem to mean "neigher," "one who neighs (like a horse)," or "crows," "caws," or "screeches." (All those are meanings of the stem *kuhu*). Alternatively, as discussed in the introduction to this part and in a note to the previous one, the word may not be a bird name at all but the name of a leafy plant.

made it hard for medicine men to bring down rain. And he made a rule that parents must teach children right and wrong and teach them not to show off and lie.

the husband, to stay until morning. She thought the girl had just gone out to visit friends and would come back.

The girl's mother went to search for the girl but couldn't find her. She followed her tracks through Snaketown.[2] She followed her hard because she intended to make her return to her first husband. She got close to where the girl was and saw her grinding corn. She thought she would get her back home immediately, but when she got to the [current husband's] house, the [current] boy's mother said she would give her corn and pumpkins. She took those gifts and went home. Once home, she knew her daughter had done wrong in acting secretly.

Noda is a word for a parent pleased over love of a son.[f]

The first husband went home and told his parents that he was married. His mother was happy and cleaned the house well. His father, Noda, went hunting deer.

The father didn't know of the desertion. He found deer tracks, followed them for a day, made camp, and sang:

> *Grey coyote is going to make a grey deer*
> *And is going to put it in a cliff.*

The next day he followed the tracks and made camp that night and made this song:

---

[f]The word is probably *noḍag*, 'dizzy', 'crazy'. If so, this is not a praise-worthy pleasure but is excessive and lacking in restraint and overly proud. In using this word, Smith is criticizing the man.

Yellow Buzzard is a medicine man
Who came here.
I am going to suffer much
I am going to cover all the earth.

He had to get the deer. Next day he went on, made camp, and sang a song that is now forgotten.

The next day the same, with this song:

In the morning
I am going to find the deer
And in the cliff
The deer will make a noise
And come out.

The next morning he did find a deer and killed him with an arrow. He carried the deer on his shoulder to his daughter-in-law's house, where the girl's mother was afraid to tell of her daughter's unfaithfulness and ashamed of her wickedness. So she told some neighbors to tell him and to ask him to take back the meat because she could not eat it. The neighbors did this, and the boy's mother came to take the meat away. The boy's parents were very sad and couldn't eat the meat. They took it to a place where there were many ants and left it there. The ants ate it.

Meanwhile the girl saw that her new father-in-law went out early in the morning and talked [to the village]. The girl was happy because the fields were full of corn and watermelons. The father-in-law told the people always to plant plenty of corn, pumpkins, watermelons, and Indian beans. The girl thought she would live here always and sang:

> *Cadigum man goes out*
> *And sends his breath in all directions.*
> *His breath seems like green wind*
> *Which is corn.*[3]

(Second verse cut in half)

> *His breath seems like green weeds*
> *Which is pumpkins.*

The girl lived there but came to Showing River (*mas akimo*) [*Ma:s akimel*] to get cooking water. A man from a ruin east of Showing River also went to where the girl got her water. His name was Her-va-chut (Bluebird).[8] He waited at the river for the girl to come. When she didn't come for a long time, he made a blue light and sent it to the girl's home. She was there making baskets.

When she saw Blue Light it pleased her. Blue Light left and started back, and the girl took a pot and followed. When she got to the river, she saw the man who was very beautiful. The girl spoke first and asked what he was doing there. He said he just wanted to see her because, "When you were living

---

[8]*He:wacud*, 'bluejay' (Saxton, Saxton, and Enos 1983: 20). See note 1, part 3, pertaining to Thin Leather's Corn and Tobacco story.

at your old home, I sometimes saw you and was very happy." She said, "That is true, for sometimes I think about you." And he said, "Well, it is all right then, leave your water pot and come to my home."

The girl obeyed. They started and did not go straight but stopped at some place and sat down. When night came they got up and started on to his home. While they walked the girl sang:

Means she was thinking of fear in the future.

Byavchuluv [the girl's name] have [has?] made
  darkness
To fall around
In which with superstitious thoughts
I am getting farther away.

Means the girl must be bad. She knows she is doing wrong. These songs tell whoever hears them that she is doing something too dirty to mention.

Byavchuluv have made the darkness
To fall all around
I am a little bit "nodag"[h]
Getting farther away.

The girl went to live with Hervachut and saw that he was lazy. When she saw this she sang two songs:

Means that Hervachut saw wind in the corn and knew that it was easy to raise corn but would not do it.

The blue Hervachut
Is lying down on top of the winds
And is shaking himself.
Look and see
That the corn tassels are tossed
By the wind.

------

[h]*Nodag*, 'dizzy', 'crazy'.

The blue Hervachut is lying down
On top of the water.
Look and see.
The pumpkin blossoms are shaking
Which is made by the clouds.

The girl ran away from Bluebird and went with another man named Ho-ho-ki-muld (Butterfly).[i] Butterfly asked the girl to marry and live with him. He said he had a farm with much corn and pumpkins, so it was hard for a woman to work there. She went with him and saw that what he said of the farm was true. Butterfly had the kind of farm known in those days as Vapik-oiduk, which meant land with underground moisture. Everything was planted in this wet land. When the girl saw this she sang:

Butterfly has a farm
Which is in a sacred place.
In that farm grows the corn
And there is too much work
For a woman.[4]

(Second verse cut in half)

Where the pumpkin grows which
Is too much work
For a woman to do.

Now we are to find why this woman got into all this trouble. Sin got into her, and it was a demonstration of what the woman is, and she was going to be a sinful woman, and she taught

So this woman went on, leaving Butterfly, and went toward the east, teaching all women wicked ways.

---

[i] *Hohokimal*, 'butterfly'.

every woman to go after her ways. So the same thing was put on man, too. For people to talk about a woman is just as much a sin for one sex as the other. (Sinful to talk of woman's sins.) Thus it is today. A woman with everything, like a home and children, will often leave to look for some better place.

The people in the east, Si-u-dom and Ka-voa-lim,[5] went all over the world teaching sin to all people.

This girl went to the east, then she returned to the west to some people that we call *Naksert*, the Mojave Indians. When the girl got to those people we call Naksert (scorpion),[j] while this [other, second father-in-law] man was living some place, we call [him?] Cadigum, he [Cadigum or his son] was thinking that the girl would come back to him. Then the girl remembered that one time she had a nice home, and she thought that some time she might go back to that home.

So she returned back, got in a certain distance, and saw one end of the mountain Komatke (Estrellas)[k] in the distance. When she saw this, she was happy and sang:

> *Before the Pimas called these mountains Komatke*
> *The old-timers called it Old Man mountains*
> *Below these mountains are fields that are green all*
> *   over*
> *Here's where this By-av-chu-luv [said to be the girl's*
> *   name] owns some fields.*
> *In those fields you see the corn tassels which shine*
> *And among those tassels*
> *You hear women laughing.*[6]

---

[j]*Nakṣal*, 'scorpion'.

[k]*Komaḍk*, 'broad', 'spread out'. This mountain is called "Estrella," the Spanish word for "star," in English. Pimas do not call it "Hu:'u," which is their word for "star."

She kept coming, and just before sundown she came to the home of Cadigum. When the Cadigum man saw all that had happened, he didn't believe it was true. When the woman found out what Cadigum was thinking, she sang:

> *I came here*
> *I came here*
> *And you sing unbelievable words*
> *And I'm shaking myself.*

So the father of the young man didn't go to the place where the people go at night to talk over matters. He didn't go for four nights because he liked the woman who came back. Then on the fifth night he went to the meeting, and the first thing he did on reaching the meetinghouse was to go to the wisest medicine man and ask for some tobacco. The medicine man answered, "I [would] have given you all the tobacco you can smoke. Why is it that for four nights you have not come for my tobacco. I know the reason you did not come to see me. It is over a bad girl who you met at your house. That is why you did not come."

The woman [meanwhile] went out and was grinding something. The women who lived around there saw her and asked what this bad woman was grinding. When she heard the other women talking about her, she sang:

What am I grinding (about herself)
I took a seed
And that seed I am grinding (she means the corn).

So from the beginning when the woman committed the first sin where she ran off from her true husband, she set an example for the women today, and that is why it is the duty of other women to talk about her and call her bad names such as that.

When Siuuhu saw this happen, he thought it was a great sin. He made another commandment to the people, and since that time it is the duty of the father and mother to preach every morning to their young men and women, to tell them what is right and wrong. So this woman lived with this man, and she didn't do anything wrong from then on, and she died there.

THERE ARE TWO MYTHS in this part. The first is really an adjunct to the stories on farming and family life. It gives an origin of the cactus wine ceremony, a topic that was treated at the end of the Thin Leather Corn and Tobacco text, above.

The cactus wine ritual is for the purpose of bringing rain. This is best seen in the chanted or orated speeches that are given during the event. Actually the speeches included in the Thin Leather Corn and Tobacco text, although attributed to Corn, are like the ones used at wine ceremonies, or "wine drinks" (*nawait i'ita*), as these events are called in Pima-Papago.[1] Taken together, all these texts, including Thin Leather's Corn speeches, normally dwell first on the obtaining of wind, cloud, rains, and seeds from the inhabitants of distant "great-houses," that is, great-houses at the edges or corners of the universe. Then the typical speech turns to rain and the seeding of the local fields. The seeds grow and prosperity comes. Wine feast speeches sometimes also mention drinking and the subsequent vomiting of cactus wine and the rumbling of people's stomachs and bowels. Thus, the humans act in sympathy with the clouds that they hope to attract.

In their prose narrative and comments, Smith and Allison do not mention the rain-bringing aspect of the wine ceremony. The songs in Smith's story allude to this, but the prose ignores the songs' hints. To Smith and Allison, the ceremony is a misuse of saguaros and an excuse for drunkenness. Siuuhu, they say, did not intend saguaro to be used this way.

The version of the origin of saguaro wine given at the end of part 3, from Thin Leather, does not mention Siuuhu or his equivalent I'itoi. Thin Leather places the origin in the Hohokam era, and if one supposes that Siuuhu was a factor throughout that time, then Siuuhu might have observed this development with dismay. But, in fact, godly dismay over human wickedness is a theme only for Smith and Allison. The other mythologies see Siuuhu as equal to the Hohokam in moral frailty, as we will discover in comparing the accounts of Siuuhu's murder.

The second story, "Origin of Irrigation," is a clear-cut man-over-nature myth. Irrigation obviates rain and therefore would obviate the wine feasts of which Smith and Allison disapprove.[2] The myth begins with a most obscure passage stating that Siuuhu expected a loss of both seawater and rains. The people notice a decrease in the rain, and they start a canal from a point actually a bit to the north of historic Pima territory but a point at which one of the longest of the actual Hohokam canal systems had its tap, into the Salt River. This system carried water as far as twenty miles. Interestingly, this Hohokam system begins at approximately the same place where the water from an immense American-built damming project enters the Phoenix metropolitan area, a place called the Granite Reef Dam. Smith mentions this, implying that the Hohokam preceded the U.S. Corps of Engineers in selecting the ideal spot to bring water into Phoenix.

The text of the myth would gladden an engineer's heart. A series of medicine men try to make water flow through the already dug channel. The first, weak, medicine men fail; the last, most magically potent one, succeeds.

Appended to this part are both the Fewkes and Lloyd versions of Thin Leather's story of the origin of canals. I include both because they are short and difficult of access at present and because the topic of canal building is of some interest. The texts are reassuringly similar, a testimony to Thin Leather, his Pima interpreters, and Fewkes and Lloyd. These versions are generally similar to Smith and Allison. Their differences are four. First, neither version of Thin Leather mentions a canal-building location near Granite Reef Dam, even though Thin Leather refers to a place in that region in other stories ("Feather Braided Chief and the Gambler" and one of his conquest episodes). Second, each Thin Leather version mentions a *pair* of communities where canal projects are undertaken, one where the canal is successful, and another where difficulties similar to those in Smith-Allison are encountered. Third, no distinction is made in these versions between the point where the fields would be watered (no doubt, close to each canal-sponsoring community) and the point where a river would be tapped. In fact, this third matter makes a difference when comparing Thin Leather to Smith-Allison. The first of the Thin Leather communities almost certainly corresponds to today's Pueblo Grande Ruin, in Phoenix, Arizona. It is also certain that this place was watered by a canal that taps into the Salt River only five miles from the site and twenty miles downstream from Granite Reef Dam (Map 2). Thus, the canal system that feeds Pueblo Grande would not be the one referred to by Smith-Allison. The second community is more vaguely located: "near Mesa [Arizona]," says Fewkes's Thin Leather; "on the south side of the Salt River" [which is true of Mesa], says Lloyd's. Any Hohokam community near Mesa would have been served by the canal system originating near Granite Reef Dam, and so this part of Thin Leather's myth is consistent with Smith-Allison. Fourth, both Thin Leather versions differ from Smith-Allison in holding that the final, powerful medicine person is actually a medicine woman, who has to be summoned from far to the west (the oceanside, according to Fewkes); furthermore, the insufficiently powerful medicine men are not ordinary Hohokam according to Thin Leather. Rather, it is Siuuhu who cannot make the canal water flow.

STORY 7

ORIGIN OF CACTUS WINE

After this sin was committed, Siuuhu thought he would make some kind of food for the people that would be delicious and healthy. He picked up a man, gave him some of his power, and ordered him to do

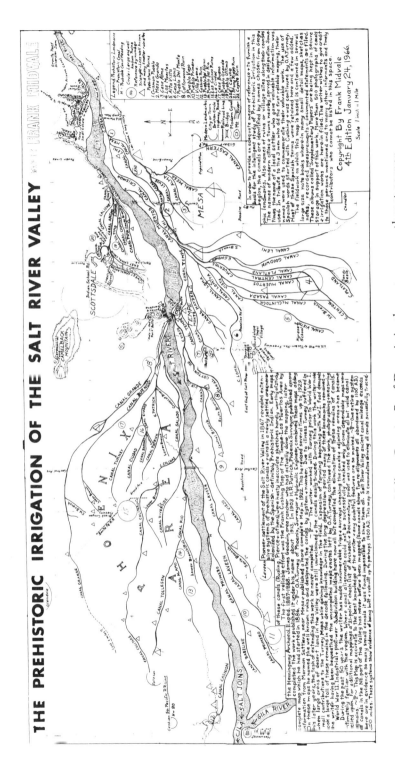

Map 2. Hohokam canals in the Salt River Valley. Granite Reef Dam is in the extreme northeast corner. (Drawn by Frank Midvale, a Phoenix archaeologist)

this thing for him. When the man received the power, he felt proud. He got his brother-in-law and went to the west. When they started to go, they sang:

> I went out
> And I'm sadly going
> Toward the west.
> I'm looking at saguaro blossoms
> And I'm sadly handling the cactus.

He went a little distance, turned back, and started toward the east. In the east, he sang:

> I am going toward the east.
> I am sadly looking at young cactuses,
> With ripe fruit on it.
> I am sadly handling them.

He went just a little ways east. He was making the cactuses, and if anyone goes that way they will see that the cactuses don't extend very far from here to the east.

This means like when a man plants a seed, he takes care of it, keeps it clean, and guards it; and when it comes up a good crop, he is happy.

When the man saw that the cactuses were good, he thought that Siuuhu was very wise. Then he took care of himself for four times four days.

When the cactus fruit was ripe, the man didn't think very right about how he would use the fruit. He made plans to make a wine that would make people drunk. So when the fruit was ripe, they gathered it, made wine, and kept it for four days to ferment.

When it was ready, they called four powerful medicine men to drink the wine. They called the people together and took one of the medicine men and sat him on the north side, another on the west side, another on the south, and another on the east. When the sun was just coming up, two men put some wine in vessels and took it and gave it to the man who was sitting at the east. They gave him four full vessels to drink. When he drank the wine, he felt pretty proud, as though he was the wisest medicine man of any of them. He sang (the "drunkard's song"):

While the man was singing, thinking that he owned all the power that was going out of him and making the earth turn yellow, he forgot that Siuuhu owned this power.

> *Some blooming, blooming wind (like pretty perfumed*
> *   flowers)*
> *I'm sending my wind (power)*
> *I'm making the earth turn yellow.*

Of the two that were distributing the wine, one next went to the north and the other went to the south. The next man to get the wine was the one that was sitting at the north. When this man drank and got drunk, he sang:

> *They have come to their blooming,*
> *Wine,*
> *I drink it and am drunk (noda)*[a]

---

[a]"Dizzy', 'crazy', or 'drunk', but there is another word, *navam*, that only means drunk.

So I am sending out clouds
And everything it's turning green.

The other one who carried the wine, who turned to
the south, gave the wine to the one who was sitting
on the south side. He drank it and sang:

They gave me that red water to drink,
And when I drink it
I am drunk,,
And I am making
Some rainbows.

Both of the two men who were distributing the
wine came to the man sitting on the west side. They
gave him the wine, he drank it, and sang:

You have given me
*Some crazy water (*nodigum schrodek*)*[b]
And you have made me drunk.
This ground is getting damp (he makes rain).

So the four people that
drank this wine, each has
made different things, and
they thought to themselves
that they owned all the
power by themselves to
make them.

All the people got drunk and were running all
around, and it happened that one old man was dead
drunk, was lying down someplace, and they stepped
on his head and smashed it.

The people that did this thing of drinking were three
different kinds, or were related to each other in three
different ways:

---

[b]*Noḑaggam ṣu:dagi,* 'dizzy [crazy, drunk] water'.

1. A-pa-pa-gum,[c] a certain way of calling father, like in English "Daddy," "Papa," etc.,[d]

2. Va-va-gum,[e]

3. O-galt.[3]

These three groups of people were there at the first drinking.

When Siuuhu saw this drinking, he didn't like it. The people did not use the fruit as he had planned for them, as food. So he changed it so it would be ripe only at one season of the year, and he commanded that the cactus would take a long time to grow before it would start giving fruit.

STORY 8

ORIGIN OF IRRIGATION

The reason Siuuhu planned this was that someday in the future the earth was going to be burned up and the water in the sea was going to be dried up.[4]

From then on, old man Siuuhu turned himself into a small child and sat someplace by the seaside. He made a hole there, and he said he was going to bring all the water from the sea and put it in the hole.

[c]*Apapgam*, the "fathers" in a certain clan or sib.
[d]Where in English one says, addressing one's father, "father," "daddy," "pop," etc., in Pima the children of a given clan or sib address their fathers by a "daddy" term specific to that clan; e.g., those of the clan called *apap-gam* address their fathers as "*ñ-apap*" ('my-apap').
[e]*Vavgam*, the fathers of the *vav* clan or sib.

He also told that the rains would not come all over the earth very often, only once in a while. And the crops that people raised would be irrigated evermore by rainwater.

The people saw that the rain wasn't coming down often as it used to, so they gathered to plan how they would make canals in order to irrigate their crops. They finally decided they would make a canal right below "Suik" (Red, the little mountain north of Granite Reef Dam).ᶠ They dug with pointed sticks and used their hands to throw out the dirt.

Being of one mind, they thought they would complete this work, but when they completed it and tried to make water run in it, the water wouldn't run. Seeing this, they got one of the medicine men and asked him to draw water in the canal. He went down and walked there, singing:

> *There lie the ditches*
> *And among them*
> *I am walking.*
> *And among them I am breathing,*
> *Leading the water.*

The water acted like it was going but didn't go. This medicine man couldn't do it. So they got another

---

ᶠS-weg, 'Red', the name of a mountain at that place, which is north of the point where today's highway from Scottsdale to Payson begins to descend to the Verde River.

medicine man, and he went down and stood in the canal and sang:

He sends dust devils in the canal to make the water go.

> *There lie the ditches*
> *And I stood in the midst,*
> *I'm making the winds blow (dust devils)*
> *I'm making the water go.*

The water acted like it was going, but it stopped and turned back to where it started from. This man couldn't do it. So they got another medicine man and told him to try. He sang:

The wind is ruffling the surface, pretty patterned water.

> *By the side of a river*
> *There lies a canal.*
> *In that canal*
> *The water is making signs of pretty decoration.*

This man made the water go, but not enough. They got another medicine man and told him to put some more water in the canal. He went down and stood in the canal and sang:

He pulled a hair from his head, put it in the water, and it moved.

> *There lie the canals*
> *And in the midst of those*
> *I stand*
> *Making water-hair snakes.*

The water flowed some more, and they had plenty of water in the canal. From there on, the people learned how to build canals in order to irrigate their farms.

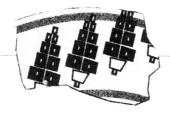

SUPPLEMENT

**ORIGIN OF
IRRIGATION
(THIN LEATHER)**

White Feather and his people lived at a settlement called Sturavik Sivanavaaki[8] near Tempe,[5] the site of which is now a large mound. According to some legends, this chief was the first man who taught the Pimas irrigation, and he showed them also how to plant corn. Through his guidance his people became prosperous, and all the Pima congregated at his settlement to trade.

The people of a settlement near Mesa could not build a canal because the ground in the vicinity was too hard, so they asked Tcuhu [S-e'ehe, Siuuhu] to aid them. He sang magic songs for four days, and at the fourth song the ground softened and the people easily excavated the ditch, but the water would not run in it. Tcuhu found he was powerless to make it do so and advised them to invite Towa Quaatam Ochse,[6] an old woman who lived in the west by the great water, to aid them. She was summoned and sent word to the Mesa people to assemble in their council-house and await her coming. They gathered and awaited her coming, but she did not appear. At night a man passing that way saw her standing at the highest point of the canal blowing "medicine"

[8]S-tua Vi:g Siwañ Wa'aki, 'White Down-feather Chief Great-house'.

along the ditch. Later there came a great wind that dug out a wide channel, and water ran in the canal. The Casa Grande people, it is said, learned the art of irrigating from those living on the site of Tempe, who were taught by Tcuhu. (Fewkes 1912: 51)

And after this [killing of the Witch, the next story in Smith-Allison's sequence] the people had long peace, increased in numbers, and were scattered all around. Some lived where the old vahahkkees [great-houses] now are in the Gila [River] country, and some in the Papago country [desert south of the Gila], and some in the Salt River country [north of the Gila until the two rivers join slightly west of today's Phoenix]. And those who lived where the mound now is between Phoenix and Tempe [probably at Pueblo Grande Ruin] were the first to use a canal to irrigate their land. They raised all kinds of vegetables and had fine crops. And the people of the Gila country and the people of the Salt River country at first did not raise many vegetables, because they did not irrigate, and they used to visit the people who did irrigate and eat with them; but after a while the people who lived on the south side of the Salt River also made a canal, and you can see it to this day.

But when those people tried their canal it did not work. When they dammed the river the water did not run, because the canal was uphill. And they could not make it deeper, because it was all in lime rock. They sent for Ee-ee-toy [Drink-it-all-up, alternative name for Siuuhu] to help them. And Ee-ee-toy had them get stakes of ironwood and sharpen them and all stand in a row with their stakes in their hands at the bottom of the canal. Then Ee-ee-toy sang a song, and at the end of the song the people were all to strike their stakes into the bottom of the canal to make it deeper. But it would not work, it was too hard, and Ee-ee-toy gave it up.

Ee-ee-toy said, "I can do no more, but there is an old woman named Taw-quah-dahm-awks (which means Wampum Eater), and she, though only a woman, is very wise and likely to help you better than I. I advise you to send for her."

The people sent for her and she said, "I will come at once." She came as she had promised, but she didn't go where the people were assembled but went right to the canal. And she had brought a fog with her, and she left the fog at the river, near the mouth of the canal. She went up the course of the canal looking this way and that to see how much uphill it ran.

When she reached where the canal ran uphill, she blew through it the breath which is called *seev-hur-whirl*,[h] which means a bitter wind. This wind tore up the bed of the canal, as deep as was necessary, throwing dirt and rocks out on each side. Then the fog dammed up the river, and the water ran through the canal.

The old woman did not go near the people but went home, and in the morning when one of the people went to see why the old woman did not come, he saw the canal full of water and he yelled for everybody to come and see it. In this way the people got water for their crops and were prosperous as the others below [downstream from][8] them.

---

[h]*Siw Hewel*, 'Bitter Wind'. This wind is an important character in a version of the Feather Braided Chief and the Gambler myth, discussed later.

PLEASE RECALL the instances of women giving birth in the previous myths. There are two, or really a negation of women giving birth and an irregular affirmation. The negation is in the flood myth. A woman thwarts her one-night-stand husband and causes him to give birth. The irregularity is the wife of Corn who gives birth normally but after an irregular impregnation, by eating a worm. The whore has no children; parenting is not the point of that story; footlooseness is.

In fact, nowhere in this mythology will there be an account of a birth by a woman nine months after she has made love with a man. Nor, therefore, will there be a single paternity of the normal sort. Men create people by molding them of earth and in other ways. And furthermore, *only* men do this. The summary for the entire mythology, then, is that women give birth as women normally do, from their wombs through their vaginas, but they do so rarely as far as the narrators are concerned and never following normal lovemaking. Men sometimes make people completely without women, as "creator gods" such as Earth Doctor and Siuuhu; and sometimes they give birth freakishly, like the philanderer; and sometimes they impregnate women abnormally, like Corn.

This does not mean that normal procreation was absent in the times covered by the mythology. It simply means that such procreation is glossed over. Myths, at least these myths, are not about normal procreation.[1] This myth and the next one (part 7) center on abnormal procreation. Here a woman is impregnated by sitting on a ball that has been kicked toward her by a man. In the next part, a man turns into an eagle by drinking a gruel prepared by a woman.

This last is a woman-induced transformation, not the birth or manufacture of creature from scratch.[2]

The witch story is conveniently discussed relative to its core, its preface, and its postscript. The core is the engendering of a monstrous female child, after the child's mother sits on a kickball; the career of that child as a clawed mass stealer and devourer of babies (she was a threat to babies analogous to the threat posed by the philanderer to marriageable girls); and the execution of the monster-witch by first drugging her, then placing her in a cave, and then burning or rather baking her there.

The Smith-Allison text is confined to that core. For comparison I give the Thin Leather version, which has a very similar core and a fairly typical preface and postscript as well. The latter is as follows. After the witch is killed, there is a feast to which a certain old woman and her two grandsons are not invited. Being excluded from the feast, she sends her grandsons to get drops of the blood of the cooked witch (it is not said what was eaten at the feast; presumably, it was not the witch). From this blood she creates parrots. The feasting community wants these parrots so much that they are willing to kill the old woman and her grandsons for them. Therefore, the old woman sends the boys and parrots (the boys' pets) to the east. There the boys release the birds. They return home to find that their grandmother has been killed. They bury her, and tobacco grows from her grave.

Thin Leather's preface also includes parrots, as follows. Morning Green Chief, the ruler of the great-house that Americans call Casa Grande, has a daughter close to whom a lizard falls to earth, apparently from the sky. The fallen lizard becomes turquoise whose mass greatly exceeds the mass of the lizard. These stones are taken up as decorations and adornments by the great-house community. The chief at a neighboring place (not called a great-house, nor was the chief called a sivañ), named Sun Meeter, desires some of the turquoise, so he creates a parrot and sends it to Morning Green's place to swallow as many stones as possible. The parrot returns home filled with turquoise. This loss provokes Morning Green to send rainstorms to douse Sun

Meeter's community. The dousing is not fatal, and the un-defeated Sun Meeter sends a young man with a kickball to impregnate Morning Green's daughter, thus ushering in the core of the story.

We have in these two flanking stories two creations of parrots, one of tobacco, and one of turquoise. And we have a rare extra-body creation, of parrots, by a woman, the grandmother.[3] Let us note some resemblances and opposi-tions among those elements and between them and some other events we have encountered. First, the lizard becom-ing turquoise resembles the flood myth by virtue of green-ness, if we can associate that color with water. In Pima-Papago, blue and green are not distinguished linguistically. Both are *s-cehedag*; and, of course, turquoise is blue-green. Second, the turquoise spreads into the ground where the lizard has struck. Let us say that the lizard-turned-to-turquoise is a flood turned to stone, not a dangerous flood but rather a blessing. Specifically, it is a blessing to Morning Green Chief who, as we note in this story and recall from Font, is the master of Casa Grande (now) Ruin and there-fore a master of rain.

This chief's opposite is Sun Meeter, a creator of parrots. The parrot eats/drinks the turquoise (ingested them to its fill; the text is explicit on this). Concerning the Font text, I speculated that Siuuhu's name "Drink-it-all-up" is solar, and I take this parrot episode as support of that speculation. The sun "drinks" water; when water (or wetness or dew) evaporates, the sun "drinks" it. The parrot does similarly, with the flood-turned-to-stone. That this parrot is green does not cancel its solarity, I submit. There could be a green sun as a kind of limiting or bridging condition between hot light and rain, and indeed I suspect that this is the meaning of Morning Green's name. He approaches sunness from the side of wetness, and the parrot approaches wetness from the side of the sun.[4]

That the postscript parrot is created from blood is also solar if I was correct earlier to align Pima-Papago mythol-ogy with that of the Aztecs (and no doubt others in the New World), which holds that the sun needs to drink warm human blood. Here, then, we seem to have a piece of that broad system, a solar bird that is formed of at least semi-human (monster, witch) blood. The postscript parrots are also released in the east, the direction of the sunrise.

Finally, tobacco. This is a plant whose burning inevitably summons rain. We learned that from the Thin Leather text on Corn and Tobacco. The tobacco woman-god of that text flees to the west, where it is always wet, the opposite of the sun parrots. Thus, one can see a tendency to place moisture in the west and moisture's enemy, the sun, in the east.[5] The problem is why tobacco should originate from a killed and buried woman, young in the story of Corn and Tobacco and old in the Witch story postscript. I praise Thin Leather for stating this origin, but I cannot interpret it.

I cannot explain the female origin of tobacco, but I do see this crop as a step in Pima mythology's progression into the cultural order of things. Thus, we may note that Siba and Morning Green Chief do not need tobacco. In their wet paradise they can have rain whenever they wish. It is only *normal* people who need tobacco since, as story 4 and its variants say, there came a time when the person Tobacco left humanity, whereafter the plant tobacco was needed.

Seen in this light, it is significant that Morning Green Chief's daughter gives birth to a witch, but the witch is not tobacco. The smoke from the witch's burning does not bring rain, nor does the burned or cooked witch's blood produce tobacco; it produces parrots. Tobacco is produced from the killing (we do not know how, bloodlessly or bloody; I imagine bloodlessly) and burial of an entire woman. In sum, I cannot explain why the plant should come from a buried woman, but one can see how that fact articulates with, and enters an opening in the core of, the Witch story.

My guess on why tobacco comes from a woman is that men admire fertile women's menstrual clocks, and they imagine that if tobacco was sprung from a woman, then the tobacco, when smoked (but why smoked?), will bring rain "like clockwork." I do not offer this as a final analysis and cannot prove it.

An additional text, not about the witch, is appended to this part. It is a text on the life and times of Morning Green Chief, the successor of Siba as the master of Casa Grande

and the grandfather of the witch according to Thin Leather.
In this story, the erstwhile commanding chief's women, including his wife, are stolen by a rival chief during a song and
dance festival. The text will come as a relief to those im-
patient with the symbolism just discussed, for this is a
story of earthly politics, Hohokam style. As such, it fits
nicely with the preliminary part of the Witch story, except
where the chiefly politics of that story were over the command of turquoise wealth, here the politics are over
women. In my view, women are no less important than the
other topics. They are what men boast about together
early in the evening, and the "symbols" are what they
awaken with in their minds in the dead of the night.

STORY 9

**HO'OK,
"WITCH"**

That's the way the people made their living for
years. As time went on, a woman lived west from
here [Snaketown or Casa Blanca, Ariz.]. She was a
Mojave [and therefore lived about 180 miles west of
Snaketown]. She was unmarried. Young men tried to
marry her, but she didn't like any of them.

Another man lived [about 15 miles] east from here,
at the San Tan mountains. He was called Yellow
Buzzard (Huamanui),[6] and he had a son. He knew
the woman that was living over there, and he knew
she was hard to marry.

He gave his son some kind of ball, so he would play
with it and come running over this way. When the

boy got close to the girl, he kicked and threw the ball so it came close to where the girl was working, making a reed mat. The ball came close, and she picked it up and hid it under her clothes. When the boy came to her and asked if she had seen the ball, she said she didn't know anything about it. All this time the boy knew that the woman got his ball, but he pretended not to know and looked for the ball around her. When he didn't find it, he went home.

The ball turned into a baby, and the woman brought out the baby inside of nine months. When the baby came out, it was not like any other baby but had claws on its fingers like a bear.

These Mojave Indians did not know who the baby belonged to. The baby grew up and was learning to crawl along, so these people decided they would meet at a certain place, sit around in a circle, and put the baby in the middle. At that time, the only way they could find out about a baby was because a baby always knew its father. So they sat in a circle, put the baby down, and the baby crawled around in the middle of the people.

Coyote sat with them and called for the baby to come to him, pretending to be its father. The people told this Coyote not to call the baby to him. Among these people was the grandfather of the baby, Yellow Buzzard. The baby crawled to him and climbed on him. Then the Mojaves knew the father of the baby.

The baby was a girl. Four years passed. The child had an uncle who would take her along when he went hunting. When he killed a rabbit, he would give it to her to carry for him. When she got the rabbit, she would tear it to pieces and eat it raw. When the uncle saw this, he was sad because he had never seen people eat rabbits without cooking them.

Four more years passed. The man took the child hunting. She lay down on a rock. He couldn't lift her up. He went home crying and sang a song.

The child got up and came east. She settled and grew up south of here somewhere in Papago country. From then, whenever she found that there was a baby at some place, she would go there and play very kindly with it, take the baby home, and eat it up. All the people were afraid, so they let her take their babies.

She kept doing this and killed a lot of children, so the people asked Siuuhu to do something to get rid of her. One man went to Siuuhu's house—at that time he was near here at Mo-ha-duk (South Mountain).[b]

When the man got to Siuuhu's home, he asked if he knew that this thing was going on, that something was eating the babies and destroying a lot of chil-

---

[a]*Ma'i*, 'older-sister's-child'.
[b]Muhadag, 'Greasy', the name of the mountain along the south edge of Phoenix. It is called "South Mountain" in English but "Greasy Mountain" (Muhadag Du'ag) in Pima-Papago. See the introduction to part 9 for more on this mountain.

dren, and he told Siuuhu that the people wanted him to kill this thing. Siuuhu said, "Yes, I know, it's *ho'ok* (some kind of evil witch).[c] Tell them to gather a lot of wood, and when the fourth day is up I will come over there.

When the fourth day was up, and the sun went down, he came. He told them to send one man to this evil person's home and tell her that Siuuhu was going to sing some songs. The man went to her house and told her what Siuuhu said, and she said that she doesn't like that kind of singing. The man went back and told Siuuhu that she would not come.

This man went over there three times and told her to come, but she would not come. The fourth time he went there, the woman said that she will come. This mean woman was very glad to go. She picked up her dress made from human bones and put it on.

One kind of tobacco in this tube, sweet tobacco. At that time the people packed the tobacco in a reed tube to make her drunk. The chuna-suk was mixed with regular tobacco.

When the man came back to Siuuhu, he told him that she was coming. Siuuhu went to work and made four cigarettes. One of them was called *chuna-suk*.[d]

---

[c] Ho'ok, actually the personal, individual name of this one female witch, or monster, or ogre. There were no others. The word is commonly translated as "witch" or "monster," however, as if there could conceivably have been more than one.

[d] Probably *jenaṣat*, the name of a lizard (it is said). The word occurs in a set of jimsonweed curing songs (Bahr and Haefer 1978), and in various "War Speeches" or "War Orations" published by Russell (1908: 339–389). It is a narcotics-related, smoke-related word. It is also the name of a Hohokam chief, according to Thin Leather. See his story of Morning Green Chief at the end of this part, and see Appendix on the conquest itineraries.

The song is untranslatable, but it mentions the four cigarettes. It uses old Pima words.[7]

Another [cigarette] was called *heo-ko-tatk*,[e] some kind of root to make her weak. The third was some kind of tobacco that is dope for sleeping; and the fourth was a weed that grows in damp places, roots of jimsonweed. He told the people that, when the woman came, he would light one of the cigarettes, smoke it for a while, and then give it to the woman to smoke. Then he sang.

The mean woman came. The first thing she did was to go and stand beside Siuuhu and begin to dance. Siuuhu lit the first cigarette, smoke it a little, and gave it to the old woman who smoked it, breathed it in her breast, rubbed her breast with her hands, and said, "I'll never get tired, I'll dance all night."

They passed this first cigarette around. The people, knowing what was in it, pretended to smoke it but were not smoking it at all. Siuuhu sang:

From here the words are obsolete and untranslatable, and Juan forgot a third song.

> *On top of this mountain (Mo-ha-duk)*[8]
> *I am singing—*

The old woman was getting weaker all the time. She would open her eyes and then close them again. Then Siuuhu sang the fourth song:

> *Old woman went to some singing*
> *And fell asleep.*
> *And this old woman was sound asleep*
> *Then.*

---

[e]Unknown word plus (Hayden's final syllable) *tadk*, 'root'.

When she was sound asleep they took her to a cave, laid her on her back, and pulled wood into the door of the cave. They set fire to the wood and burned her to death. From then on the children grew up and the people lived happily for many years.

[Preface]

At the time Elder Brother [Siuuhu] transformed Vantre [the Gambler—story 10] into an eagle, strange things happened to the people of Casa Grande [great-house]. There is a game called takal [*toka*] played by the women. One day the women were playing takal, and among them was the daughter of Sial Tcu-utak Sivan [Si'al Cehedag Sivañ, 'Morning Green Chief']. Suddenly a strange little green lizard dropped in front of her while she was standing among the other women. The earth about the spot became like the green part of the rainbow. They dug there and found some green stones (*stcu-uttuk hatai*),[f] which became very useful for necklaces and ear pendants.

----

[f] *S-cehedag hoḍai*, 'green stone' [literally]; turquoise.

There were people living at some tanks [ponds] on the east side of the mountains [Ta-atukam]^g north of Picacho [a town in Ariz.], and among them was a man named Tarsnamkam,^{h} Meet the Sun. He saw the beautiful stones used at Casa Grande and wished to get some of them; but how was he to do it? He made a fine green bird, stu-utuk o-ofik,^{i} parrot, and sent it to Casa Grande, telling it to swallow all the green stones it could find about the houses.

The parrot went to Casa Grande and was found one day by the daughter of Sial Tcu-utak Sivan. The bird was kept for several days, but it would not eat, so it was turned loose. It went about until it found a piece of turquoise, which it swallowed. The daughter of Sial Tcu-utak Sivan saw this and told her father, who directed her to give the bird all the turquoise she could find in the house. The people gathered to see the bird that ate stones, but as soon as it had eaten until it was full to the mouth, it flew away. Tarsnamkam was glad to see it come safely home. The parrot vomited the stones, which its owner gave to the people to use, and there was plenty for all.

Sial Tcu-utak Sivan was angry when he learned that the bird had been sent to steal his turquoise. He sent the rain for four periods, or sixteen days, to destroy

---

^{g}Ta:tkam, 'Feeler'.
^{h}Taṣ Namkam, 'Sun Meeter'.
^{i}*S-cehedag u'uhig*, 'green bird'.

Tarsnamkam, but the latter also possessed magic power and was not injured. At the end of the sixteen days Tarsnamkam sent a man with a fine football (*rsonyikvol*),[j] directing him to give it to Sial Tcu-utak Sivan's daughter, whose name was Pia Konitam Ofi.[k]

[Core]

The messenger went near the woman's house as she was at work and kicked the ball so that it rolled close to her. She took it up and hid it under her dress and told the man there had been no ball there when he came to inquire about it. He declared that it stopped close by her, but she again said no, she had seen no football. When he came back she searched for the ball, but it could not be found. It had gone into her womb and become a child. When this child was born it was a strange-looking creature. The people wanted to destroy it, but the mother said it was her child and she wished to care for it.

The people wished to destroy the child because it had long claws instead of fingers and toes; its teeth were long and sharp like those of a dog. They gave it the name Ha-ak, meaning something dreadful or ferocious. This female child grew to maturity in three or four years' time. She ate everything she could get her hands on, either raw or cooked food. The people tried to kill her, because she killed and

[j] *Şoñgiwul*, 'football', 'kickball'. This word would yield to etymological analysis, but I have none to offer at present.
[k] Pi Kuñkam Ufi, 'No Husband-having Woman', 'Husbandless Woman'.

ate their children. She went to the mountain Ta-atukam[1] and lived there for a while in a cave. Then she went to Baboquivari[9] for a time and then to Poso Verde,[10] where she was killed by Elder Brother.

As Elder Brother and the people were preparing to overcome the magic power of the Ha-ak they sang together [20 lines of song, comprising five songs or stanzas].

[Postscript]

When Elder Brother killed Ha-ak a great feast was made, just as when Eagle was killed [story 10], and to this day the cave remains where Ha-ak was killed. . . . After Ha-ak was killed the people were invited to come and partake of the feast which had been cooked there. One old woman and her two grandsons were not invited to come. When the feast was over she told her grandsons to go and see if they could find any of Ha-ak's blood and if so to bring it to her. After the boys had brought a few drops of blood which they found among the rocks, she put it into a dish and told them to look at it after four more days. When they looked they saw two little birds, at which their grandmother told them to look again at the end of four days. When they came to look they found two very beautiful birds. After four days the people came and tried to destroy the grandmother and the boys in order to get the birds. The old

---

[1]Ta:tkam, 'Feeler', near Picacho and Eloy, Ariz.

woman told her grandsons that after another four days the people would come and take their birds away. So they must take them at night to a distant land and set them free there. She said that when they returned they would find her dead, as the people would have killed her.

After the people had killed Ha-ak they followed the tracks of the boys, who had gone toward the east with their parrots. The pursuers raised a cloud of dust as they went along, which betrayed their presence on the trail to the boys, who exclaimed, "What shall we do!" At length they set free the parrots, which flew up into the mountains, where they concealed themselves in the forest. Following their example, the boys hastened to the same place, where they successfully eluded the pursuers.

After the people had abandoned the search, the boys went back to their former home and found that their grandmother had been killed. She had left directions which they carried out. They gave the body proper burial in the sand. At the end of four-day periods she had told them to visit her grave until they saw a plant growing out of it; four days after it appeared they were to gather the leaves, and in time they would learn what was to be done with them. The boys obeyed her commands and obtained tobacco, which they learned to use through the instruction of Elder Brother. (Russell 1908: 221–224)

SUPPLEMENT

**HOW A CHIEF
FROM ANOTHER
"GREAT HOUSE"[11]
ENTICED THE
WOMEN FROM
CASA GRANDE
(THIN LEATHER)**

Morning Green, chief of Casa Grande, invited Chief Tcernatsing[m] and his women to visit him. Tcernatsing lived in a great house situated by Gila Crossing, which is so far away [40 miles downstream] from Casa Grande that he found it necessary to camp one night en route at the settlement on the Gila River opposite Sacaton [present-day Gila River Reservation headquarters]. When the visitors arrived at Casa Grande a dance was held in the open space north of Compound A, somewhere between it and the circular wall enclosing a reservoir or "well."[12] Here the women who accompanied Tcernatsing danced with those of Casa Grande, singing the song:

> *Ta sai nu wu wu*[13]
> *Sun shade sing with me*
> *My body will become a hummingbird.*

When Tcernatsing came and witnessed the women dancing, he shook his rattle and sang a magic song, which enticed the women of Casa Grande to follow him to another dance place, nearer the Gila. Morning Green, who also sang a magic song, found it powerless to prevent the departure of the women, and he

---

[m]*Jenaṣat*, the name of a lizard species. See footnote d.

went back to his house for a more powerful "medicine," after which he returned to the dance and ordered his women back to their dwellings; but they were so bewitched by the songs of Tcernatsing that they could not, or would not, obey him. Farther and farther from their home Tcernatsing enticed the women, dancing first in one place and then in another until they came to his compound. Among the women who abandoned their home was the wife of Morning Green, who refused to return even after he sent a special messenger to her.

The sequel of the legend is that Tcernatsing married Natci,[n] a daughter of Morning Green, making him so angry that he sent a spider to bite his own grandson, offspring of the union. When the boy was sick unto death, Tcernatsing invited Morning Green to visit his grandson before the boy died. Morning Green relented and sent his daughter an herb (the name of which is now lost) powerful enough to cure the spider's bite, and thus the child's life was spared. (Fewkes 1912: 45–46)

---

[n]Possibly the same name that is sometimes encountered in myths and ceremonial speeches as Nasia. The word does not sound like Pima-Papago, and there are no myths with this person as a central character. She only appears in cameos. See note 6 for part 9 for more on her.

ALTHOUGH THERE IS another procreation episode in this story—a young woman causes a young man to become an eagle—procreation is not the focus of the text. The origin of war ceremonies is the main issue, and, as was stated in the introduction, it is interesting that this origin occurs among the Hohokam. They are killed in Siuuhu's war, but in some sense they also invented the practice.

A moment's review will establish that there has been neither warfare nor war ceremony in the mythology so far, that is, in the first nine stories. In the last part, there were magical battles between chiefs, and a witch and an old woman were killed. What, then, is warfare? For this mythology as I understand it, war is the intentional, face-to-face, bloodletting killing of a male by a male. This is lacking in the previous stories, and when it occurs in this part, a postkilling, purificational ceremonialism also begins. Thus, war is men killing men and being purified afterward.

There is one killing complete with purification in the Smith-Allison text, and there is that one plus another in a text that I include as a supplement to the Smith-Allison story. This time the supplement is from the Papagos, from a narrator named Sivariano (Cipriano, in Spanish) Garcia. His text was obtained by the musicologist Ruth Densmore in 1929.

These mythical killings only approximate the above definition of war. In the Smith-Allison text (and Garcia has this, too), the killer is Siuuhu. The enemy is a young man who has been turned into an eagle. The postkilling purification is done for Siuuhu by an old woman. The eagle has been a menace to society, carrying off people as food for his family. He has captured a human woman as his wife, and he has children by her. He supplies his family with human meat.

The other killing also occurs in both texts, but only Garcia makes it the occasion for a purification. This time the man who is killed is a normal but old Hohokam, that is, a man from the killer's community. The situation is this. A boy being raised by his grandmother takes the figurative commands of his male elders literally. After a series of such fiascos, the elders station him for a deer drive, so they can drive deer past him, and they order him to shoot "the old man." He shoots a human old man. For this he is banished from society, or he leaves voluntarily. In the Garcia version, while wandering he comes to a person called Bitter Wind, far in the west. Bitter Wind, who has magically directed his literal foolishness, purifies and initiates him into the status of warrior on the strength of his having killed the old man.

The boy's act of killing and his subsequent purification come at the beginning of this quite long myth, and Siuuhu's killing and purification come at the end. The remainder of my introductory remarks will treat three questions. First, how does the story progress from the young boy as killer to Siuuhu as killer? Second, where does the character Feather Braided Chief enter the story? And third, why would an old woman officiate in the purification of Siuuhu?

Concerning the first question, the Smith-Allison text drops the young boy after the old man/deer killing episode, without connecting his story to the myth of how Siuuhu killed the eagle. In the Garcia version, the boy returns to society after his initiation, and he resumes residence with his grandmother. He is now a ripe and respected man, but it is never said that he marries. Soon a friendless, wandering, and always losing young gambler comes to him. The ripe young man gives him dice sticks that render him invincible in gambling (see the note on the game gins, in story 4). The Smith-Allison text substitutes Lightning for the returned ripe young man. It is Lightning who pities the loser and makes him invincible.

The texts agree that the gambler is a menace to society. He threatens to win everyone's property. People cannot refrain from trying to best him. In the Garcia text, Siuuhu (called "Elder Brother") observes this and decides to intervene. In the Smith-Allison text, the intervention is by a person whose name I cannot understand. This name is translated as "tall fellow medicine man." In any case, the interventions follow the same course. An intervener gets a young woman to tempt the gambler to a waterhole before his next bout. There she gives him a gruel of feathers mixed with corn. When the gambler drinks it, he becomes an eagle, flies away, and commences to kill people as already stated.

In the Smith-Allison text, the people turn to Siuuhu at this point; in the Garcia version, Siuuhu has taken an interest since plotting to turn the gambler into an eagle. The texts agree on what Siuuhu does to the eagle. He seeks him where he lives with his wife and child on the top of a mountain, and he kills him with the wife's connivance and to the child's horror. Humanity is saved. The uneaten stored dead are revived (which gives origin to the white people); and Siuuhu is initiated by an old woman into warriorhood.

Second, who is Feather Braided Chief? According to Thin Leather (Russell 1908: 218; Lloyd 1911: 62; Fewkes 1912: 51), Feather Braided is the name of the literalist boy who becomes the benefactor of the gambler. As an adult, according to Thin Leather, Feather Braided Chief lives in the northernmost of the great-houses conquered by the Pimas. We will hear of him later in that context, not in great detail but merely by way of affirming that the characters represented at this stage of the mythology were indeed Hohokam, that the Hohokam chiefs comprised a small world, and that all these chiefs fell, according to Thin Leather (also Smith-Allison), to the Pima-Papago. (Feather Braided Chief is not one of the two great adversaries mentioned in the discussion of the Font text. He is neither a rain god nor a sun god but is merely one of the many Hohokam caught up in the sweep of conquest.)

Third, the old woman who took care of Siuuhu. There is no mistake that this sex and age were intended, because Smith-Allison and Garcia agree on them.[1] I can no more explain the selection of an old woman here than I could explain the selection of the earlier one as the source of tobacco. I can only show some correlates and consequences of the selection.

Thus, I suspect that because an old woman was selected,

no war oratory is derived from this particular episode. Recall from the introduction that the Pima-Papago accompanied the purification of their successful warriors with oratory, that is, with word-for-word memorized speeches. We will find those speeches recalled but not actually delivered as texts in the Garcia narrative of Feather Braided's purification. There the purifier is Bitter Wind, a male. We will find one other Hohokam era event from which the Pima-Papago derived war oratory. This is the death, resurrection, and underworld entry of Siuuhu. There the purifier is Earth Doctor, another male. But the purification that we are now interested in, administered by a woman, has no speech making. I do not think this is coincidental. The officiants and speakers at "actual" war purifications were men (Underhill 1946: 185–210; Underhill et al. 1979: 89–139). Quite probably, men would not give a speech originally mouthed by a woman.

If that is true, it is all the more interesting that a woman performs this function for Siuuhu. If we cannot say why it is a woman, we can at least say how, for the texts are quite clear on that. This woman has an exceptional ability to sense that Siuuhu has survived his encounter with the eagle (the encounter is described in very suspenseful terms; Siuuhu does not seem invincible). With kindness and modesty, quite as a mother we may say, she nurses him to health. There is nothing aggressive or ecstatic in her action, as there is in the purifying actions of Bitter Wind upon Feather Braided and of Earth Doctor upon Siuuhu (part 8). She makes clay pots and prepares a corn gruel for him, which in this context seems more like baby food than like the wicked refreshment that turned the gambler into an eagle. According to Smith-Allison, she holds Siuuhu like a baby and suckles him.

One cannot help comparing this scene with the Pietà, Michelangelo's sculpture of Mary holding Jesus after the Crucifixion. Both scenes show a woman's tenderness to a man-god. Siuuhu, however, has just rescued the Hohokam, and his problems with them will come later. This woman holds a victor, while Jesus' mother holds him dead.

STORY 10

THE BOY
GAMBLER, THE
MAN-EAGLE,
AND THE
ORIGIN OF
WHITE
CULTURE

In a certain year a baby was born. It was never quiet but always crying. Its mother tried in every way to keep it still but couldn't do it, and its grandmother also tried but couldn't. Finally they went to get some cactus thorns and made holes in its ears, so he[2] might die and they would be rid of him, but the baby did not die. When they saw this, they sang:

> *The naughty baby*
> *The naughty baby*
> *The mother is trying*
> *To scold the baby*
> *But he is still naughty (repeat, substituting*
> *"grandmother" for "mother").*[3]

When Siuuhu saw this, he made a rule that every woman, when raising children, must show them the right way. When a child is naughty, they must get a stick and spank the child in order to make him understand. Before he made this rule [in response to this abused, naughty child], all the children were perfect, and there were no naughty children.

This baby was a boy. Soon he grew big enough to go out hunting with the young boys. Sometime then the older people made plans to go out and hunt deer and mountain sheep. The leader of these hunters told the boy that he must go to a certain place where there was a gap in the mountain and wait for a deer. The boy went to the gap and stayed there. He gathered all the rocks that he could find loose, and he made a wall to close the gap. He worked all day. Then it was time for the hunters to go home.

That evening all the hunters brought some kind of meat they had killed, and this boy didn't have anything. His mother asked him why he didn't kill anything. He told her that the hunters told him to go to work and close the gap in the mountain [they meant that he should hide there, not build a wall there], and that is the reason he didn't kill anything.

So the people told each other that they must not tell this boy to do that again. The next time they went hunting, they told him to go and stay someplace and watch out for the "*cule*"[a] (slang for buck deer; the old people did not kill anything but the oldest animals). So he went and stood someplace and watched for a cule to come along, but instead of an old deer, it was an old man that came along, and he shot and killed him.

When the people saw what he did, they saw it was a great wrong, and they decided to leave him alone, to leave him go. So they did, and he went on. At that time there was a man who was fond of a game called *ginss*.[4]

Four numbered sticks five inches long, thrown in various combinations, flat

---

[a]*Keli,* 'old man'.

sides down. One stick is called *ginss*—15. One is called *see-i-ko*, 14; then 6, then 4.

This man always lost everything he had. Once he lost all his dishes, cooking pots, and dippers. His mother had to use spoiled pots for cooking. When she finished cooking, she fixed something like a dish scooped in the ground, put the food in it, and told the man to eat the food. She said, "I have fixed this for you and you must eat out of it," and she scolded him that it is not right for him to gamble and lose her cooking pots.

The man was very sorry. He ate his food with the dust. When he finished eating, he went to a man who had the power of lightning, and who was called Lightning. The man asked what he wanted and also told him that everyone was afraid and would not come close to him. The man told Lightning about the trouble he had in playing the game, and he asked for help.

Lightning told him it was all right, he could help him out and do something for him. He made a lightninglike symbol for the ginss [15] stick. He did the same, only halfway, for the see-i-ko, and he did the same for the other sticks, six and four. The man took these sticks and went back to the people he had played with. This time his luck changed. He won all the time, was getting wealthy, and was happy. His mother was also happy because he was doing nicely. The place where they lived was east of the San Tan mountains. It was and is still called Two Tanks.

One day the men were going to play again, starting in the morning. With them was the man who had been the naughty child. Now he was called Huik-eene (tall fellow medicine man).[b] He saw the man [helped by Lightning] playing and was jealous. He went and got some corn, mixed it with feathers, and told one of the women to grind up the mixture. Then he told her to go and sit at a place where there is water.

When Huik-eene saw that the other man was preparing to play ginss, he put the thought in his head to go drink some water before playing. The man did this. Huik-eene also planned for the man to drink some pinole before playing. So the man told the woman, "It is all right. I know I'll be hungry at the time when I'm playing." After he swallowed a mouthful, he began to feel funny and began to shake all over. The second time he drank the pinole, little feathers came out from his body, just like a young bird. The third time he drank it, the feathers became longer. The fourth time his feathers were full grown, and he was like an eagle.

Meanwhile the people had gathered to play. When the man didn't come, they began to ask each other why he was slow. They sent a young man to tell him to come right away so they could start the

[b]I do not understand this word or phrase. It is not the normal way to say "Tall Medicine-man" (Cew Ma:kai). This man corresponds to I'itoi/Siuuhu of the Garcia text. That is, he is not the young man who did everything literally.

game. This boy went to where the water was, and at that time the man-eagle was sitting by the water cleaning himself and playing with is feathers, as you see birds doing sometimes. The boy went back to where the people were and told them in a very sad way that the man had turned himself into an eagle.

The people told one another that something terrible was going to happen, that they must prepare their fighting weapons that very day. They gathered their bows and arrows and surrounded the eagle. The man-eagle began to rise slowly while the people shot arrows at him. He caught the arrows in his claws and went northeast (*see-a-tak-uk*, an old Pima word).[c]

Then Siuuhu spoke to the people and told them that the time that he had told them about earlier was getting near. He told them to remember that the earth, the people, and the mountains were all spinning around.

A Pima visitor, a schoolboy, listening to this telling, spoke up to say that this is the Appalachian range next to the Atlantic Ocean.[5]

The man-eagle made his home at a place where there is a steep, high mountain that no one could climb.

The man-eagle got food by killing deer. Soon the deer got afraid and moved down this way to live. The next things the man-eagle killed were young children. Then he began to kill grown people for food. Once he got a young woman who had never

---

[c]*Si'alig* is the normal, present-day way to say "east," and the *see-a-* of this word seems related to that.

married. He didn't kill her but kept her for a wife. The next thing he got was a female dog which he kept for a pet.

Siuuhu did this so man would receive more understanding. He knew the man was coming, for he is one of the gods, and he only acted asleep. This was a symbol that some people would come out [at the end of this story], not Pimas, but wiser than Pimas, as he had told them before.

When the people saw this, they held meetings on how they could kill the eagle. They thought they would ask Siuuhu to kill him for them. One man was sent to Siuuhu's place which at that time was at South Mountain [by Phoenix]. When he came, Siuuhu was lying down asleep. The man tried to tell him to get up and listen, but Siuuhu wouldn't wake up, so the man got a burning coal and put it on his chest. When the coal went out, he got another one and put it in the same place. Then a third, then a fourth one. Siuuhu finally woke up and got up and sat down. The man asked him if he knew what trouble was going on, if he knew the people were being killed and only a few were left, and he asked him to kill the eagle for them.

Siuuhu told the man to go back to his people and tell them that he would come inside of four days, and they must get four saguaro ribs. When the man returned, he told the people that Siuuhu would go to the house of the eagle, and, if he was not killed, they would see a white cloud rise over the mountains.

Siuuhu lit one of the sticks [obtained from the people], and that was his light in the night as he went on [toward the eagle]. When he went a certain distance, morning came, and he hid himself. He stayed there all day, and, when the sun went down, he lit another stick and went on all night. Then when daylight came he did the same as before and stayed hidden all day. The eagle could not see him as he flew above where Siuuhu was hiding.

When the sun went down for the third time, he lit another stick and went on all night, and the next morning he did the same as before. Then, when the sun went down, he started out with the last stick in his hand. All night he traveled, and sometime before dawn he came to the bottom of the mountain where Eagle lived. He hid himself there, as it was Eagle's custom to go out very early in the morning. That morning he saw Eagle go out.

So Siuuhu came out and went around the mountain looking for a good place to climb it. He saw it was impossible to climb, so he called a man by the name of "Nowtchuk."[d] This man had been alive since the time of the great flood.[e] So when this man Nowtchuk came, he brought some gourd seed with him. He made a hole at the base of the mountain and planted the seed there. Then he sang and, while singing, danced:

> A cliff is coming out
> A cliff is coming out (repeat, as you please).

---

[d]*Nawicu*, the "clown" figure in the Pima-Papago *wi:gita* "prayerstick" or "harvest" ceremony. This is one of the rare myths that gives an account of that person. Saxton and Saxton [1973: 270–304] give two versions of this story, one with and one without the *Nawicu*.

As he sang this song, the seed started to grow. It began to climb the cliff and went up until it reached Eagle's nest on top. Nowtchuk did this to make a place for Siuuhu to climb on, but a strong wind blew the plant back to the ground. Nowtchuk couldn't do it [successfully help Siuuhu]. Then Siuuhu spoke up and said, "If it was my desire, I would just say that the Eagle might die, and he would die." Then he looked around and got a kind of wood called *vass* (Juan doesn't know what this wood is),[e] and he sang:

> *I am* Heetoi[f]
> *Vass, I have stuck*
> *The vass,*
> *And I walked on them*
> *And killed the eagle*

So Siuuhu climbed on these [vass sticks] and came to where the eagle's wife was and asked her what time the eagle would return. She told him he would return at noon. Then Siuuhu asked what he does after he gets back home. The woman told him that when Eagle comes back, he looks very carefully among the meat that is there, and if he finds any living creatures, such as flies or spiders, he kills them.

---

[e]*Va:s*, apparently broomweed (Mathiot n.d.: 215—*Vass* entry, no Linnaean name given), or broom snakeweed (*Gutierrezia sarothrae*—Parker 1972: 292–293; no Pima-Papago equivalent given). The latter, Parker says, is a native perennial half-shrub that grows both in gravelly and clayey soils. Saxton, Saxton, and Enos (1983: 61) give "a species of plant used for pink dye (unidentified)" under their *wa:s* entry (= Pima *va:s*). Saxton and Saxton (1969, 1973) lack this word.
[f]I'itoi, another name for Siuuhu.

After he finds that there is no danger, he lies down and goes to sleep. When Siuuhu heard this he was afraid.

It happened that Eagle had a son. Siuuhu asked the woman if the son could talk. She said that he understands well enough to tell his father that somebody came there. So Siuuhu stuck his hand in ashes, took it out, and rubbed his fingers on the young boy's mouth, meaning that his mouth would be tied and he couldn't tell his father what had happened. Then Siuuhu turned himself into a snake and crawled into a crack in the stone. He asked the woman if she could see him there. She told him that she could see him and that the Eagle could find him.

So Siuuhu came out and turned himself into a fly. He went way underneath the oldest pieces of meat and was out of sight. In a little while the Eagle came. He brought the people that he had killed. Some were completely dead, and some were groaning. The young child ran to its father and was trying to tell him that someone had come, but he couldn't do it. He could only say, *"a-papa-chu-vitch"* (meaningless).

The eagle told his wife, "Someone has come here, and this is what this son of mine is trying to say." The boy kept repeating the same word. The Eagle spoke to his wife for a second time, "If someone has come, you must tell me." The woman said, "You know very well that nobody can come here because everyone is afraid of you." And, "You know when a child is learning to talk, he will be trying to say something and someday he will tell us what he is trying to say."

The Eagle went out and began to look over everything and to kill anything that showed it was alive. He didn't feel easy, and it took him a long time to go to sleep, for he knew that troubles were coming and his time was getting closer. The woman got the eagle, placed him on her lap, and began to nurse him to put him to sleep. She sang.

The Eagle fell asleep, and the woman whistled for Siuuhu to come out, but before he came out, old man Eagle woke up. The Eagle said to the woman, "I believe someone is around here, that's why you are trying to call him." The woman spoke back, "You know very well that nobody can come up here. I'm just making this noise because I'm glad we have fresh meat to eat."

She sang the same song again:

Hai yaka hai yaka hai mona *(last line)*.[8]

At the end of the song, Eagle fell asleep again. This time she whistled and Siuuhu came out. He took something that they called *chu mos* (something to cut with, Juan doesn't know its appearance), stuck Eagle's neck with it, cut the neck off, and the eagle flopped until he died. Then he did the same thing to the young child. Then he sprinkled some hot water over the bodies of all the dead people that were lying around, as many as Eagle had killed since he started killing people. The last human beings that he brought back to life, when he finished, were the white people.

His purpose was that, when he threw the dogs into the hot earth, they would turn into human beings and would be the Negroes.

Siuuhu spoke to the white man and asked him where his home was. The man wouldn't speak because he didn't understand Siuuhu's language. Siuuhu thought very hard over this white man, and he began to work hard. At that time a dog that was the Eagle's pet had brought up some pups, and they were making a lot of noise. Siuuhu gathered the pups and threw them down into some earth that was very hot (*stoin ju-ut*).[8]

The reason he gave this writing to white people was that, if they ever forget what happened long ago, they must have written it down and can look it up, then they can remember.

He did this because he didn't want any noise while he was planning what to do with the white people. He pulled one of the feathers from the Eagle and cut the end off the feather with his right thumbnail. He dipped the pointed end into the Eagle's blood and took a deerskin and wrote something on it just like white men do today.

The purpose was that someday the white people were going to come out here among the Indians.

He picked up one white man and one Indian and placed them face to face. He told them that when the white man nods his head, that will mean "yes," and when the Indian shakes his head side to side, that will mean "no."

---

[8] S-ton Jewed, 'Hot Earth', 'Hot Land'.

Then he sang a song for the white people:

I have made a people out of you
You are brightening my people (teaching)
You are making your home
In the home of the morning.

When he brought the white people down from the mountain, he sang:

The reason he spoke this in his songs is so the white man will be wise and invent wonderful things.

I am bringing you down
I am sending you among bright ways.

He set the white people down and placed his hands on their shoulders, just like a father does when he sends his son someplace. He sang:

I am making you go
To the star that never
Moves around.

Siuuhu spoke to them and said, "You will make your home on the other side of the ocean." He told them that what he had said to them [about the inventions and knowledge of the New World and the North Star⁹], these things would come in the future. He also told the Indians that they must know that there is another world on the other side of the ocean. When the end of the world was getting closer, the white man would cross the ocean and come over to this side. When they come, they will give the Indians things the white people use for food, such as sweets, and they will both eat the same food together. After the understanding of the white people goes higher, there will be trouble for them. When the day comes that the earth will pass away, Indians will raise up children white, white women will have Indian children and white men also do it. But the white man can't create another world like Jeoss did.

Those were all the words Siuuhu spoke to his white children. Then he worked on old man Eagle, pulled off all his feathers, placed him over his shoulder, and started home. When he came over the tops of mountains, the soft white eagle feathers rose over the mountains and showed the people what he had told them before he went: to watch for white clouds over the mountains, and they saw them there.

STORY 11

ORIGIN OF THE PURIFICATION CEREMONY AND THE STRENGTHENING OF MEDICINE MEN

When the people saw the clouds they were happy. One old woman worked to make a dish and a water cup for Siuuhu, so when he got home, he would eat from the platter and drink from the cup. Others made a shade [ramada] for him, so when he got home he would go under it to rest. And when he came home he did so, because it was the season they call *moo-ee-he-bik* (burning heat).[h]

He stayed four days under the shade without drinking water or eating food, and the nights were four without water or food. When the fourth day was about finished, Siuuhu was ready to pass out. The old woman came and saw him in that condition. She put some water in the cup, placed it beside him, then put her hand under his head, and raised it. She sang:

> *I'm going to give you*
> *Some bright water*
> *Which will make your heart shine.*

She raised his head onto her knees and sang (same as before). Then she raised his head still higher, onto her shoulder, and sang (same as before). When she finished the song, she made Siuuhu drink the water. Since his strength was almost gone, the water nearly choked him, and he almost passed out. When he came back to consciousness, he told the people about the mountain where Eagle lived, and how there was much blood on the mountain, and how it has a bloody smell. He told them to call it "Cliff that smells like blood."

From that time, there were two kinds of medicine men. He gave the long feathers to the medicine

Then he made a rule for the Pimas and Papagos, that whenever they have wars with the Apaches, when

---

[h]Unknown, unless it is *mu'i he:pidk*, 'much cold'.

men who knew how to heal—*sy-juukum*[i]—and the soft feathers to the medicine men who knew how to pray for rain—*makai*.[j]

one of them kills an Apache, he must go without food and water for four days. And at that time he prepared some eagle feathers for Pima medicine men to use in working over a sick person. He also prepared the fine, white, soft down feathers and gave them to the medicine men to use in praying for rain. When he completed all this work, he started for home.

From then the people continued to multiply, and the understanding of the sy-juukum and makai increased.

SUPPLEMENT

STORY OF THE GAMBLER (SIVIRIANO GARCIA)

[After his adventures as a literalist, the boy left home]. He traveled a long time, always going toward the west. The reason for this was as follows: His strange actions had been caused by an evil medicine man named Beater Wind,[10] who lived in the west[11] and compelled the boy to come toward him. Beater Wind had foreseen that the boy would do something like the killing of his grandfather, so he made a

---

[i]*Sai ju:kam*, 'very doers'.
[j]*Ma:kai*, 'medicine man', 'shaman'. Most people use this word for all those who can divine and "see" magically, whether for rain forecasting or curing or any other purpose. Thus, the distinction made here between the two kinds of medicine men is not universally made.

new house for the boy near his own and was living in it when the boy arrived.

All the time that the boy was going toward the west, Beater Wind lay in the new house with his back to the door. Someone came in the door and sat down. Beater Wind could feel it and turned over and said, "I did not build this house for you to enter first. The person for whom I built it is coming." The man who entered was Brown Buzzard.[12] The house was full of "medicine," which was said to be something like the heat vibrations that rise from the desert in the summer.[13] Beater Wind had put his medicine in the house for the boy, but Brown Buzzard was so angry at Beater Wind's words that he spread his wings against the house and took out every bit of medicine of every sort.[14] He sang this song:

> Am I an eagle?[15]
> My feathers are filled with mysterious power.

When Beater Wind found that Brown Buzzard was doing this, he turned to him and said, "I do not mean any harm. You can enter this house if you want to." Brown Buzzard was already offended, so he walked out the door and flew over the highest and the lowest mountains and dropped onto each mountaintop some of the medicine that he had taken out of the house. Because of this some of the mountains became full of medicine, as the house had been. Brown Buzzard said that because of this medicine there would be a roaring of wind or noise of thunder and a shaking inside of these mountains before a storm, and this would be a warning to the people.

The boy approached the house after Brown Buzzard had flown away. He went inside and sat down by the door. Beater Wind turned over, saw the boy, and said, "Have you come?" The boy replied, "Yes." Beater Wind took him in front of the house where he had cleared a big circle. He put the boy in the middle of the circle and went over to one side. Then he went back to the boy, took him up, and threw him to the east. He went again to the boy, took him up, and threw him to the north. Then he threw the boy toward the west and toward the south.[16]

[Commentary from the Densmore text:] Garcia said that a speech should be inserted at the point where Beater Wind picks up the boy. He said that he had heard the story many times, but the speech was always omitted because there was no one present who could give it correctly.[17]

He thought that the boy must be dead, and yet he knew that he had not fully killed him. Beater Wind went home and lay down for a while. Then he thought he would go back and see if the boy was getting up yet. The boy was "coming to" but lay there, his long hair tangled and filled with sticks or whatever was on the ground. Beater Wind picked him up and carried him to the place where they sat down together.

While they sat there Beater Wind fixed the boy's hair as it was when he arrived. He cut several sticks four or five inches long and pointed at the end and told the boy to use these instead of his hands in scratching his head or body. Beater Wind put these sticks in the boy's hair and told him that henceforth it would be the custom that if a man killed an enemy he must use one of these sticks until he had gone through a certain manner of purification.

[Commentary from the Densmore text:] The following acts of Beater Wind were the beginning of the custom which was later called the Limo[k] and used throughout the tribe.

Beater Wind took the boy quite a distance from the house and fixed a place where he was to stay four days without food or water. At the end of four days, the boy was as though he had been sick for years. On the fifth day Beater Wind came to him with a little food and one swallow of water. From that day on, for four days, he got about the same amount; then for four days he got about double that quantity of food. This was followed by one more period of four days during which the food was double that in the third period. After each period Beater Wind had the boy bathe and come nearer the house. Beater Wind was doing this all the time to "straighten out" the boy. While the boy was fasting, Beater Wind was thinking all the time, keeping watch of the boy, and seeing that his mind was clearing. At the end of sixteen days (four periods of four each), Beater Wind saw that the boy was going to be all right, so on the seventeenth day he allowed him to enter the house and gave him a full meal.

---

[k]*Limhu*, 'purification', 'offering'. The word may be from the Spanish Catholic *limosna*, 'offering', 'charity', which is present in Pima-Papago as *limhuṣa* and is used in reference to food offerings left for the dead on All Souls' Eve. Or *limhu* as used in the context of warrior purification may have a completely different and strictly Indian etymology. The word does not sound like Pima-Papago, however, and it does sound like *limhuṣa*.

The boy stayed in Beater Wind's house quite a while, and then he decided to go home. Beater Wind said, "All right. I have done what I wanted to do. I have straightened out what I wanted to straighten out in you. It is all right now for you to return and live like other people."

The boy came out of the house and started toward his own home. As he went along he entered every mountain and learned songs. The four kinds of songs he learned are called komatan and koop (used in treating the sick),[18] kohemorle (used in the rain ceremony), and hicuhcolita (songs that come from the ocean).[19] He learned these and knew that all these songs would in the future be used for curing the sick and performing other remarkable acts beneficial to the people. These were very powerful medicine songs.[20]

After entering these great mountains the boy reached the village, went into his own house, and lived as Beater Wind had taught him, staying at home all the time and not mingling with the people. There was much gambling in the village. There was one young man who constantly stole, gambled, and lost, then he would go to another village, steal, gamble, and lose again. This had gone on for a long time. The fellow was very rough in all he did. He gambled all the time and was called "Wanta," meaning "gambler."[1]

---

[1]In fact this word does not seem to mean 'gambler', but simply to be the person's name. It does not seem like a Pima-Papago word.

[Deleted here are the sections of the story on Wanta's be-
friending the now grown boy, Wanta's invincibility in gambling thanks to gaming sticks supplied by the grown boy,
Elder Brother's success in turning Wanta into an eagle, the
eagle's ravages, and Elder Brother's success in killing the eagle. These are all rather like the Smith-Allison text. We resume the story with the account of Elder Brother's purification by the old woman.]

Before Elder Brother had left the old woman's[21]
house [to hunt the eagle], he strung a string across
her room, saying, "If this breaks, you will know I
am dead, but so long as it is not broken, you will
know I am alive." The shock of the earthquake
[caused by the eagle's death throes] broke the string,
and Elder Brother's people began to fear that he had
failed.

. . . Back at the house where his string was broken,
the old woman had medicine power, and she knew
that Elder Brother was alive and had killed the eagle.
So she sang and danced.

Before Elder Brother went away [to hunt the eagle],
he told the people to watch a certain chain of mountains. He told them to watch a low place in it and
said that if he had been killed by the eagle there
would be white clouds over that place. So the people
watched the old woman dancing and singing, and
they also looked for the clouds in the low place. At
last something appeared that looked like clouds, but
it was Elder Brother's hat decorated with tufts of
eagle down. Then they remembered his words and
said to each other, "It must be that the old lady

knows more than we know and Elder Brother has killed the eagle."

After Elder Brother came down from the high place where his hat showed, he did not come home at once but went to a quiet place for several days. The old woman was out walking and came upon him, asleep from exhaustion. After she found him she went home and began to make an olla [pot] to cook gruel for him, a little olla for him to drink from, and a plate, and a little spoon for the gruel. When she finished making the dishes and had made the gruel, she got some water, took it over, and sat it beside him. This is her song.

> *You have done it right, you little bit of an Elder Brother.*
> *Henceforth the villages will be safe and I am on the ground, I will get along better.*[22]

After giving him the food, she cared for him for sixteen days. She had also made ollas to carry water for his cold bath, and she cared for him in every way, as Beater Wind had cared for the boy at the beginning of the story. . . . At the end of the third period of four days she took him inside the house and continued her care until the end of the fourth period of four days, when he took a bath and was entirely free. Then he lay around the place for a while. He knew everything was settled and that everything would go on the same as before the gambler was made into an eagle. (Densmore 1929: 36–39, 52–54)

AT THIS POINT in the mythology, war ceremonies, crops, marriage, and a host of other things have originated, and the two mortal menaces, the witch and the man-eagle, have been eliminated. All this occurred in the era of the Hohokam, so it is clear why I call the mythology "The Hohokam Chronicles." In truth, nearly everything of mythic import to the Pima-Papago occurred in the Hohokam era.

That time nears its end in the present part, because the Hohokam kill Siuuhu. Following our normal method of augmenting and contrasting Smith-Allison with Thin Leather and with a Papago source, we will find this time that Smith-Allison's version of Siuuhu's death is generally Christian and specifically like the neo-orthodox Protestant theology of Reinhold Niebuhr.

According to Smith and Allison, the Hohokam "thought they understood more than Siuuhu," and they spent four days asking him presumptuous and embarrassing questions: Who is God, and who are God's son, father, and mother? What is Siuuhu's status as son of the earth (see story 1)? Why does Siuuhu permit weeds to grow, and why did he permit the Corn child to die (story 5)? Why is cactus used to make wine (story 7)?

In the introduction I said that the figure of Siuuhu is like Jesus because both are killed and resurrected. This is true, but prior to his death, Smith and Allison's Siuuhu acts more like the Old Testament God than the New Testament Jesus. Thus, on the Old Testament analogy, the Hohokams' interrogation of Siuuhu equates with humanity's fall from grace in Eden. The Hohokam interrogation is humanity's first, and also fatal, disobedience to God. All the sin that we have seen heretofore in the mythology was done in innocence of this one Great Sin.[1]

It is fairly clear that the above was Smith and Allison's position, but it was not the position of Thin Leather or Dolores's Papago narrator. They and nearly every known Pima-Papago source (the key exception being the Font text) have Siuuhu killed, but they trace the killing to something quite close to the story of Chief Jenaṣat's theft of Morning Green Chief's women. To them, Siuuhu is an ardent attendee at the Hohokams' celebrations for their girls' coming of age, that is, their puberty ceremonies.[2] At these ceremonies he sings very attractive songs, and according to Thin Leather, he absconds with the girls.

Smith and Allison must have known this other, earthy explanation for why Siuuhu was killed. It is easy to imagine that Smith and Allison found that explanation to be lacking in dignity, but I suggest that they also found it lacking in theology. Thus, I think that they wanted to reform their mythology in the direction of a Protestant sense of Original Sin; and they correctly understood that this Protestant sense is not tied to an episode with an apple but to the *idea*, which I find in Niebuhr, of vain human disobedience to God.[3] Smith and Allison express this idea in the Hohokam interrogation of Siuuhu.

In effect, Thin Leather, Dolores, and most other Pima-Papago narrators humanize Siuuhu at this point in their mythologies, while Smith and Allison deify him. In either case, it is important to realize that at this point in the mythology Siuuhu has finished his creating and monster killing. Thrilling and significant as those accomplishments were, they are now finished.

Siuuhu has always lived in isolation from the Hohokam settlements. Although he resembles a Hohokam chief in attending song fests and contesting for women, according to Thin Leather, he is not a normal chief because he will not marry. If he had married, had started a great-house, and had raised children, perhaps the Hohokam would not have wanted him dead. But he would also not be a god; or rather he would have stopped being one if I am correct that "gods" in this mythology are people who cannot marry and reproduce normally and who in not doing so are gifted with greater than human powers of creation. This, then, was Siuuhu's dilemma in the mythologies: what will he do when the era of creation is over‽ Thin Leather and Dolores answer that he will become a pest at fiestas.

Smith and Allison answer differently. They deny any social visits by Siuuhu to humanity, except for this last visit when humanity questions his past actions. Smith and Allison make him into a god like Jehovah, into whom humanity can and should not probe.

The texts divide differently on the means used to kill Siuuhu. Smith-Allison and Thin Leather have humanity try successively but unsuccessfully to kill him. According to them, humanity ultimately resorts to the god Buzzard. Dolores, however, has the killing accomplished by a human Siwani, that is, a great-house chief. We will take up more of this Dolores text in the next part, for it not only simplifies the killing of Siuuhu but renders the Hohokam conquest as a very brief affair.

STORY 12

SIUUHU'S DEATH AND RESURRECTION

The medicine men thought that they understood more than Siuuhu, and the people were mad at him. They used an old word for madness, *i-a-no-ty-kik*,[a] against him because they thought they knew more than he did.

They asked Siuuhu questions, "What is Jeoss‽" and "Whose son is Jeoss‽" (There are different Pima words for "son," one referring to [the son of a] father and one to [the son of a] mother—so "Who were

---

[a] *I noḑagig*, 'to be dizzy', 'to be crazy'.

Jeoss's father and mother?") Siuuhu answered, "When you put the corn seed in the ground, nobody knows where it gets its life and how it comes out from the ground. Only Jeoss, and nobody else, knows this. That's why there is a rule that nobody can find out where Jeoss came from."

Siuuhu told the people that Jeoss was the father of the heavens and earth. Then the people said, "Why did you kill this corn baby?"[4] Siuuhu answered that it is Jeoss's duty to do his own will, whatever is right. Then the people asked, "Why do you make all of the weeds among the good things in our fields, weeds that are not good to eat?" Siuuhu answered that one reason why these weeds were made is because people had done a great wrong.

Then the people asked, "Why did you make the good fruit on the saguaro and make it into a strong drink which makes the people drunk and they make pleasure of it?" Siuuhu said, "The reason these things happen is because, when a man has a little son, who doesn't have any sense, who is about to fall in the fire, it is the father's duty to grab the son and drag him from the fire so he won't get hurt."

From that time, these two loves went on until today. Today there is one kind of love for the righteous people and another for the unrighteous. The two cannot work together. The

The people argued with Siuuhu for four days, asking him all these questions. Then they left him. They held meetings by themselves to plan how they would kill him. When he found out the thoughts of these people, Siuuhu said that one love had split into righteous love will work one way and the unrighteous the other. He called this unrighteous love *ya-wult* (the devil).[b]

two, meaning that one was a righteous and one was an unrighteous love.

The next morning some of the people went to where Siuuhu was. They said to him, "You have done something that is not right. You are the son of the earth and we are going to kill you." They struck him on the head and killed him.

The next morning Siuuhu was alive again, but his head was ruined. When night came, the people held another meeting and explained how things were and said they would kill him again. They went and came to Siuuhu again and struck him on the head and killed him. Then they took his bones apart and cut the flesh from them and threw it in different directions.

The next morning he was alive in his regular form. At night they had another meeting and said they would kill him again. This time they went and killed him and cut his form into smaller pieces which they threw a farther distance than before, and they ground his flesh into hamburger, cooked it, and mixed it with dirt so it looked like nothing. This was the third time they killed Siuuhu.

[But he came back to life again.] Then the people had meetings for four days and argued as to how they could kill Siuuhu and be rid of him. One of them spoke up and said, "I am going to kill that

---

[b]*Jiawul*, from the Spanish *diablo*, 'devil'.

man." The man who spoke was the one who had fixed the earth and the mountains and was the Buzzard (*mnui*).[c] When the people heard this, they put their desire as one with this Buzzard and told him to go ahead and do it.

When night came, this man [Buzzard] went out and went straight upward into the air. There are four kinds of winds in the sky, which he went through, and finally he came to the sun. Then he sang:

> *I am climbing and*
> *I am meeting.*
> *I am climbing*
> *I am climbing.*

He got some heat that was stronger than Siuuhu's life, and he also got a bow, and he came down. When he had gone down some distance, he saw the earth under him and sang this song:

> *I am going and*
> *Below I could dimly see the earth.*
> *In this earth the breath of Siuuhu*
> *Is coming out blue.*

Means as when you pull the string of a bow back and let it go but don't shoot anything off.

At the end of the song he shot with his bow to the earth.

At that time, on the earth, Siuuhu felt his heart begin to get queer, and he went out and walked

---

[c] *Ñu:wi*, 'buzzard'. The initial "m" in the transcript is probably from *s-uam*, 'yellow', as this character's full name is "S-uam ñu:wi," Yellow Buzzard.

about. Then Buzzard came a little closer to the earth, to where he could see mountains, and he sang:

> *I am going down and*
> *Below me*
> *There stands the mountains*
> *Which are blue.*
> *In them the mind of Siuuhu*
> *Is going out blue.*

At the end of the song he snapped his bow again. At this time Siuuhu's heart was getting hot, and he went to dip himself into some cool water. When he got in the water, he found that it was hot, too, and he came out. Buzzard came closer to the earth, and he sang:

> *I am going down,*
> *And underneath me*
> *Lies the earth which is grey.*
> *And in that*
> *The heart of Siuuhu*
> *Is coming out blue.*

At the end of the song he shot again. Siuuhu was looking for a cooler place, where there was water with ice in it. When he got there he found that it had turned to boiling water, and the worst was yet to come. As Siuuhu was looking for a land where there was nothing but ice, Buzzard came down, passed through those four kinds of wind, and sang:

I am going down
And underneath me stands the mountains
In those mountains the mind of Siuuhu
Is going out blue.

At the end of the song the Buzzard shot nothing but lightning and it hit this place where the ice was. When Siuuhu reached the place, he died right away. When the man [Buzzard] came to the place, he took Siuuhu and left him on dry ground. From that time, everything was open and the people could freely go ahead and do the wicked things that they wanted to do, such as drinking strong drinks and getting drunk. They were happy.

STORY 13

SIUUHU'S JOURNEY OUT

Siuuhu died for four years. All this time he wasn't really dead, but he went and stayed with the life of the earth. Where his dead body lay, small children used to play on him. Four years passed, and he came back to life again.

So this wrong, what the people were doing, began with the creation of the world and went on. Across the ocean it [the wrong] came to the people who lived on the other side

When the children started out to play one day, they went and saw Siuuhu sitting with his face all painted black and with a sharp stick sticking in his back, to use for scratching it. The children also saw that he was fixing his canteen. They went back to their of the ocean, called the white man.

That is why the Indian and the white man are the same. They all like to show off. So, the white man is a liar. White people learned to kill a human being and how to get drunk. We are all alike, and the white man will also do the smaller sins just like Indians.

father and told him that that man was alive again, that they saw him with his face black and a pointed stick in his back.

The fathers of these children told them that something terrible was going to happen. While Siuuhu was sitting there, sometimes he thought he would not punish the people and sometimes he thought that he would punish them. He was crying for the great wrong they had done, and he sang:

> *I am going to do this to my people*
> *Which will be very sad.*
> *The sun has died halfway.*

When he finished this song, the sun came up, but it didn't shine like it used to and darkness fell over the earth. When the people saw this, they didn't understand for they had not seen anything like it before.

Then, while sitting, he sang another song:

> *I am going to do this,*
> *To spoil everything*
> *That was made so good*
> *When the moon comes up*
> *It has died halfway.*

The reason he did this was to put the power of the medicine men in the ground, so their understanding wouldn't be so strong.

Then he stood up and placed his right foot down very hard.[5]

Then he took a step with his left foot and placed it down harder. This was to lower the understanding of the *sy juukum* (the healers). Then he took another step with his right foot and pushed it harder. This pushed down the power of the bravest man [in war]. Then he took a step with his left foot and pushed down the power of the sharpshooters (fourth step).

He went to the East. At that time the sun was just coming up, and he came to it. He went upward with it, and they got right in the middle of [above] the earth where there was some kind of timber that knows how to talk. He talked with this timber and asked him for some of his power. He took some branches which were leaning toward the west, toward the setting sun, and he took a leaf from one of the branches and made a shield from it. He also took a limb and made a tomahawk. Then he kept going west and sang:

> A talking stick
> I have broken
> And I am taking four steps
> And I am going.

He sang another:

> A talking stick
> I have broken
> And I am taking four steps
> And I am running.

He went on and got to a place toward the setting sun and sang:

> It is the sun's route
> I am following

NAS 301: AMERICAN INDIAN RELIGION AND PHILOSOPHY
Discussion Questions

Week 2:
The Short, Swift Time of Gods on Earth

Keep the following questions in mind as you read the assigned text and be prepared to discuss them in class. You will also need to prepare and turn in a one (1) page response to one (1) of these questions. The written assignment is due in class on Friday.

1. What is the theme of the story titled "The Whore" and what ethical issues are addressed in it?
2. What social or ritual activities are chartered by the story of the origin of wine and what ethical/moral issues does it address?
3. What is the theme of the story on the origin of irrigation and what ethical issues are addressed in it?
4. What social practices or beliefs are chartered in the story of Ho'ok and what ethical issues does it raise?
6. What ethical issues are raised in the story of the gambler?
7. What social practices are instituted by the story of the origin of the purification rite and what are their origins?
8. How and why does Siuuhu die and how and why is he resurrected? What ethical issues are raised?

It's the land of the setting sun
I am going down.

And he sang another:

It is the walking of the sun
I am running in it.
There stands the mountain
Upon which the sun lies down.
In this slide
I am sliding down.

Means he is now on the other side of the earth. In the west there is a mountain like a slide, and when the sun gets there, it slides down.

When he went a certain distance, he came close to the home of his brother, Earth Doctor (Juut Makai). (Earth Doctor had gone through the earth, and now he had made some people on the other side of it.)[6] Siuuhu changed himself into a young child. His face was all dirty, and his hair was like that of a naughty child who doesn't take care of himself, all mussed up. He came to Earth Doctor who asked why he had come there.

With his powerful wind, Earth Doctor blew Siuuhu and threw him away, four times. Then Siuuhu said, "My fellow old man, you know how my people are [bad]." Then Earth Doctor told Siuuhu to sit down. When night came, Siuuhu told one of the elder people, who was the town crier, to tell his people to come and smoke his cigarette. All the elder people came together and smoked Siuuhu's cigarette. Then he took out four sticks that he had cut from the talking tree and showed them to the people.

Ee-ee-toy [I'itoi, 'Elder-Brother'] lived in the Salt
River Mountain, which is called by the Awawtam
[Pima-Papago] Moehahdheck,[d] or the Brown Mountain, and whenever the girls had ceremonial dances
because of their arrival at womanhood, he would
come and sing the appropriate songs. And it often
happened that he would tempt these young girls
away to his mountain, to be his wives, but after
keeping them a while he would grow tired of them
and send them back.

The people disliked Ee-ee-toy because of this. And
when they had crops, too, Ee-ee-toy would often
shoot hot arrows through the fields and wither up
the growing things;[7] and though the people did not
see him do this, they knew he was guilty, and they
wanted to kill him, but they did not know how to
do it.

The people talked together about how they could
kill Ee-ee-toy. And two young boys there were, who
were always together, and as they lay at the door of
their kee [house] they heard the people talking of
sending bunches of people here and there to kill Ee-
ee-toy, and one said, "He is only one, we could kill

---

[d]Muhadag, 'Greasy'.

him ourselves." And the other one said, "Let us go and kill him, then."

So the two boys went to Moehahdheck, and found Ee-ee-toy lying asleep, and beat him with their clubs, and killed him, and then came back and told the people what they had done. But none of the people went to see the truth of this, and in the morning Ee-ee-toy came again, just as he used to do, and walked around among the people, who said among themselves, "I thought the boys said they killed him."

That same night the people went to Moehahdheck, and found Ee-ee-toy asleep, and fell upon him and killed him. And there was a pile of wood outside, · and they laid him on this and set fire to the wood and burned his flesh. And feeling sure that he was now dead, they went home, but in the morning there he was, walking around alive again.

And so the people assembled again, and that night once more they killed him, and they cut his flesh up into little bits and put it in a pot and boiled it, and when it was cooked they threw it all away in different directions. But in the morning he was alive again, and the people gave it up for that time.

But after a while they were planning again how to kill him, and one of them proposed that they all go and tie him with ropes and take him to a high cliff and push him off and let him fall. And so they went and did this, but Ee-ee-toy was not hurt at all. He just walked off when he reached the bottom and looked up at the people above him.

The next scheme was to drown him. They caught him and led him to a whirlpool and tied his hands and feet and threw him in. But he came up in a few minutes, without any ropes on, and looked at the people, and then dived, and so kept on coming up and diving down. And then the people, seeing that they could not drown him, went home once more.

Then Nooee [Buzzard] called the people together and said, "It is of no use for you to try to kill Ee-ee-toy, for you cannot kill him. He is too powerful for me to kill. He has power over the winds, and all the animals, and he knows all that is going on inside the mountains, and in the sky. And I have power something like him." So Nooee told the people to come in, that evening, to his house. He said, "I will show you part of my power, and I want everyone to see it."

Nooee lived not far from where Ee-ee-toy did, south of the Moehahdheck mountain, at a place called Nooee Vahahkkee,ᵉ and that was where he invited

ᵉÑu:wi Wa'aki, 'Buzzard Great-house'. On my theory, since Buzzard is solar power, this place should not be called a wa'aki. I stay with the opinion that an association with water is primary to the meaning of wa'aki. I think that this place is called by that term because of its important role in Hohokam mythical history. And I will wager that no one calls Buzzard a siwañ, 'chief', that is, no Pima says "Ñu:wi Siwañ Wa'aki," Buzzard Chief Great-house.

the people to come. When the people assembled there, Nooee made earth in his habitation, and mountains on it, and all things on it, in little [miniature] as we say, so that the people could see his power; for Juhwerta Mahkai [Earth Doctor] had made him to have power, though he had not cared to use it. And he made a little world in his house for them to look at, with sun, moon, and stars working just as our sun and stars work; and everything was exactly like our world.

When night came, Nooee pushed the darkness back with his hands and spread it on the walls, so that the people could see the little world and how it worked. And he was there four days and four nights, showing this wonder to the people. After this Nooee flew up through the openings in the roof of his house, and sat there, and saw the sun rise.

As soon as the sun rose, Nooee flew toward it, and flew up and up, higher and higher, until he could see Ee-ee-toy's heart. And he wore a big nose ring, as all the brave people did, a nose ring of turquoise. But from his high view he saw that everything looked green, and he knew he could not kill Ee-ee-toy that day.

The next day he did the same thing, only he wore a new nose ring, made of sparkling shell. And when he got up high enough to see Ee-ee-toy's heart he saw that the ground looked dry, and he was much pleased, for he knew that now he would, someday, kill Ee-ee-toy. And he went home.

The third morning Nooee again put on his nose ring of glittering shell and flew up to meet the Sun, and he flew up and up until he came to the Sun Himself. And Nooee said to the Sun, "You know, there is a person on earth, called Ee-ee-toy, who is very bad, and I want to kill him, and I want your help, and this is the reason I come to you." And Nooee said to the Sun, "Now you go back, and let me shine in your place, and I will give just as much light as you do, but let me have your vi-no-me-gaht,ᶠ your gun, to shoot with when I get around to your home." And the Sun said, "Moe-vah Sop-hwah,ᵍ that is all right. But I always go down over yonder mountain, and when you get to that mountain, just stop and look back and see how the world looks."

And Nooee took the Sun's place and went down that evening over the mountain, stopping as he was told to see how wonderful the world looked; and when he came to the Sun's home, the Sun gave him the weapon he shot with.

The next morning Nooee rose in place of the Sun, and after rising a bit he shot at the earth, and it became very hot. And before noon he shot again,

<hr />

ᶠWainom Ga:t, 'Iron [or perhaps any metal except gold] Gun.' *Ga:t* means either "bow" or "gun" (= lethal shooting device). Note that Smith-Allison have Buzzard use a bow, made of unspecified material.
ᵍ*Am o wa s-ap'e*, 'It's good', 'It's OK'.

and it was still hotter. And Ee-ee-toy knew now that he was going to be killed, but he tried to use all his power to save himself. He ran around and came to a pond where there had always been ice, and he jumped in to cool himself, but it was all boiling water. When it was nearly noon Nooee shot again, and it became terribly hot, and Ee-ee-toy ran for a rock which had always been cold, but just before he got there the heat made the rock burst. And he ran to a tree whose cool shade he had often enjoyed, but as he came near it the tree burst into flame, and he had to turn back.

Now it was noon and Nooee shot again. Ee-ee-toy ran to a great post, all striped around with black and white, which had been made by his power, and which had a hollow that was always cool inside. He was about to put his arms around it when he fell down and died.

So Ee-ee-toy was dead, and Nooee went down to his setting and returned the weapon to the Sun and then went home to his vavahkkee. (Lloyd 1911: 125–130)

[While I'itoi lived in the land of the Papagos,] Siwani ['Chief'] also lived where the Pimas now lived. Siwani was a very important person, and people would always listen to him and believe him. He had many friends, and they were always doing different things with him. When Siwani wanted something, he would tell his friends, "Let's do this," and they would have to do what Siwani wanted.

Siwani had a daughter, and when she reached puberty, I'itoi found out and was going to come and sing. But Siwani got angry and told his friends, "Wait for me until I am ready, and we will go have a puberty celebration." But they started the celebration without him, over by a big pond. People came from every direction and were there with I'itoi.

In the middle of the night, Siwani came with his friends. Before long, Siwani argued with I'itoi, saying, "You aren't good for anything. You always go about peoples' homes looking for food, but from now on people will not be troubled by you." I'itoi said, "I go everywhere singing because now I am going to die and I will not be here any more. And when people remember me they will sing as I sing now."

Siwani said, "You have already covered the earth with your songs. Now it's good if we stop being troubled with you." When he had said this he took out his club and struck I'itoi and knocked him down. The people were frightened and ran off in all directions. So I'itoi lay there dead, and no one went to see him because they were afraid of Siwani.

Before dawn, as the sun's rays were on the horizon, some women who were water-carriers arrived and saw him. Suddenly I'itoi got up and looked eastward, then sat down and sang this song:

> *The sunrise I'm going with.*
> *The sunrise I'm following.*
> *With zigzag lines I'm painted.*
> *Following the sun,*
> *With zigzag lines I'm painted.*

He sang this song four times. Then the sun rose, and he just disappeared. The women went and told the people that I'itoi had come back to life and had gone away somewhere. Just as the sun went down, I'itoi began the puberty song again. Even though that's why they killed him, when he came back to life he made another puberty celebration. So many people gathered and joined I'itoi.

In the middle of the night Siwani came again. Right away he took I'itoi out and killed him again. So again he was there, dead, until morning. Then it happened as it had at the first. When the sun went down, he came again and began the puberty song at the pond. After that, it was just his luck to have happen what had happened on the first night.

So you see, they had killed I'itoi three times, and he had come back to life three times. The news spread far that something important was happening. Many said Siwani was already defeated, but many others said that now the time had come that they would really kill I'itoi. Even though some lived far away, they wanted to see what I'itoi's fate would be, so they came and gathered here at the pond.

Just as the sun went down, I'itoi came and sang there again. Then more people gathered and joined him. And even before the night was half over, he made the dancers run because he knew it was about time for Siwani to come again. As he stepped up the pace with his rattle, I'itoi said many things so that through this the people would learn that he truly had supernatural powers.

Sure enough, Siwani came with his friends and took I'itoi out and knocked him down and beat him until morning. The sun was already up in the sky when Siwani left him, saying, "Whoever takes this corpse, I'll do to you just what I did to him."

The people were afraid of Siwani, so no one touched the body. Many said, "In four days I'itoi will come back to life." So they were watching. But after four days he was still dead. Finally his flesh rotted and disappeared and only his bones were left. So the report went in every direction about how Siwani had killed I'itoi. After that everyone that heard about it always did what Siwani told them, thinking that no one was greater than he. And he really did know more than anyone.

When they killed I'itoi he was just a young man. Many years passed, and his bones were scattered where they had been. One day the children were going to play at the pond, and when they got there they saw a little old man sitting there, knitting a carrying strap for a water jar. The children said, "Where do you come from, little old man?" He didn't tell them but just said, "Hah. Run along children. A startling thing is going to happen."

So the children ran home and told their relatives that a little old man was sitting at the pond and they tried to ask him where he came from, and he just kept saying, "Run along children. A startling thing is going to happen." Then some of the adults went, saying, "We will see who the old man is sitting there and why he says something startling is going to happen." So they went there and found that it was I'itoi, but he had gotten old. He was singing:

> *What characteristics are mine,*
> *What characteristics are mine,*
> *What can you do to really know.*

Little people that I have made.
They did a dreadful thing to me.
Like the sun, I die repeatedly.

Great are my characteristics.
Great are my characteristics.
The poor little people I made
Treated me cruelly.
Like the moon, I die repeatedly.

Just then he finished the water jar strap and went off toward the east. There were many people along his route, but he just passed by because he knew that they would surely help Siwani. Over in the east there were many people. I'itoi arrived there and asked them where their chief[8] lived. They told him, and away he went to see him.

As I'itoi was going along he was singing this song because he wanted the people to hear that he was the one that had made them, yet they killed him four times, and he came back to life four times and really knew something. Just then he finished his song. Then he arrived and sat down with the chief and said right away, "An Apache-like people have done something maddening to me so I'm going about pleading for help." Then the chief said, "I may not be able to do anything for you. My older brother lives to the north. Go and see him. Whatever he says, I'll do." So he left and traveled on.

Far to the north there was a big village. He came to their chief and said right away, "Apache-like people have done something maddening to me so I'm going about pleading for help." The chief said, "I may not be able to do anything for you. My oldest brother lives in the west. Go and see him. Whatever he says I'll do."

So he went out and traveled on. He arrived in the far west. There were many people there. I'itoi went to the chief and said, "Apache-like people have done something maddening to me so I'm going about pleading for help." Right away the chief said, "I may not be able to do anything for you. My older brother lives in the south. Go and see him. Whatever he says I'll do."

So I'itoi went out again and traveled on. The people in the far south had a big village, and I'itoi came to their chief and said right away, "Apache-like people have done something maddening to me so I'm going about pleading for help." The chief said, "Young men, run and tell the people below[9] that whoever wants to prove his manhood soon, come and we will help this man. It's true that he has suffered many things." (Saxton and Saxton 1973: 150–162)

T HERE ARE THREE more parts in the mythology, two on the conquest and a final one in which the victorious Pima-Papago experience their first individualized death and then meet an insuperable enemy to the west of Hohokam country. They return to the land of their victories, and, after a brief dash to the present, the Smith-Allison text ends. These introductory remarks concern the structure of the conquest according to Smith-Allison (parts 9 and 10) and how that conquest compares with other versions of the end of the Hohokam.

The table in the appendix (see page 283) compares the chiefs and places given in Smith-Allison's text with the chiefs and places in one or another of Thin Leather's long conquest narratives. Thin Leather is the only other narrator of record to give an account of numerous battles in the Gila and Salt River valleys. As will be seen, Smith-Allison and Thin Leather, while not identical, are really quite similar.

Not entered in the table but excerpted at the end of this part is a longish conquest account by the Papago Mattias Hendricks (Densmore 1929: 25–34). I call this account "longish" because it covers greater distance in space—greater than Smith-Allison or Thin Leather. But this account seems incomplete and even garbled, as if it was given or taken too hastily. Geographically, where Smith-Allison and Thin Leather describe a generally east-to-west march down the two river valleys by the Pima-Papago, Hendricks gives a quadrangular march to the north, west, south, and then east. The points of the quadrangle are not perfectly clear (they correspond to mountains of partly uncertain location), but the area within them surely includes both the territory covered in Smith-Allison and additional land to the south (appropriate for a Papago-based text).

Also given at the end of this part is a short, complete, and reliably recorded single battle version of conquest. This was collected by Dolores and is actually the continuation of the Dolores text on the killing of I'itoi given at the end of part 8. This text teaches us how modestly the conquest can be conceived. Interestingly, the single battle occurs in Pima country at a place called Rattlesnake House, that is, at a place that might well be Snaketown, the location of the archaeological excavations and the telling of the Smith-Allison narrative. Also of interest is the fact that I'itoi (the equivalent of Siuuhu) gathers most of his army on the surface of the earth. It is literally as if he has been killed by one Hohokam chief (called Siwañ; see my remarks on this term in introducing the Font text), and he carries out his vengeance by means of neighboring chiefs (called "ones-made-big"—*ge'ejig*—not *sisiwañ*).

With Hendricks and Dolores to remind us of the diversity in conquest narratives,[1] let us now review the key points held in common by the two longest and richest versions, Smith-Allison and the various renditions of Thin Leather. These points are three, and they occupy a physical space of about sixty miles along the course of the Gila River. From east to west, the points are (1) the ruin at Casa Grande National Monument, that is, the home of Font's Siba and Thin Leather's Morning Green Chief, (2) a ruin thirty miles to the west of Casa Grande, near the present Pima village of Casa Blanca, and (3) a location without a known ruin about thirty miles to the west of Casa Blanca. The Casa Blanca location is the home of a "chief" (siwañ) who is identified by Thin Leather as "Black Sinew Chief" (Cuk Tataikam Siwañ). The final, most westerly location is the home of Buzzard, who is more a god than a man. Like Siuuhu, he does not have a normal home and family. He lives alone in a house where, according to Thin Leather, he performs most exceptional acts of cosmic, not sexual, creation (Thin Leather's account of these is given at the end of the previous part). My impression is that no Pima in Thin Leather's or Smith-Allison's time and area could point to exactly where Buzzard had lived,[2] but many, like Thin Leather, were confident that he lived not far from the Gila River where that river traverses south of the mountain called "Greasy" (Muhadag) in Pima and "South Mountain" in English. (According to these Pimas, Siuuhu lived on that mountain. He was Buzzard's godly neighbor.)

We have, then, two identifiable ruins and one mysterious location. Before pursuing the complexities of the names of the chiefs associated with the two ruins, let us note how the three places fit in the overall story of the conquest. Simply, Buzzard is an important conquest because it is he who has previously killed Siuuhu. His conquest is the climactic act of vengeance in the mythology according to both Thin Leather and Smith-Allison. In Thin Leather, Buzzard is dealt with after the conquest of the chief and great-house at Casa Blanca, but in Smith-Allison he is dealt with before (see the Appendix). Following Smith-Allison, our part 9 ends with the conquest of Buzzard, and our part 10 ends with the fight against the chief who lived near Casa Blanca.

Now, who is this other chief, and how was his killing also climactic? Thin Leather calls him Black Sinew Chief and Smith-Allison simply call him Chief (Siwañ). I take him as emblematic of the whole of the Hohokam, not only because of his unadorned name "Chief" in Smith-Allison but also because of his mastery of moisture. As both narrators state, this mastery does not avail. The chief's powers of night, fog, mist, and mirage do not protect him from the Pima-Papagos' light and heat. Interestingly, Siuuhu stays out of this contest. The unstoppable solar powers are wielded by Pima-Papago medicine men who are now fully fused with Siuuhu.

Now a complication—but not a contradiction. The master of the great-house at Casa Grande National Monument was called Siba by Font, and although the published texts do not show it, some Pima-Papago call the master of this place Chief (Siwañ), and they call the place Chief Great-house. (Thin Leather locates Morning Green Chief at this place, and Smith-Allison put a pair of brothers there.) In short, these other narrators use the same names for this chief and place as Smith-Allison use for the chief and great-house at Casa Blanca. Some may do so in awareness of the fact that the same names are used for both chiefs and places, but some, I am sure, use the name strictly for the national monument, without knowing of any mythic battle at Casa Blanca. Thus, some Pima-Papago think of Casa Grande great-house and its master as the premier, even the sole, Hohokam great-house and chief (see n. 1).

From this we could either conclude that Thin Leather's distinction between Morning Green Siwañ and Black Sinew Siwañ is an elaboration on a simpler and earlier myth or that the simpler versions are contractions from an earlier complexity. The Font text implies the former, since it only deals with one great-house and chief, but we must suppose that Font's narrator knew stories about Casa Blanca and other locations. It is just that we do not know what Font's narrator would have said. The conversation broke off prematurely, as Font himself noted.

Thus, something equivalent to the complexity of the Thin Leather and Smith-Allison texts must have existed in Font's and Manje's time, for all of the places mentioned by the later narrators existed then, and the places should have held fresher memories than in 1900 and 1935—fresher but still three hundred years old. I cannot, and we may never, guess this earlier mythic or oral historical complexity. Let us revert to what we can do and assess the importance of Casa Grande National Monument, the easternmost place, in the mythologies of Thin Leather and Smith-Allison. The assessment is simple. This place and its ruler are of lesser importance than the two westerly places and rulers. According to Thin Leather, Morning Green Siwañ, the subject of several pre-conquest era myths, lived there and was defeated without difficulty early in the Pima-Papago march of war. According to Smith-Allison, two brothers, Wing-feather Running and Down-feather Running, lived there, and they were defeated early and without difficulty. I conclude then that Casa Grande National Monument is of secondary and possibly demoted importance within Thin Leather's and Smith-Allison's *conquest* mythology. It is obviously secondary, but we cannot say it was demoted because we have no earlier conquest myth in which Casa Grande National Monument is prominent (save possibly Manje's, if Apache pressure counts as a conquest). And I note for emphasis that the secondary importance in the conquest does not mean that Casa Grande National Monument is secondary in Thin Leather's and Smith-Allison's narratives of preconquest Hohokam times. In those myths, Casa Grande is the most important great-house and Morning Green was the most talked about chief.

What historical conclusions or hints can we draw from Smith-Allison's and Thin Leather's myths of the Hohokam conquest? There are two hints, general and specific. The first is that the totality of places named in Thin Leather and Smith-Allison may correspond with the final Hohokam phase clay-walled settlements of the Gila and Salt River valleys. I cannot pronounce on that, as I do not know the full registry of final phase archaeological sites.[3] The second hint is that the Casa Blanca great-house emerges as central to the Thin Leather and Smith-Allison myths, and one wonders how this site registers archaeologically. To my knowledge it has neither been surveyed nor excavated. It is five miles from Snaketown, but as history had it, archaeology picked Snaketown, which is not mythologically prominent (save in the most simplified Dolores text), rather than Casa Blanca, which is.[4]

STORY 14

**SIUUHU'S
JOURNEY BACK**

When the people saw the sticks, they agreed it was all right for them to go to these (upper) people and make war on them. The four sticks meant that when four days were up, they must be ready to go and make war. They must prepare the food to use as they go along.

Siuuhu spoke to them and said that his white people are out of this question. He meant that the white people were not against him.[5]

They asked one man to go over the [underworld] land and find out what it was like toward the east. He went and found four places where there was good water, so they could stop at those places to drink.

When the four days were up, the people started to come, not only the men but also the women and small children, and so their journey was started. In their carrying baskets they took their fighting weapons such as bows and arrows and everything they must fight with. With the power of Earth Doctor, these carrying baskets walked by themselves. Earth Doctor spoke to Siuuhu and told him, "If you get to a place where it is impossible, you must remember me and I'll help you out."

When they started their journey, they had a broad road. When Earth Doctor saw this road, he sang:

> *Toward the morning*
> *Bright roads have been made.*
> *And bright carrying baskets*
> *Are being set.*

They went on and came to the first place where there was good water to drink, and they camped there. They started and came to the next water hole and camped there, and the third and camped there, and the fourth water hole and camped there. From this place they sent the same man who had found the water holes, and he came out over the edge of the earth and was looking out into the west.

The people [emerging] from beneath are called *"wooshkam"*:[b] the people above, *"hohokam."*[c]

He returned back, and when he got to the people he said, "When I looked over the earth, I saw many *wahpo ki* (houses, called *"ki"* now),[a] and it seems that they extend right across to the setting of the sun."

He told that among these [upper] people were old and young, and men and women, who talked wisely and bravely, so it seemed impossible [to defeat them], and [he said,] "If we go there, the only thing we can do is take a shot at those people and go back home." But this [same? different?] man, who had received power from Earth Doctor, was sitting with his head down, and then he straightened himself and said, "We'll kill them and we'll get them," and he sang:

> *We are going to kill them.*
> *We are going to kill them.*
> *It sounds like we*
> *Are going to burn them up.*

And another song:

> *We are going to get them,*
> *We are going to get them.*
> *It sounds like we*
> *Are going to like it.*

---

[a]*Wa'aki* (sing., pl. *wa:paki*), 'great-house'; *ki:*, 'house' (of present-day people). Notwithstanding the first emergence in Europe (below), this seems to be a vision of the Hohokam great-houses soon to be conquered in today's central Arizona.
[b]*Wu:ṣkam*, 'emerger', 'something-that-came-out'. Later in the mythology, Hayden spells this word as "Wooshkum." I retain his spellings.
[c]*Huhugkam*, 'finished-ones', 'those-that-are-ended'.

So they kept coming this way, and as they were coming over the top [edge] of the earth, they sang:

The earth is grey in which
I am coming out
And the earth is getting damp (means that they were
coming out with clouds).

So this is the way the songs were sung and is why they call them wooshkum, that is, "coming out":

A song with unknown [forgotten? untranslatable?]
words that speaks of mountains coming out
someplace.

Another song, not understood, that speaks of the
people coming along some mountains.

When they first came out, they settled way back east, farther than the [Atlantic] ocean. Then they sang:

I'm coming out of the east
We are getting closer to the
People we are mad at (vay pay shut[d]—Hohokam).

Another song:

I'm going now to the other side of
The setting of the sun.

This song asks the power of Nassya[6] (not a woman, not a human, but something that Jeoss created). It [not she] was love of woman in spirit form. Jeoss

From the place where they last camped [somewhere in Europe], they were getting ready to see what was

---

[d]*Vipiṣat*, 'great-grandparents', 'great-grandchildren', an alternative name for the Hohokam, that is, for the prehistoric dwellers of Pima-Papago country.

made it as a rule for every woman to have that love. Juan doesn't know where the name "white eater," *to quai-dum ox,*[7] came from. It may be a Maricopa name, or from some other Pima story. [In any case] Nassya is mentioned only in poetry [songs or chants-prayers-orations], which is written [said] in the old, hard words used by Pimas since the creation—White Eater, Nassya, [the one an] old Pima word, the other a Maricopa word.[8]

going on over here. They put one of their medicine men to look as far as the ocean was and find out what was there, and they sang:

> *You have done a sad thing to me*
> *You have fixed the earth*
> *And in this earth*
> *You have put me down.*
> *And I'm looking ahead*
> *And I'm seeking everything right.*

He was sitting. Then he arose and was standing, and he sang:

> *You have done a sad thing to me*
> *You have fixed the earth*
> *And in that earth*
> *You have made me stand.*
> *And in front of me*
> *I have learned the mountains.*

STORY 15

SIUUHU'S REVENGE: SOFCH KAH AND THE WATER CROSSING

The medicine man looked as far as the ocean and saw that there was no danger up to there. They [he?] could also look across the ocean, and on the other side they saw some people living called Sofch kah. They came and destroyed their enemies the Sofch kah, but they weren't as wise and powerful as the people who lived beyond them. They came [to them] and arrived at the [Atlantic?][9] ocean [to reach these next people?], but they couldn't get across and so they stopped.

Siuuhu came out and stood at the edge of the ocean[10] with his cane in his hands. He said he would strike the water with his cane. Then he remembered what Earth Doctor had said, and he thought that Earth Doctor would help as they went through this great water. The ocean turned into a large river, and the water didn't reach as far as it did as an ocean. It became narrow because Earth Doctor had made the ocean [shrink]. Siuuhu sang:

> *The river is getting low.*
> *I am striking the water with my cane.*

When he finished the song, he hit the water with his cane, and the water gathered on two sides and made a path for the people to pass through.

STORY 16

SIUUHU'S
REVENGE:
OMENS AT
MESQUITE
VAHKI

After crossing the ocean, the people settled down just where they had come out, and they sang:

> *The land is getting closer,*
> *And my enemy is getting closer.*

And:

> *The mountains are getting closer,*
> *And our enemies are waiting for us.*[11]

The man who was sent to look over the land worked like a gopher, and he sang:

> *Yellow Gopher is going and comes out.*
> *Four times*
> *My enemies' arrow feathers*
> *He chewed up, which makes them go straight.*

Then he sang:

> *Yellow Gopher is going and comes out*
> *Four times.*
> *My enemies' bow strings he has chewed up*
> *Which makes them go straight.*

When the [upper world] people [who were to be attacked?] saw this gopher, they did not know what it was because at that time there were no gophers here, and the gopher belonged to the underworld.

When the sun rose, they [attackers; see below] put something with it which is called the medicine man's stone, and the brightness of this stone shone all over the earth in different colors. At that time there was a man living somewhere northwest of Glendale [Arizona] at a place called Vahki[e] in the

---

[e]*Va'aki*, 'great-house'.

Mesquites, and this man's name was Sivain,[f] a strong medicine man. He found out that some enemies were coming to destroy them, so he was sad and afraid.

He told one of his sons to go to a man who lived at Casa Blanca and ask if he felt or knew anything about what was going to happen. The boy got to the man and told him what he was sent to find out. The man said, "I am well and happy here at my home, and there is only one thing that I know that is happening, which I think must be good luck. When the sun came up over my house, there was a bright pink light. I believe it's a sign we'll have plenty of saguaro fruit and squaw berries (*qua wult*)[g] to eat, and so will you."[12]

The boy returned and told what he'd been told. Sivain said there was some kind of trouble behind those signs. He felt sorry because his brother [at Casa Blanca] didn't understand them. Then he sang:

> *The sun is coming up*
> *And it is shining*
> *Through the houses.*
>
> *The sun is going down*
> *And the lights are shining*
> *In blue streaks.*

---

[f] *Sivañ*, 'chief'. Note the use here as a personal name. For Smith there was only one Sivañ.

[g] *Kwawul*, a shrub (*Licium fremontii*) that seems to grow particularly well in Pima rather than Papago territory and is a popular Pima wild food item.

While he sang, one of the Wooshkam[h] dreamed
what he was singing about. These Wooshkam were
divided into two parts, called Ap p ki kan and Ap pa
pa kan.[13] These people[14] lived together close to the
ocean for one year.[15] During that year they practiced
how to shoot and how to use their shields for protection, and they practiced a power called *chu dun ki,*[i]
which is more powerful [than bows or shields], and
their medicine men also used lightning (*weu pa ki*)[j]
and thunder (*Wee hun*).[k] The man [must be Siuuhu]
who was taking care of these people, who had
brought them up to fight the earth people, watched
and sang these songs:

> *In the rising of the sun*
> *We are coming out*
> *And the sound of our weapons*
> *Sounds frightening.*
>
> *Toward the west*
> *We are shooting*
> *And the sound of our shooting*
> *Is frightening.*

[h]*Wu:ṣkam*, 'emerger', 'emergent', the people brought by Siuuhu from the underworld.
[i]Unknown word, probably related to *ceḍeñ*, 'to thump', 'to hit'.
[j]*Wepgi*, 'lightning'.
[k]*Wuihom*, usually also considered to be a kind of lightning, especially the crashing, flashing, white lightning that strikes things in rainstorms, as op-posed to the glowing red lightning (normally called *wepgi*) that one sees in the distance.

While they stayed there [by the ocean], they told one of their medicine men to look over this way and find out the shape of the land and mountains. The medicine man sang:

The first song means that the powerful medicine men over here [in the land to be conquered] look like babies, and the second means that the bravest sharpshooters look like sissies or women.

*I am now sitting down
And ahead of me
Is the land that looks like day
And in that are our enemies
That looks like babies.*

*I am now standing up
And in front of me
I saw the mountains dark
And among them our enemies
Looked like women
And I have found out what I have found out.*

When his work was done, they told a second medicine man to look and see if he could see anything. He sat and looked and saw an Apache in a certain place. He could see them plainly leading a dog. He sang:

*Coyote is running
It seems to be him
Waving his tail.*

When the Coyote heard this, he was all excited and started running around. Then the medicine man sang:

> It is the Coyote's road
> It seems to be true
> Waving his tail.

The Coyote was ready to kill, but he couldn't do anything because the songs were about the dog and not him. So two of their [emergents'] young boys came over here [to the present Pima country] and killed the Apaches. Then they were going to get everyone to start, and they sang two more songs:

> I am coming out
> And I am going
> And the sound of my moving
> Is terrible (frightening).

> I am now jumping out
> And running
> And the sound of my running
> Is frightening.

After he saw the people start out, one of the medicine men made some kind of plume, out of some kind of feathers, which meant that whoever wore it would die. Song:

> I am a medicine man
> And sadly my understanding.
> My nephews are wearing the plumes.

The plumes are called *Buch po ka,*[1] and the hat is like a conventional [powwow] Indian war bonnet.

I have an understanding
And my nephews are sadly wearing
Hats of peacocks' tails.

STORY 18

SIUUHU'S REVENGE: JACKRABBIT EATERS

They moved on and made camp at four places. At the last one they asked the medicine men to look over this way. He sat down and saw some Jackrabbit Eaters (*do a quoi duk*).[m] He saw one of their sharp-shooters go out and kill a deer, and he sang:

Who was this man that
Killed the deer?
It was the man wind
Who is coming
In a black shadow.

Who was this man
Reached the deer?

---

[1]Possibly *baiyoka,* 'bead', 'pendant', 'necklace'. In any case, this does not look like any word that I know for feather, plume, peacock, or parrot. Recall, however, that Thin Leather's story of the Witch has both turquoise and a parrot in its preliminary portion; and turquoise would be the prime material for beads, pendants, and necklaces.

[m]Probably Tua Kuadag, 'White Eaters', because one kind of jackrabbit is commonly called "white jackrabbit" (*tua cu:wi*). These people, commonly called Cu:wi Kuadam, 'Jackrabbit Eaters', are a kind or subgroup of Hohokam, that is, a subgroup of the prehistoric inhabitants of Pima-Papago country. Another possibility for this expression is To:bi Kuadag, 'Cottontail [rabbit] Eaters', but Allison's translation negates this.

It was the cloud man
And there he shines.

Among the Jackrabbit Eaters was a medicine woman
as powerful as the medicine man [of the emergents]
who saw them. She knew that trouble was getting
closer, so she worked to make wind to make trouble
for them. She sang:

I am calling the wind
And that wind
Is going to twist them.

I am calling the clouds
And that cloud
Is going to dampen their arrows.[16]

It is true that wind and rain came, and everything
was soaking wet. Then the woman gathered all her
relatives and went toward the south. One of the
Wooshkam medicine men saw this and told his boys
to go for four days; inside of four days they might be
able to meet them. He sang:

Right now you are going
Where the sun is right
Above our heads.
You are going to meet
The enemies.

Right now you are going to run
And find out

And before the setting of the sun
You will find the enemies.

So the Pimas know that there is a kind of Indian who live in Mexico who are Pimas [and these are the descendants of the Jackrabbit Eaters].

So they tried to catch the enemies, but they disappeared and were saved. Some others [searchers?], going straight, came to [some others of?] the Jackrabbit Eaters and destroyed them all.

When they had destroyed all the [contacted Jackrabbit?] people, they made their home there.[17]

STORY 19

CIIIIHII'S
REVENGE:
BUZZARD

The older [emergent] people held a meeting because some [Jackrabbit Eaters] had escaped. They worked and made a *Kal da kum*,[18] a bird, something like a nighthawk, and sent him over here [present-day Pima-Papago country]. They did so because it was this bird's habit to land in the winter and lay there for the year [season?] without any food or drink. The medicine man who made the bird sang:

> *The Kal da kum bird*
> *Is going*

And he is going
To lay for my enemies.

The Kal da kum bird
Is running
And he is going
To lay for my enemies.

The bird came here among the [enemy] people, and they heard him singing this song at night. When winter came he lay down, and the same happened to these people. They all wanted to lie down because the bird held down their strength.

Another Wooshkam [emergent] made a bird called *gi i sop*,[n] a small bird that makes a nest like a basket with a hole in the side. He sent him here, and he sang:

Blue oriole
You are going
With some understanding
To have found the enemies
And are putting them to sleep.

When this bird got here, he made a nest before sundown and went in the nest and went to sleep. So it was with the people, everyone went to sleep.

---

[n]Gi:supi, 'black-phoebe-bird'. See footnote j, part 3, on Thin Leather's Corn and Tobacco story. These birds are like orioles in that they build mud nests, but in my experience Pima-Papago have a different word for orioles, *wajukuk*. The latter are yellow and black, while the phoebes are gray and black. Smith's song, however, is about a blue "oriole/phoebe," which, I take it, is a mythical magical bird that we cannot see.

Meanwhile the Wooshkam planned to split into four
companies. They would not go all together this
time. They sang:

These are not really songs,
for Sivain was crying.

> We are now going
> We are going to split up
> Into four companies
> You see the lights
> And you call it a whirlwind
> Though you don't know.

The Wooshkam came down this way and asked
another medicine man to look ahead and find out
what was going on. He sang:

> Now I am seeing you
> I am now holding a soft feather
> And I can clearly see
> My enemies
> And with this
> I am lighting the earth.
>
> I am seeing my enemies
> I have strung out some beads
> And with these beads
> I am running
> I am looking at my enemies.[19]

The medicine man looked over here. He saw the
men go out, and he saw Buzzard go out and straight
up in the air. The medicine man sent some people

with the power of eagle and hawk to catch Buzzard in the air, for he knew he was headed for a hole in the sky and liberty.

Meanwhile Sivain [not Buzzard] created fog to cover the earth, so the Wooshkam got another medicine man who had power with his cane. The cane man pointed this way [toward Siwain's settlement], but he couldn't see anything for the fog. He sang:

> *My bright cane*
> *I am pointing*
> *And it could not shine.*

He rubbed the cane with his hand and pointed it again, but he still couldn't see. Then they asked another medicine man to try. This man made an owl which he sent this way to the [enemy] people, and he sang:

> *The grey owl*
> *Who is a medicine man*
> *He went*
> *And found our enemies*
> *And he don't feel like sleeping.*
>
> *The grey owl is now running*
> *And he found our enemies*
> *And he spoilt your memory.*[20]

So it was true, the owl came close to the Hohokam houses making a noise that they didn't know. They were superstitious because the owl didn't belong there.

The Wooshkam traveled and made a camp at sunset. They asked for another medicine man. This one looked and saw some people and saw their chief [Sivainʔ] who had clothes called *soan kam ko tam*. (Nobody knows what that means.) He also had some *nom kam* cloth.° The [Wooshkam] medicine man sang:

> *After I got here*
> *And from here I looked over*
> *And I saw my enemies.*
> *Hohokam kotam I see.*
>
> *After I got here*
> *From here I looked over*
> *And I saw my enemies*
> *Hohokam nom-tam [not "nom kam," as above?] I see.*

As those Wooshkam moved on, some of them would be killed.

They moved down and came to these people and destroyed them all and made their home there.

They decided to spare some of their [present] enemies' lives, but they would make them fight for them. So, Buzzard had been traveling up, but just before he reached the hole in the sky, his enemies

---

°The "soan kam" of the first phrase could include *s-uam*, 'yellow'; and the "nom kam" of the second could be *namkam*, 'meeter', 'one-who-meets-something', but these are just guesses.

[Wooshkam Eagle and Hawk soldiers] caught him alive.

They brought Buzzard to the Wooshkam camp, and tied his hands and feet together, and set him among the people. All the people made fun of him and called him a powerful medicine man to make fun. The women came and spit on him and burned him and called him names. (They burned a wooden splint and stuck it in his flesh.) They sang songs for him:

> *(First word not understood),*
> *Why are you going to die?*
> *We are going to hang the skin on your head.*
>
> *(Next song is hard to say. It means the same as*
>   *before, and mentions Sivain and curses Buzzard.)*

Meanwhile the elder people held meetings to discuss the punishment of Buzzard. Some wanted to drown him, and others wanted to burn him alive. Buzzard prayed to the people who asked them not to punish him too hard. He said, "If you leave me alive, I might be of some use to you." The majority of the people agreed because they knew of his great understanding, but some still wanted to kill him.

They argued for four days, and those who didn't want his death won. So they set Buzzard in the middle [of the ground] and cut around his head. The skin slid down to his neck and that is why his head is red today. They cut his head [hair or feathers] and hung it on a stick, that is, the top of his head was skinned and put on a stick. They gave Buzzard a rattle and told him to sing to the skin of his head. This was his punishment for killing Siuuhu.

Buzzard did not really mean to help the people, and he had a plot against them. He breathed on his hand and put it on the rattle, and the breath was the sign of his wicked scheme. Then he stood up and rattled the rattle and sang two songs (which are not understood or translatable).

Buzzard sang for four days and nights. This was a great joy for the Wooshkam. They did not give him food or drink for eight days, four days of arguing and four days of dancing. He sang and danced all that time without any rest. This was to suffer for what he had done.

The people dancing with Buzzard took turns to eat and rest. At that time it was the same month as now [when this story is told, April 1935], and the squawberries were plentiful for food. It happened that a young woman went to her home to eat berries. When she finished, she got up and returned to the dance. Her husband asked her if she was going to dance again, and she said that she was.

Her husband thought that maybe she didn't do right at the dance but might be going with another man. This thought came from the breath that Buzzard

These were some of the songs that were sung for good dances. One row of dancers faced another, and they swayed toward and away from each other in a dance called "straight dancing" (*chei le nea*).[21]

had made on the rattle handle, which caused jealousy. So the husband said bad things about his wife. The language was so bad that it must not be repeated.

But the sin of Jealousy that was committed at that time was carried on to the present. It spread all over mankind. Thus, at Pima dances today there is sure to be trouble, and it is the same with whites.

One of the chief medicine men found out that Buzzard did something, and he told Siuuhu. Siuuhu said he knew what Buzzard had done, and he remembered that Earth Doctor said he must give permission before something is done to Buzzard. He remembered because Earth Doctor had promised to help him. So Earth Doctor gave Siuuhu something with which to take away all of Buzzard's power. It made him into something useless that must eat rotten stuff for food and that is easy for anyone to kill.

SUPPLEMENT

A SHORT CONQUEST (DOLORES)

[I'itoi had gone to a series of earth surface chiefs to ask for aid in revenging himself against Siwani.] The last chief, to the south, sent word to "the people below" [who will now emerge from the underworld to conduct a short conquest of Siwani under I'itoi's direction and on his behalf] . There were two gopher boys who guarded the doorway [to the earth's surface] of the people below. They went down [tunneled to the underworld], and before long they returned saying, "You [in the south] must weaken the enemy by singing. Four days from now the people from below will come to help you."

So in four days these gopher boys opened the doors and many people came out. I'itoi began to lead them.

But Siwani found out that there was going to be a big battle, and he invited the people to help him. Not many came, but Coyote came and Siwani sent him to go and find out how many people were going to help I'itoi. Coyote ran and climbed up Baboquivari [a tall mountain in Papago country, 80 miles south of the Gila River] , and from there he saw the earth open up in the south and many different people come out. Coyote also had this power, that if something displeased him he would laugh at it and it would change. So he was watching them. The number of people was increasing greatly, and he said, "Ha, ha, ha! Oh, won't the peoples' tail ever break off?"

So the opening closed right up on the rest of them. But many people had already come out and gone on. Coyote ran back from there and returned to Siwani's house and said, "The land opened in the south, and many different people came out. Who knows how many would have come, but I laughed at them and the earth closed up. However, many had already come out and are coming this way."

I'itoi led the people, and wherever there were a lot of [earth surface] people they would immediately go along to help. So the people increased and reached quite a number by the time they arrived near the house of Siwani and camped.

I'itoi said, "In the morning Siwani will come out and whoever kills the first man, I will let him choose whatever land pleases him to be his home." When Rattlesnake heard this, he went in the evening and sat in Siwani's road. In the morning the people [of Siwani] came out and Rattlesnake was the first to kill someone. Then they wrecked Siwani's house and destroyed his people, and Rattlesnake chose the land for himself which is now called Rattlesnake House.[22]

Those who now live along the [Gila] river lived far to the south [in today's Mexico] and were farmers. So they took the land along the river. From that time on we call them to River People. Those that were hunters took the land below Baboquivari because there were many mule deer and plenty of other food there. From that time on these were called the Desert People. (Saxton and Saxton 1973: 163–168)

The people emerged from the east and traveled toward the north, then to the west, and south, some completing a great circle and returning to the east. On this journey they continually fought the earlier inhabitants of the land. From time to time groups of people left the company and settled down, the Papago remaining in the Sacaton Valley. As they journeyed Elder Brother gave names to the mountains. He would listen to the people as they talked about the beautiful mountains, then he would tell the name of the mountain in a song.

It was said that the people saw a little cloud on top of a mountain and said, "We thought we had everything with us. We thought we had all the clouds. What can be the name of that mountain that has a little cloud inside?" Elder Brother sang the following song, telling the people that the mountain they saw was Raven Mountain (Hawantohak).[p] The whole crowd said to themselves, "That is Raven Mountain," and it is called by that name to this day.

> Here we are on our way and see the distant mountain.
> See, the mountain far away from us that has the cloud
> is Raven Mountain.

---

[p]Hawan Duag, 'Raven [or Crow] Mountain'.

A mountain at each of the cardinal points was named from some circumstance on the journey. When they were journeying in the north a man had his lunch in a frog skin and threw it away on a mountain which is called Frog Mountain to this day.[23] When they were in the west they named the mountains "Crooked Mountains." When they were in the south a man killed a big bird, cut off the head, and left it there. This mountain is still called Head Mountain. A mountain to the east of the present site of Tucson was named Turkeyneck Mountain.[24] One of the men cut the skin from around the neck of a turkey, turned it inside out, and put his lunch in it. He finished his lunch when on this mountain and threw away the skin of the turkey neck, from which the mountain was named.

A beautiful picture of the multitude is suggested by the words of the following song. The people were looking for a good camping place. Some favored one place, and the others said, "Come, we have found a better place," so they swayed from place to place. Elder Brother looked upon the swaying crowd, and in a song he told them what they resembled.

> *Downy white feathers are moving beneath the sunset*
> *and along the edge of the world.*

(Densmore 1929: 25–27)

The fourth incident [of conquest that Hendricks recalled] was the encounter with Brown Buzzard. When the Papago came to Brown Buzzard's house they caught him and were going to kill him, but he said, "Do not kill me. I will do something so that your evenings will pass pleasantly." He removed his scalp and fastened it at the end of a pole. When evening came he held up the scalp and sang all night. This was the beginning of the custom of taking scalps and dancing the scalp dance. This is also the reason why the buzzard has no feathers on top of his head. (Densmore 1929: 33)

And they went on again to the place where Noo-ee lived, called Wuh-a-kutch. And Ee-ee-toy said, "When you come there, you will know the man who killed me by his white leggings, and when you find him, do not kill him but capture him and bring him to me, and I will do what I please with him."

And Ee-ee-toy had the Eagle and the Chicken-hawk go up in the sky to look for Noo-ee, for he said he might go up there. And the Eagle and Chicken-hawk found Noo-ee there, and caught him, and brought him to Ee-ee-toy who took him and scalped him alive. And Nooee, after he was scalped, fell down and died, and the women came around him, rejoicing and dancing, and singing, "Oh why is Seeven dead!" And after a while he began to come to life again and lay there rolling and moaning. (Lloyd 1911: 159)

T HE FINAL TEXT of this part is the earlier mentioned conquest of Siwañ, or Black Sinew Siwañ, at a great-house near the present village of Casa Blanca. The story as told by both Thin Leather and Smith-Allison has a feature not mentioned in the introduction to part 9, namely, a bridge into post-Hohokam, specifically Apache, war-burdened times. The bridge is as follows. Both Thin Leather and Smith-Allison state that the Hohokam chief had a son who was taken in by the Pima-Papago. According to Thin Leather, the boy was called Kokoñip;[a] Smith-Allison do not state his name. Also according to Thin Leather, the boy married a Pima-Papago woman named Pu:l, or Hu:l, Ha'akam;[b] Smith-Allison do not tell this part of the story. While she was expecting their first child, Thin Leather continues, Kokoñip went deer hunting alone and was killed by Apaches. The son grew up to be a vengeful warrior named Paḍ A:ngam.[1] His career is recalled in war oratory published by Russell (1908: 353–356), Lloyd (1911: 180–182), and Saxton and Saxton (1973: 178–182; 183–186).

Thus we have a story that runs for three generations, the first and only in the entire mythology. It is far from a normal family history. The vengeful warrior's grandparents are Hohokam on one side and Pima-Papago on the other. His father is a Hohokam orphan, and his mother is Pima-Papago. He is himself an orphan due to his own father's

---

[a] A name I cannot translate or analyze etymologically. Although it sounds like Pima-Papago, it does not seem to have linguistic or lexical meaning. Most personal names do have such meaning, e.g., Elder Brother, Earth Doctor, etc.

[b] The first word is untranslatable, which is perhaps why it was recorded differently by Russell and Saxton and Saxton. The second word means "Has-pottery," or "Pot-haver."

death. There is no reason to believe that the mixed parentage was regretted or disapproved of by the tellers, but there is good reason to believe that they regretted the double orphaning: it is a sad boy who loses his father, who also lost his father, to warfare.

In this already long book, I will not reproduce the texts that express that sadness. They include war oratory as well as prose. I do, however, underscore the change of mood between the Hohokam conquest stories and this story with its two generations of doomed fathers. The Hohokam chief, the first of the doomed, flees with his son from his destroyed great-house. The pair are hunted down by the Pima-Papago. The chief tells his son to hide while he faces his death. He does not die boastfully but is pitifully dispatched once his magic power has run out. It is a merciless fugitive death story.

The son's doom comes similarly. While out hunting, he is scalped and disemboweled by Apaches. In other words, gone are the days of the massed army, castle-busting Hohokam conquest, and begun are the days of the killing of isolated hunters and gatherers. The post-Hohokam era, when it was dangerous for individuals to leave home alone, has begun. This was the era that the Europeans actually observed, starting with Manje.

STORY 20

SIUUHU'S
REVENGE:
MESCAL
PAINTED
CHIEF

The Wooshkam went on and made camp and asked the medicine men to look ahead. At this stopping place they [rather than the medicine man] sang some songs for a medicine man who was going to work and find out what was ahead of them. He found out that among these [enemy] people was a chief who was going to grind mescal,[2] get the juice out, mix the juice with red paint, and paint himself with it. That is what the Wooshkam medicine man saw. He sang songs about what he saw and told his people about it:

> *Toward the rising of the sun*
> *There lies some land*
> *From there I looked over here*
> *And saw a man*
> *Painting himself.*
>
> *Toward the setting of the sun*
> *There are mountains with steep cliffs*
> *And on these cliffs*
> *I saw a man with stripes of paint*
> *On his face.*

They came down to the place where they saw this man and destroyed some of the people, but some of them they captured to themselves.

STORY 21

**INTERLUDE:
WATER PLUME
AND HIMMULT**

After they destroyed everything there, they made camp for a while, and they had a little trouble among themselves. The trouble was this. In the world where these Wooshkam came from, people lived in different, separated groups just as we do here now. There was one leader for each district, or group. Now, it happened [after the emergence] that the leader of one group was named Schroduk see oo da kum, "Water Plume."ᶜ He was very good at hunting, a sharpshooter, and so his people knew he had the power to kill.

As the people traveled, these [Water Plume's] people were killing the best game, deer and birds, and they were selfish in their understanding toward others. Then the other people took this power away from them [Water Plume's band or tribe], and they took it away from another tribe, too.

Juan doesn't understand the words, but he knows it's a prayer to the medicine man to get back what he knew before, how to kill. And he knows that these people who had lost that power had become sleepy and lazy. The song asks for the medicine man to give back their former understanding [and power?].

The name of the leader of the other group was Himmult. When these two chiefs found what had been done to them, they went to a medicine man and told him their troubles in prayers. One of them gave the medicine man a soft feather, and the other gave him a bead. Then Water Plume sang a song.

Juan doesn't understand the words, but their meaning is the same as the preceding.

Then Himmult sang.

The song has old Pima words, and Juan doesn't remember their meaning.

The medicine man got the soft feather and bead and held them up in his hand. He held the hand on his

---

'Ṣu:dagi Siwudkam, 'Water Plume-having', 'Water Feather-having', or 'Water Flame-having' ("*siwud*" can mean "plume," "feather," or "flame"). This water-associated chief does not violate the rule that the conquering army lacks wetness power. This man's water power is stripped from him.

But roughly the song means that the medicine man is glad for what these [two] people had told him about their troubles and about their sad prayer to him, and he was happy to hear this from them.

breast, and then he straightened up—he'd been bowing down.[3] Then he sang to Water Plume.

Then he sang to Himmult (song means same thing), and then he restored their understanding. They went away and hunted and killed and were free from then on.

STORY 22

SIUUHU'S REVENGE: HAT MOUNTAIN PAUSE

The whole Wooshkam [tribe] moved on and came down to a certain mountain which is called Wonnum (Hat).[d] (Its location is unknown.) They were getting close to where we [telling and recording this story] are today (Snaketown). When they stopped at Wonnum, they placed some of their youngest medicine people, who had never performed because they were very young. These young ones sang a song:

> *I am acting*
> *Like a medicine man*
> *I am surrounding many people*
> *With beads.*

These two young medicine people looked over here and saw that among the [Hohokam] people there

---

[d]*Wonam*, 'hat', perhaps from Spanish "sombrero."

was a leader who knew that some trouble was coming. He was getting ready. He would go each morning to look at the rising sun, and he had two of the rocks that the Hohokam medicine people used at that time. These rocks shone bright and were terrifying.

So one morning he went out and stood on top of his house and sang:

> *It was a white morning*
> *In this I came out*
> *With a shining heart.*
>
> *The green evening (*hod nuk*)*[e]
> *It is shaped like a windbreak (*oon ma, *old word;* uk*
> *oa, now word)*[f]
> *And in that I came out*
> *With the green mind.*[4]

This man looked dangerous, like fire, to the Wooshkam medicine men.

Remember, now, that the Wooshkam had sent an owl to find out what was ahead [story 18]. All this time the owl had been among the Hohokam making noises at night and making signs that they would be destroyed soon. Also remember that the

And all this time Earth Doctor, who was left on the other side of the world, knew that the Wooshkam were scared of the Hohokam and that they were staying a long time at this place [Hat Mountain] where they had stopped. He got his cane and shot it through the earth. It came out where the Wooshkam were camping, and it had eyes on it, like a person.

---

[e]*Huḍñig*, 'descent', 'sundown', 'evening', 'west'.
[f]*O:nma, u:kṣa*, two words for roofless, windbreak enclosures.

Wooshkam sent a gopher among the Hohokam to destroy all the fighting weapons that they had [story 16]. All this time the gopher was working among the Hohokam, breaking their bowstrings and chewing the feathers on their arrows. When a man sat down to make a bowstring, the next morning it would be all chewed and broken.

When the Wooshkam people saw this cane, they sang:

Come all you people
And see
A green cane has come.

The cane went back in the ground and came out over here, under the Hohokam, looking around. The Wooshkam then sang another song:

My crooked stick went
And came out toward the setting sun
And it came out
Over there.
And my enemies saw it
And they talked about it
And they laughed at it.

Then:

It was my thin stick
Which went toward the setting sun
And came out over there
It was my enemy, a woman
Who came and saw it and
Laughed at it.

That's why some of those rocks are found here [Snaketown archaeological site]. They don't look dangerous anymore because the power has been taken away from them, so they don't look like they did.

When it came out over here, it destroyed all the power of the medicine men who had the two terrifying shining rocks.

The next thing they [invaders; Siuuhu's people] sent here was a rattlesnake. It went on top of the house where the medicine man went every morning. The next morning, when he went to look for the Wooshkam, the rattlesnake bit and killed him.

Just before the Wooshkam started to come this way, they told their children how they should live if they [parents] were killed or destroyed, and they set a rule for their children and wives. And they sang:

> Sivain i vah ki *(Siivan, man; vahki, house; so*
>   *"Siivan's house")*[8] *is*
> *Making me mad*
> *It is far away*
> *We have many days to go yet.*
> *Siivan i vahki, you are*
> *Making me mad*
> *Away ahead of us*
> *We can see dimly*
> *Many mountains.*

They hadn't moved yet. They asked two more medicine men to work for them. One of them made a raven which he sent to the Siivan, and he sang:

> *You have made a raven out of me*
> *I am now hanging above vahki*
> *And I am making my enemies' heart*
> *To go to sleep.*

---

[8] *Sivañ*, 'chief'. This is the same word that was spelled "Sivain" earlier in the manuscript. There it appeared to be the personal name of a man living in Vahki in the Mesquite, near Glendale, Ariz.; *wa'aki*, 'great-house'. In this passage, it seems that the Pima village Casa Blanca is identified as a chief's great-house.

The raven came down where Siivan was. The siivan had some sons who ran out of the house and tried to shoot the raven down, but this raven was not a real bird.

The other (Wooshkam) medicine man worked and pulled some *komitch kaduk* (hair from the temple, an old word) and made a snake out of it. He sang:

> *You have made a snake out of me*
> *I am tying*
> *The hands of my enemies.*

This snake came down where Siivan was and tied his hands together.

The evening before they were to start, the Wooshkam held a meeting to plan how they would fight the people down here. Some said that they must kill all the people that they had already captured, or these people might turn around and help the Hohokam. They finally decided they must not kill them but watch them very carefully Then they [invaders] asked another medicine man to work for them. He had the power of the bluebird and sang:

> *Bluebird medicine man*
> *You called me*
> *To the land that lies before me*
> *I am breathing.*
> *I am tying the hands*
> *Of my enemies.*

There were two [enemy] men living at the house that today is called Casa Grande Ruin, and they had wives. When they got up one morning, the men's and women's hair were tangled, and they had to break loose from each other.

That was a sign of good luck and a way to drive away bad luck. At that time Indians used to say that when a man was sleeping at night, if he dreams of the dead, it is a sign of bad luck. So they breathe on their breasts to drive away bad dreams.

When they [enemies? Wooshkam?][5] were ready to start [for home? on a journey?][6] at night, after a meeting, everybody breathed on their [individual?] breasts.

And they sing:

> I am now going around
> And the enemy are scared
> They are leaving their quivers
> And running away.

> I am running
> And my enemies are afraid of me
> They are leaving their sons
> And running away.

The people with their hair tangled were brothers. As they got ready [for the coming trouble], the oldest worked and created a big whale.[7] He put it in the direction that the Wooshkam were to come, for protection. When the Wooshkam came to where the whale was lying, it acted very dangerous. They didn't come any further, but stopped right there. The younger brother also put one in their road. (The older brother's name was Han de mutch, Feather running. The younger's name was Vee ky mutch, Soft feather running.)[h]

When one of the Wooshkam medicine men found what these men were doing, he sang:

> *Running feather*
> *You've made a whale,*
> *Close to this whale*
> *The wind is twisting.*
>
> *Soft feather running*
> *You've made a whale*
> *On the back of this whale*
> *The clouds are twisting.*

When the songs ended, they sent some young men to these whales. They stuck a bunch of sticks in one whale's mouth and killed it.[8] The other whale they would kill by hanging.

The people who lived at the house at Casa Grande ruins came out of the house and went to a mountain called *kok chut* (curled up). The Wooshkam found them there and destroyed them. That is why the house [today's national monument] is not wrecked like the others: they did no fighting there.

---

[h]Probably A'an Melc, 'Wing-feather Cause-to-run', and certainly Wi:g Melc, 'Down-feather Cause-to-run'.

When they killed all those people, they came to a place just east of Casa Blanca (where there is a small mound). The man who lived there was a sharp-shooter who always hit his mark, didn't know what missing was, and always killed what he hit. His name was Suam veek sil da kum—Yellow soft feather plume.[i] When they got there, they surrounded his house, but they didn't come very close.

The man came from his house, and he shot arrows and killed people. The Wooshkam told their captives to go first, so the man was killing his own people. They saw that his arrows were as fast as lightning. They were frightened and sang:

> *Another land,*
> *Yellow soft feather plume,*
> *Around your arrows*
> *Are flying fast.*

> *Another mountain*
> *I give you a white bead*
> *In that a striped bow*
> *Is running near.*

---

[i]S-uam Viːg Siwdagkam, 'Yellow Down-feather Plume-having'. These shooting skills would seem to place this Hohokam on the solar side. He is a background adversary, not one of the principal ones.

Then a medicine man who had the power of thunder worked and killed the sharpshooter, but he had killed a lot of people.[9]

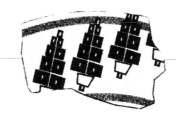

Now they came to Siivan i Vahki at Casa Blanca. The man Siivan went into his house with all his people. The Wooshkam watched him and said, "You come out like a man. You're not a woman to stay in the house." Some of them said, "Maybe he's not home, and that's why he doesn't come out."

Four different kinds of fog surrounded the vahki so the Wooshkam couldn't see it. They told one of their medicine men to roll a cigarette and breathe and find out if he [Siivan] is in there. The medicine man did this and saw Siivan inside with his hands tied by a snake and unable to do anything. The medicine man sang:

> *Vahki is built of clay*
> *In it I saw*
> *A medicine man.*
> *He is afraid of me*
> *He is staying in there*
> *The vahki is made of clay.*[10]

The people inside the vahki were shooting their arrows through holes made in the walls for that purpose, and they were killing the people outside. They fought for four days. Then they [Wooshkam] searched for a child who had become an orphan, whose [recently] dead father and mother were powerful medicine people.

Meanwhile the people inside the vahki looked out and said [insultingly] that the "plate-licker" (*was a a viñ oo ma dum*)[i] couldn't do anything. Then the child pulled one of his hairs, held it between his hands, and threw it crossways to the vahki, which it hit and broke. The vahki fell down, and that was the end of Siivan.

After they killed this man, who lived here at Casa Blanca, they came to his body to search it and make sure he was dead. They asked a medicine man to work over the body and be sure he was dead, because they had heard a lot about the power of these Hohokam people. The medicine man sat down to work and sang:

> *I am now sitting down*
> *And my power is shining forth*
> *I saw rainbows.*

The medicine man said that the man was dead, the understandings that he had were gone, and the

---

[i]Huas-ha'a Wiñumdam, 'Pottery-plate (literally "basket-pot," a post-Hispanic neologism used to describe European-style pottery table goods) Licker'.

things that he used were just shining dimly. All that the medicine man could see [of Siivan's things] were just colors like a rainbow. The people cried out that they must destroy this last little bit of understanding, that shows in the rainbow colors. Then the medicine man sang another song:

> *I am holding my hand*
> *And with my cane*
> *I have destroyed the understanding*
> *Of this medicine man*
> *And the stones that he used*
> *Are now coming out in black colors.*

STORY 26

SIUUHU'S REVENGE: DOWNSTREAM

From there the medicine man looked over this place here [Snaketown] and saw that some people left here and went west, but some remained. So they [Wooshkam] moved down this way, came here, and destroyed everything that was here. Then they gathered some big rocks and placed them on the ruins of the houses. This was to show that the people who had lived here were powerful. No one [Wooshkam] was killed.

The Wooshkam made camp here [Snaketown] and then saw that ahead of them lay a great body of water that no one could cross. The man who had made this water lived just north of here (perhaps the "tanks" north of Higley, Ariz.). The Wooshkam asked a medicine man to find out why the water was there. The medicine man was named Judum nam kum (a man that has the power of a bear).[k] He worked and found that there was a house there [at the water?], and the house foundations were made of ocotillo (*mul-luk*).[l] He sang:

> *I saw ahead of me*
> *A house which has*
> *A foundation of muhluk.*
>
> *I saw a house ahead of me*
> *I have now learned*
> *That this house is there*
> *And the roof of this house*
> *Is made of ocotillo.*[11]

The Wooshkam went down and found that there really was no water between them and the house. The man who lived at the house had fooled them to

---

[k]Judum Namkam, 'Bear Meeter'.
[l]*Melhog*, 'ocotillo' (a kind of cactus).

make it look like there was water, which was really a mirage (*coʼo at ju ki*).[m] When they got to this house, they fought for four days and nights with no food but with water to drink. Finally they destroyed some of the people there and captured and made prisoners of the rest.

STORY 28

SIUUHU'S REVENGE: GUADALUPE AND PUEBLO GRANDE

Namkum means that a person sleeps at night, and if he is very interested in something, such as birds and animals, and if the bird or animal knows that, then it comes to him in his dream and shows him how to act like the bird or animal. That's how medicine people get their power, by learning from different things [creatures] that they are interested in, in their dreams. That's what *namkum* means.

They made camp there and asked another medicine man to work for them. He had the power of the bluebird, Huh wut jut nam kum.[n]

The bluebird man found out that ahead of them lived a chief with many people, at a mound that is somewhere a little north of Yaqui Village (Guadalupe, Ariz.). (The medicine man sang two songs, but Juan has forgotten them.) The house at this mound was destroyed.

The bluebird man worked some more and looked in the same direction and saw that it was raining very hard at a spot just across the river from where the previous enemy man was (Guadalupe). This spot

---

[m]*Ku:jegi*, 'mirage', 'heat wave' (as over a road) (Saxton, Saxton, and Enos 1983: 35).
[n]He:wacud Namkam, 'Bluejay Meeter'.

was where Yellow Buzzard (Huam a nui)° used to live (Pueblo Grande).¹²

Every Hohokam village had a medicine man, called *makai* (doctor), as a leader.ᴾ

This man had made his house from solid rock, so it seemed impossible for the Wooshkam to hurt it. He had done this because he didn't want any of his people to run off and leave him. They must all stay in this house with this medicine man.

It wasn't really a stone house, but the leader made it look like solid rock.

At that time there was evil in the minds of the people who used to live here. They wanted to kill and destroy everything, which is like selfishness. This same evil has been carried on until today.

The bluebird man fooled himself by saying that the house was made of rock, and he couldn't do anything with it, so they asked another man who had the power of thunder to see what he could do (Chu din nam kum). He sang:

> *It is a hard house*
> *It is a hard house*
> *It is a hard house*
> *Do you see the foundation?*
> *It is made out of rock.*

Then he told the people that it [destruction?] would be easy for him, and he sang:

> *I saw that he is*
> *Too light for me.*

°*Uam Ñu:wi*, 'Yellow Buzzard'.
ᴾ*Ma:kai*, 'medicine man', 'shaman', 'doctor'. This is a different word from *siwañ*, 'chief'. Smith is not alone among narrators in holding that the Hohokam had "medicine men" as well as "chiefs." The contemporary Pima-Papago, however, and also those who emerged from the underworld, had only medicine men. They have no chiefs, that is, no sisiwañ.

*It is like a windbreak (*oksha*, four walls, no roof,*
shelter for cooking)
Made out of these ocotillos.

It was true. The thunderman came down over the house and smashed it to pieces. When this happened, the earth quaked and it knocked down a house that was close to the city of Phoenix (La Ciudad?).[13]

STORY 29

**INTERLUDE:
ARROWS FROM
THE SOUTH**

After they destroyed this house (Pueblo Grande) where Huamanui lived, they made their camp there and asked another medicine man to find out what was ahead of them (Juan doesn't remember what power this man had). He looked west and saw a distant cyclone or whirlwind that was pulling out trees by their roots. This frightened the Wooshkam. They decided to stay there for a while and make plenty of arrows to prepare to fight the people who were ahead of them.

All this time there was another company of Wooshkum who had gone south from here [see story 18] and were not fighting very hard. They had plenty of weapons with them because there were not so many people in that country. Among this group was a medicine man called Siu duk wy nam kum, Power of the blue deer.[q] He saw that the people who had come this way [now resting at Pueblo Grande] had been fighting hard, that their weapons were getting scarce, and that most of them were killed. He sent a woman to bring them some arrows.

When the medicine man (one of those to the north) saw her coming with arrows, he knew they were for the Wooshkam, and he sang:

> *The woman is getting closer*
> *The woman is getting closer*
> *Don't you see her?*
> *All you people?*

She brought the arrows, and they distributed them.

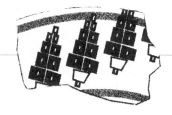

SIUUHU'S REVENGE: SIVERN, HIS BOX, AND THE HANDSOME YOUNG BOY

During all this time, the man Sivern [probably the same as the Siivan of story 25], who was living there [somewhere], was getting ready, and he told his child to get his *va sha* (box).[r] He got the box, and somewhere where Sivern had a piece of land, where

[q] S-cehedagi Hwai Namkam, 'Blue Deer Meeter'.
[r] *Vasa*, 'covered box', 'suitcase', 'oblong-plaited-basket-with-cover'.

he planted his crops, Sivern took the child and the box. He put him somewhere and covered him up. He left the child, telling him, "You must lay here all the time. You will notice the wind blowing. If it keeps blowing, I'm alive, but if it stops, you will know I am dead. Then you go and look for my body. When you find it, cut me open, and down in my heart you will find a shining stone. Take it. Then you must follow the Wooshkum people. Wherever they camp, you go and circle their camp till you find out where there is a small group gathered separately. You go and make company with them. Then you'll find out if they'll keep you or kill you."

There were four [Wooshkum] medicine men who worked and made the strong cyclone, or wind, [of Sivern] become gentle. It was easy for them. But the medicine man, Sivern, got half of the power of the strong wind and closed it in his box. The other half was the wind that the Wooshkum saw [story 22?]. In the box were also some feathers from the man-eagle [story 10].

When Sivern saw that the power of this wind was going down, he spoke, "I thought I was more powerful than anybody else, but now I see that there are people more powerful than me." Then he cried and sang while crying:

> *Way off you can dimly*
> *See the wind standing*
> *In that my heart is dying.*

The clouds are all gone
My mind is all gone.

While he sang, the clouds came close to the earth, and the Wooshkum couldn't see where this man was. They got the man who had dreamed the song of this Sivern when they first came to the ocean from the east [story 16]. When this man was ready, he sang:

I am now sitting down
I am now singing the song of Sivern.

I am now standing
I am learning the song of Sivern.

Then he sang the song which is Sivern's:

The sun is coming up
It's shining through the va pa ki *(houses).*

He saw that Sivern went out of his house and was moving in some direction. The Wooshkam made lightning to kill Sivern, but it did not hit him. (*Sivern* or *Sivanyn*, a word meaning medicine man). He went underground somehow and came up someplace. They tried to hit him again, but he went down, and they couldn't do it. Then he came up close to where he went down. This time thunder tried to hit him, but he went down again. Then he came out again, and this time he was walking. He was not a medicine man anymore but just like any other person.

Then it was not a medicine man who went after him, but some of the people who were good with bows and arrows. They went down [there] and killed him.

The fighting went on for four times four days (a sacred number, with a special word, *"gee ko chiu moi duk"*).[s] After they killed this man, the sun went down, and they made camp for the night. The wind stopped blowing where the child was with the box, and he came out and did what Sivern had told him to do. He circled the camp and found a group of people by themselves. He came to them, and it happened that one was a medicine man, sitting by the fire. This man said to the people who were there with him, "Look behind me. Somebody is standing behind me."

When the people looked they saw nobody standing there. The man told them to look four times, and they still couldn't see anything. Then he reached with his hand behind him, and surely there was the child with the box.

The people saw that he was a handsome young boy (*skugut viap pwuh*).[t] The people talked among them-

The people who received the child were those that we call Ho ho la.[u] They live at Ak Chin and Gila Bend, a mixture [today] of Pima and Papago blood. So [too?] the Pimas are mixed Wooshkum and Hohokam. There were originally three kinds of Hohokam, collectively called "Kee a kum":[v] *ma ma gum, va va gum,* and *oh ga gum.*[14] And there were two kinds of Wooshkam.[15]
Today all five are living here, and everyone knows who they are.

Today the Hohola people have that box, and nobody else is allowed to see or take care of it.

---

[s]Probably *gi'iko ce:mo'oidag*, 'four-times completion', 'four-times permeation'.
[t]*S-keg viapoi*, 'handsome (or 'good') boy'.
[u]Hu:hu'ula, a "dialect group" of Pima-Papago. They live in the northwest part of today's Sells (or Papago) reservation and are the core residents of today's Ak Chin and Gila Bend reservations.
[v]This word is probably *kiikam*, which simply means "resident." Thus, it is probably not, as one might hope, a hitherto undisclosed name for the Hohokam.

selves and said they must not tell everybody about this lad that had come. They must keep him secretly.

The next morning the [entire Wooshkum?] people talked and decided to rest for a while, because they were worn out. They asked a medicine man to look around where they were and see if there was any danger close by.

SUPPLEMENT

**BLACK
SINEW CHIEF,
HIS BASKET,
AND KOKOÑIP
(THIN LEATHER/
RUSSELL)**

[The Pima-Papago army moved toward the great house at Casa Blanca, home of Black Sinew Chief.] They then attacked Tcotcuk Tatai Sivan,[w] who was the most powerful of all the chiefs who ventured to oppose them. He knew that they would defeat him, yet he struggled bravely to save his people and at the last to save himself.

He first took some soot from his chimney, powdered it in the palm of his hand, blew it into the air, and darkness immediately fell so dense that Elder Brother's warriors could see nothing.

Tcotcuk Tatai Sivan then threw down his dwelling and made his way through the midst of his enemies.

---

[w]Cucuk Tatai Siwañ, 'Black Sinew Chief'.

But the god of darkness [i.e., the lightmaker, working for the invaders] dispelled the night, and the escaping leader was seen in the distance. Elder Brother's warriors succeeded in getting ahead of him and were about to surround and kill him when he wiped the tears from his eyes and blew the drops among the men about him. This produced a mirage which concealed him from view. But the god of mirage [the heatmaker, evaporator of moist mirages] caused the veil to lift, and again he was seen fleeing in the distance.

Again Tcotcuk Tatai Sivan was headed [off] and in danger; but this time he took out his reed cigarette and blew puffs of smoke, which settled on his pursuers like a heavy fog through which he continued his flight. The god of fog [dispelling] drove it into the sky and he was seen escaping.

He now realized that he had but one more chance for his life. When the fog had formed clouds in the sky he took his belt and threw it upward and climbed up and laid himself against the clouds as a rainbow. It was impossible for the god of the rainbow unaided to bring him down; he made several unsuccessful attempts before he hit upon the expedient of making some spiders, which he sent after the rainbow. They formed a web over the bow and brought it to earth and destruction.

Elder Brother's soldiers were so astonished at the prowess of Tcotcuk Tatai Sivan that they thought he must have a strange heart, so they cut it open to see, and, sure enough, they found within it a green stone about the size of a bullet. The stone is kept to this day in a medicine basket which they captured with his grandson.

Before he had undertaken his flight he had told the boy, Kakanyip, to go with his basket and hide under a bush; after the grandfather should be killed the lad should come, touch him, and swallow the odor of the body, and he would acquire the power of the Siwañ. But a warrior named Shohany discovered the little Kakanyip, and after a time sold him to the Papago chief Kak Sisiveliki,[x] Two-Whirlwinds. The box is yet kept by the Papagos living 30 miles south of Gila Bend. If it is disturbed a severe storm is produced and cold weather prevails in Pima Land. (Russell 1908: 227–228)

HE GREAT DOCTOR'S END (THIN LEATHER/ LLOYD)

And then they [invaders] went on to where the Casa Blanca vahahkkees now are in ruins; and the great doctor who lived there [Black Sinew Chief], the same who had sent his boy to inquire of the proph-

---

[x]Go:k Sisiwelig, 'Two Whirlwinds'.

ecies [on the coming invasion], drew a magic line before his place, so that the enemy could not cross. And when Ee-ee-toy's men came to the line the earth opened, and they could not go further till one of their great doctors, by his power, had closed it, and then they could pass it.

And they had a great battle there, for the place was very strong, and hard to get into. And there was a doctor among them called Nee-hum Mahkai,[y] and they asked him to use his magic power to tear the place down, and he tried but could not succeed. And they asked another, called Tchu-dun Mahkai,[z] or Earthquake Doctor, and he tried and failed also. And then they asked another little man, not supposed to have much power, and he took a hair from his head and held it up by the two ends and sang a song and turned it into a snake. And he sent the snake, and it struck the house and shook it so it broke and fell down from above. And then Ee-ee-toy's men took the place and killed everybody there except Tcheu-tcickadahtai Seeven,[aa] who escaped and ran on.

And one of Ee-ee-toy's warriors pursued him and was going to strike him with a club, when he sank down, and the place where he sank was filled with fog, so they could not see him, and he got out on the other side and ran on. But they had a doctor called

---

[y]Probably Wuihom Ma:kai, 'Lightning Medicine Man' [or 'doctor'].
[z]Ceḍeñ(¿) Ma:kai 'Thumping(¿) Medicine Man.'
[aa]Cucuk Tatai Siwañ, 'Black Sinew Chief'.

Ku-mi-wahk Mahkai,[bb] and they had him clear away the fog, and then they could see him and chased him again.

And again, when about to be struck, he sank down, and a mirage filled the place so that they could not see him, for things did not look the same. And he got out beyond and ran on. And they had a Saskatch Mahkai,[cc] or Mirage Doctor, who cleared away the false appearance, and again they chased him and were about to kill him, when again he sank.

And this time a rainbow filled the place and made him invisible, and again he ran on till their Kee-hawt Mahkai,[dd] or Rainbow Doctor, removed the rainbow. And then once more they were about to strike him when he sank, and the quivers which heat makes, called coad-jook,[ee] filled the hole, and again he got away. But they had a Coadjook Doctor, and he removed it, and then they chased him and killed him. (Lloyd 1911: 156–158)

[bb]Ko:mhaiwa Ma:kai, 'Fog [wet, misty] Medicine Man'. Here and in the next two instances, a person who *counters* the thing in question, e.g., who counters fog.
[cc]Şaşkaj Ma:kai, 'Mirage [waterlike] Medicine Man'.
[dd]Kiohoḍ Ma:kai, 'Rainbow Medicine Man'.
[ee]Ku:jegi, 'mirage' (as waves over a paved road), 'heat waves'.

NOW THE END, which is self-explanatory or at least understandable from the footnotes and earlier introductory statements. Just one text is given to supplement Smith-Allison. This is from the long but poorly recorded Hendricks version of the conquest. It describes the death of an old woman among the conquerors, and it is clearly the same story as Smith-Allison's story 32. Thin Leather lacks a version of it. I include it to show that more narrators than Smith-Allison follow the conquest, which is almost bloodless for the victors, with an origin of death among the victors.[1]

STORY 31

ENDING: BIG
MOUNTAIN

The makai [medicine man] worked around where these people were and found out that the Hohokam were going toward a mountain that they call "Gu do ak" (Big Mountain),[a] all frightened and running. There was no danger. Then he sang:

> *I am looking very sad (*hu matchum*)*[b]
> *Feather water (*an schrodek*)*[c]

---

[a]Ge'e Duag, 'Big Mountain'.
[b]Seems to be *hemajim*, 'kind', 'gentle', 'tame', 'sympathetic'.
[c]*A'an ṣu:dag*, 'long-feather water'.

I am going to big mountains
To the big mountain
Enemy woman looks good.

I am now looking sadly
At soft feather water
To the big mountain
Some of the children
Of my enemies
Are pretty.

That's the way he saw the mountain and the pretty woman, how it came to his mind. They weren't going to hurt these people. They just came to destroy the ones that lived by Snaketown, because they killed Siuuhu.

STORY 32

ENDING:
FIRST GRAVE

When they saw there was no danger close by, the [Wooshkum] people decided to make their home close to Komatke[d] mountain. Then the medicine man sang two other songs:

A sandy land I saw
And in this land
I make my home.
A sandy land mountain
I learned
I am going to make my home there.

---

[d]*Komatk*, 'Broad'. Pima-Papago name for Estrella Mountain, southwest of Phoenix, Ariz. Also the name of St. John's village, which is near the mountain.

While they made their home there, a leader of the other company [of Wooshkum] died. This man's wife was an old woman. She began to lead the people, who were called Chuch ma mike Oh tum, or horned toad people.[e] She took sick and was going to die.

At this time the people staying at Komatke were planning to leave again, and they told the other group, "When this old woman dies, you can leave and go on. We don't think there will be any more trouble."

So some were going to leave, and some were going to stay there. Then they said they would do something to show that the owl (*chu kut*)[f] does not belong here [in Pima-Papago country]. They made a rule: when a big bird builds its nest someplace, the owl will come and fight with the bird, chase it away, and lay its eggs in the nest.

So it is true today. No one ever saw an owl build its own nest anywhere.

This was true. When the owl found the nest of another bird, he fought the bird and took away its nest and laid its eggs there.

Early in the morning, before sunup, the people got ready to start their journey, and they sang:

> *I am leaving you and*
> *I am going*
> *The morning shining across.*

---

[e]Cecmamaig (sing., *cemamaig*) O'odham, 'Horned-toads Pima-Papago'.
[f]*Cukud*, 'owl', 'ghost'. In this story, the "ghost" as well as the "owl" meaning is present.

I am leaving you
And running away
The setting of the sun
Is shining blue.

Part went on their journey and part stayed, but they were all afraid because this part of the land was dangerous. When the old woman found out the thoughts [plans to stay and leave] of the people, she sang:

She's telling the people she's sick, and when she walks the ground doesn't feel hard but springy.

Over ahead of me the land
Seemed like a piece of rubber
I want to lead my people
But I cannot do it.

Ahead of me there are many
Mountains.
In these mountains
My mind is getting weak.

The people taking care of this old woman were her grandchildren. They sang:

Our grandmother
I wish you would die.
And everything will be all right.
Ahead of you the land
Seemed to be springy.

Grandmother,
We wish you'd fall pretty soon.

Ahead of you there are
Many mountains.

Juan says he doesn't know how it is today. Maybe it is spoiled, but it still shows.

The old woman died, and they arranged her body in a grave like she was sitting down, close to these Komatke mountains. From that time, the grave where she was, was kept clean by the Pimas.

STORY 33

ENDING: RAVEN AND GEEHODUK

Soon after the old woman died, the people [who had stayed behind] moved closer to these [Komatke] mountains, where there were lots of bushes or trees in a thicket. There a raven and a bird they call *geehoduk* (like a pigeon)[g] had a fight. The raven was a Wooshkum and the geehoduk was Hohokam.

The bird like a pigeon made a noise like a pigeon, and the [Wooshkum] people were afraid. It wasn't long since the old woman had died, and they were sad all the time. They sang:

> *We have arrived*
> *In the land of the thicket*
> *In this the geehoduk*
> *Is gladly singing.*

---

[g]Unknown. *Gi'ihodag* means "thinness," "leanness."

We have arrived
In the land of the thicket
In this the raven
Is gladly singing.

STORY 34

ENDING:
TURKEY MAN

Soon after they sang those songs, the people moved west. Soon they came to the other [Wooshkum] people who had been ahead of them. They were getting close to the man that went before these people who used to live over here.[2] His name was Tovacule, "Turkey man."[h]

When he saw them coming, he turned himself into a skeleton. When they saw him, they were afraid. He sang:

> *I am turning myself*
> *Into a dead person.*
> *Your tomahawks are*
> *Breaking all to pieces.*

The reason why the child rolled on the ground was that he was going to change himself into a hawk.

The Wooshkum hunted for the child who had destroyed the house at Casa Blanca [story 24]. When they found him, they asked him to kill that man.

---

[h] Tova Keli, 'Turkey Old-man'.

The child lay on the ground and twisted himself in every way. When Tovacule saw this, he made fun of it and said, "You ashes dumper, *ma ta ya wa tum,*[i] you can't do a thing to me."

When the child's grandmother heard Tovacule say this, she was very mad, and she sang a song:

> *That is my poor boy*
> *You have called him my poor boy*
> Pi vi cum *(hawk)*[j] *bird is mighty strong.*

So it was true. The child turned himself into a hawk and killed the old man Tovacule.

STORY 35

**ENDING:
DEFEAT AT
THE OCEAN
PEOPLE**

They fought those [Turkey Old-man] people and destroyed them all. They moved to the west, and whenever they came to a group of people, they destroyed them easily. They reached and crossed the red river, Wik Akima.[k]

At that time there were some people living close to the ocean. They knew these [Wooshkum] people

---

[i]*Matai iawatam*, 'ash dumper'.
[j]Unknown, not a known hawk name.
[k]Weg Akimel, 'Red River', equals the Colorado ("Red" in Spanish) River.

were coming and that they were destroying everyone they came to. The people by the ocean worked
to make them thirsty and to make them lose their
way.

The Wooshkum got thirsty and sang:

> *Ahead of me lies mirage*
> *Ahead of me the land*
> *Is nothing but mirage.*

They got out of the heat that these people sent out,
but then they lost their way. They sang:

> *Ahead of me lies nothing*
> *But fog.*
> *Don't you see?*
> *Ahead of me mountains*
> *Are covered*
> *With fog.*

They went on and came out of the fog. Then they
came to where these people were living, and they
found that they were small people. They also found
that their country was awfully cold. Snow fell all the
time, and their houses were built into the ground.
On top of them was nothing but snow.

They had a fight. The [ocean] people would come
out from their houses, shoot at them, and go back in
their houses. The Wooshkum couldn't do a thing to
them because they were from a warm country and

could not stand the cold. The thunder tried but couldn't explode because it was too cold, and the chu dunk tried and couldn't do anything for the same reason.

The thunder sang:

> *Thunder,*
> *I'm like the thunder*
> *It hits*
> *But it slips*
> *To the other direction.*

The chu dunk sang:

Chu dunk is a heavy rock with fire. Long ago, you sometimes saw a streak of lightning like a shooting star, tied to thunder.[1]

> *I am chudunk*
> *I look like a chudunk*
> *I am coming*
> *From above.*

After the Wooshkum couldn't do anything to these people, they held a meeting and decided not to bother them. If they kept on fighting, they might lose all their people, so they decided to turn back. They all came and turned their faces away from the [ocean people¿] and sang:

> *The sun is going down.*
> *I am now going back*
> *On the road where I came from*

---

[1] Apparently the same *cedeñ* ('thump')-derived word that we encountered earlier, where it was said to mean "earthquake."

I am holding my cane
Against my breast.

The sun is going down
And I am returning
On the road that I came from
I am now running
I am holding my cane on my breast.

END: STOP THE WAR, SPLIT THE WATER, DEPART THE GOD

The Wooshkum started back to where they came from. When the people who lived there [cold ocean shore] saw this, they came from their houses and yelled and made fun of them, saying many things in their language that the Wooshkum did not understand because their languages were different.

The Wooshkum moved back this way sadly and came to a place where the ground was boiling.[3] They said they would fight this land, and that might make them happy. They sang:

I have gotten this far
With a shining rock
I have gotten this far.
And I have now folded the land.

I have gotten this far
With a shining rock
I have gotten this far
I have folded the mountains.

The bravest people tried to destroy the boiling water, but it acted very dangerous. It boiled, and all around it hot water splashed at a certain distance so no one could get close to it. Then the Coyote got his shield and tomahawk and went near to it. It splashed on him and turned into arrowheads which went all over into his flesh. He came out and said, "I did this so the people can learn how to kill their enemies with the shield and tomahawk."

Then he went to the ocean to doctor himself, singing:

Don't you think
That I am a real man?
I have gone to the edge
Of a large body of water.
I met a medicine man.

Am I
A real, true medicine man?
On the edge of a large body
Of water
I met a Nassya (White Eater).[4]

After this happened, Siuuhu sang to state that the war was all over:

I have placed myself
And I saw.
I have killed the enemy
I am carrying it across.

Let us run and see
It was Siuuhu who killed
And he has brought it.

The people moved on down this way. They came to
the red river [story 34], and its waters were now
very high. They couldn't go further. They camped
there. Then they talked to a man who understands
his arrows thoroughly. They asked him to help them
get across.

He stood up and got one of his arrows and sang:

You called me
That I have the power
Of an arrow.
I have put my arrow
In the water.
And with [it] I am going
To break the water
In two.

This man couldn't do anything, so they stayed there
all night. The next morning they went to a man
with the power of thunder. He went and stood at
the edge of the water, told the people to get ready,
and sang:

You called me
That I have the power
Of thunder.
I am now standing in the middle
and with this
I am breaking the water
In two.

This thunder exploded and he went down into the water, and the water split in two and made a road. But just about the time the people were ready to go through, it came back together again.

So the thunder man couldn't do anything, and the people stayed there all night. The next morning they asked Siuuhu to try for them. He went down and stood at the edge with his cane in his hand and sang:

A bright morning cane
With it
I am breaking the water
In two.

Those people who went after this child are called Sa up makum.[m] They are like Pimas, but their language is slightly different.

He hit the water with his cane, and sure enough the water rolled back on both sides and made a road for the people who went down and came out on the other side. But among the people was a small child who was naughty. He cried and started back for the other [far] side, and his relatives went after him.

---

[m]Could be S-a'ap'emakam, 'Those-that-seem-normal', perhaps 'Those-that-try-it-out'.

When the waters closed ahead of them, they were left on the other side.

The ways that these [Wooshkum] people went through were very wicked from the beginning of the story. The cutting of the trees is a symbol of the wicked ways of the people of this earth, that sometimes a man gets in deep sin and he must cut out the sin and begin a new life.

Siuuhu looked back to the people who were left on the other side. He told them it would be all right to make their home there, and they would become relatives of the Yumas. Then he told the rest of the people [who had crossed] that they must go to the land that they had won and make their home there. He also told them about the trees in this [present Pima-Papago] land, that when the trees get old they must chop their limbs off so they might start a new life again.

He also told the people that the Wooshkum and Hohokam must love each other and work together. He said that the five kinds of people ["sibs"] must get together and fight their enemies together, and he spoke especially about the Apache Indians who would be their enemies in the future. Then he spoke about the time when the war between Apaches and Pimas would stop, and they would make friends.

After he told them these things, Siuuhu went back to his home which is called Chok we cum (the place where the olla is, in which Siuuhu enclosed himself during the flood).[n] The people lived and made war with the Apaches until one time when this was

---

[n]Probably Cuk Wi'ikam, 'Black Remainder', of story 2. Most Papago stories say that he went to live at Ba'boquivari Peak, the highest point on the Papago reservation.

stopped and they made friends with each other. Apaches would [at one time in the past] come to visit the people here and eat with them here with whatever they raised on their farms.

So at one time a [Pima] woman was gathering mesquite beans somewhere, and she had a baby somewhere [with her]. The baby was crying, and just at that time some Apaches were close by and heard it. They went where it was and tried to nurse it to stop it from crying. They didn't mean any harm.

The mother came and was scared and went to where the Pimas were and told them that the Apaches got her baby. The Pimas went over and killed the Apaches, and they began to fight one another again.

They went on fighting, and finally a chief of the Apaches and a chief of the Pimas met together, talked things over, decided to stop the fighting, and did stop the fighting. From that time, the Apaches did come every once in a while and made friends with the Pimas and shared the things that the Pimas raised over here. Everything went on in peace.

At another time, there was a white man living at a place called "Vow pek" (Many wells, Maricopa Wells).° The Apaches stole some mules from him. He told the Pimas about it, and the Pimas went and

---

°Waiwpiak, 'Many-wells', near today's Maricopa, Ariz.

killed the Apaches. From then on they began to fight again. Then it came down to where the Government stopped the fighting, and the Apaches are our friends again.

That is why the old people say that this story is all true, what Siuuhu has done and said to the people from the beginning.

In the great throng of people who traveled with Elder Brother after he emerged from Ashes Hill,[5] there were two brothers who had their old grandmother with them. This little group could not keep up with the crowd when it was moving, and at evening they always camped a distance behind the others. The two brothers had to go in the evening and overtake the party to find what the people would do the next morning. They built a big fire and left their grandmother near it. They kept doing this for a long time, and at last they grew tired of it. The older brother said, "I guess we had better kill our grandmother and be able to travel with the rest, so we will know what is going on all the time. Perhaps we will meet some of the people we are going to fight, and we would not be able to see them because we are always behind."

The younger brother said, "All right, but we must tell our grandmother and see what she will say about it." They told their grandmother and said, "Well, grandmother, we would like to know what you think of this plan that we kill you, because you know that we are always behind and do not know what is going on over there. So we thought we would kill you and keep up with the crowd." She said, "Well, grandsons, it is all right because I have been living a long time and have seen many things in this world. I would like you to be with the crowd and see what is going on." She sang the following song, but she felt so badly that she was crying rather than singing. (This quality of tone was imitated by the singer when recording the song.)

> *Oh! I have seen many things in this world and I have been in this world a long time.*

The old grandmother said, "After I die, find some fine sand and bury me in it. When you come back this way, stop and see what you find." The boys then sang the following song. They sang it four times, and when they came near the end of the fourth time, the grandmother began to die.

> *Our grandmother says it will be all right if she dies, Because she has been alive a long time.*

That is why she does not mind dying,
Because we cannot keep up with the crowd.

The boys buried their grandmother in the sand and joined the crowd on its journey. As they were returning they came to the place where they had buried her, and they saw a plant growing. It was tobacco. Ever afterwards they did not smoke because they said the tobacco was the flesh of their grandmother. (Densmore, 1929: 27–30)

BY "MYTHOLOGY," I mean "a collection of texts, organized by one person, stating the origins of the things of this earth." I think that few would dispute the three phrases that constitute this definition, but some may object that the definition fails to distinguish mythology from history and, relatedly, fails to exclude the secular from the province of myth. My defense is simple. In the first place, the Pima-Papago mythology that we have dealt with intends to be historical, and our problem is to understand how it is so, that is, how it is preoccupied with Pima history and yet makes almost no reference to Pima and white relations. Second, except for a feeling conveyed by the narrative that what happens is happening for the first time, I find little that seems sacred in the sense of perfect or blessed in the mythology, while there is a good deal that is frightful and earthy. This feeling of origins seems essential, but I would as willingly call it magical as sacred, the magic of first times. Thus does the mythology approach but not embrace sacredness, as a matter of narrative feeling or tone.

I will now comment briefly on the relevance of the rest of the definition to the Smith-Allison text and, finally, on the relation of the text to the current production of literature by and about Native Americans.

"Collection of texts." The issue here is whether this mythology is one text or whether it is an anthology, or a conglomerate. Smith gave it as one text, and as noted in my introduction, the story and part divisions and titles were supplied by me. It is not difficult to see how it is one text. The events have a temporal order; the mythology is a linear chronicle. Still, years are not counted, the story is silent about the European period, and one character, Siuuhu, is in action through practically the entire narrative. Frankly, although I call the whole narrative The Hohokam Chronicles, the whole could equally be called *The Deeds of Siuuhu*. The subjects come together, as we know, because Siuuhu created and terminated the Hohokam. We also understand that most of the recalled origins of things fall into the Hohokam period, which makes a double impression, that the Pima-Papago who lived by and with all those things are culturally quite like the Hohokam and that the period of origins and therefore the formative time of the universe was very short, within a young-into-middle-aged man-god's time span.

In my view, there is a definite progression through the events of the mythology as a whole, and this progression gives the depth of the work. The pre-Hohokam period was a time of Genesis-like man-god creations (including acts by God himself), the Hohokam period saw the origin of human families in which man-gods could not participate, and the Hohokam conquest period was really the aftermath of that incompatibility. The conquest was the coming of the Pima-Papago, but it was also the expulsion, or the occasion for the departure from human affairs, of the god Siuuhu. On this reading, the Hohokam conquest is a literary device or, let us say, a mythic truth. It was motivated by a need to separate humanity from god.

"Organized by one person." Throughout Native North America, if anyone knew one myth, that person was bound to know others, meaning, I think, that the proper unit for mythological study, whether as history, imaginative literature, or theology, is not the single myth but the full set or corpus of one person's tales. Thus I would also define mythology as "all of the tales that one person tells, in the order that he or she tells them." Now, that definition certainly applies to the Pima-Papago. They had the idea that mythologies could and should be told by single narrators during the longest four nights of the year, in December. And as we saw in Smith-Allison and also in Thin Leather, the only other Pima-Papago mythologist whose entire work was recorded, the mythology gains integrity through association with Siuuhu. Nearly every story involves him in some way, even though one could imagine the story with a male character other than him. I suspect that this is the exception rather than the rule in Native American myth collections. More commonly, there are complete shifts of characters between major myths, and the overall order, if any, is chronological and/or thematic but not as in this case also biographical, the biography of a god.

Really, there are three questions: What is the totality of myth stories or myth types extant among a people? To what extent are these stories brought into order by individual narrators? And to what extent do these individual synthetic works duplicate or replicate each other? I do not know the answers to these questions, and I am not aware that anyone does. And if they point to a new field of study, the key to it is the concept of the single narrator, multimyth mythology. Through it, the concept of author comes into Native American myth studies. Mythology is not only the study of myths but also the creation of meaning and order between and within them.

Finally, we must note that the time of these native mythological authors may have—seems to have—passed. We need not grieve over this, if we can understand the time as a phase. Literary and cultural production have not ceased among Indians, nor has religion, nor has the potential for interest in the work of the past authors. Indeed, if the last fresh mythological syntheses have been made, those works can be viewed as Scripture or masterpieces, or both. A piece of Native American literary history, the age of mythology making, comes into view. American civilization needs to know this piece because that civilization was not only a negative force but also a stimulus and ingredient for many of the mythologies.

There is an almost perfect cleavage between what Indians have written in the last thirty years and the subject matter of the mythologies. The mythologies are silent about post-Europe, that is, about the white colonial or invasion era; and the new writing is silent in its novels, poems, and essays about the pre-European era. I do not mean totally silent, but I mean voiced from today and reaching back with wishful thoughts to pre-Europe. The Smith-Allison mythology, as we saw it, is voiced from pre-Europe, and it reaches up to now. This is why the songs are so wonderful: their "I's" are Hohokam. The "I's" in the current writing, not inappropriately, are of today, the essayist's "I," the same as I use.

If Smith and Allison seem to be unusual Indian literary persons to readers of today, that is the reason. They were late practicers of a mythological tradition that sought its inspiration solely in pre-European events. Their counterparts were the archaeologists such as Hayden who, if I understand them correctly, would love to know Hohokam events with the precision contained in but not provable outside of the mythology. If creation in that mythological tradition is now past, let it be. It was a great age.

APPENDIX: CORRELATION OF CONQUESTS IN THIN LEATHER AND SMITH-ALLISON

LIKELY PLACE-NAME	LIKELY CHIEF NAME	NEAREST PRESENT-DAY LOCATION	THIN LEATHER DATA	SMITH-ALLISON DATA
Unknown	Unknown	Europe		Place not named, peopled by Sofch Kah (story 15).
Wa'aki, 'Great-house'; or Kui Wa'aki, 'Mesquite Great-house'	Siwan	Northwest of Glendale, Arizona		Vahki in the Mesquites, headed by Sivain (story 16).
Unknown	Unknown	Eastern Arizona		Apache Indians (story 17).
Unknown	Unknown	East-central Arizona		Jackrabbit Eaters (story 18).
Unknown	Siwañ, 'Chief'; Nu:vi, 'Buzzard'	Central Arizona		Place not named, headed by Sivain and Buzzard (story 19).
Unknown	Unknown	Central Arizona		Place not named, chief painted himself with mescal juice (story 20).
Wonam Du'ag, 'Hat Mountain'	Uninhabited	Central Arizona		Hat Mountain, uninhabited place where Pimas camped prior to battle for Chief Great-house (story 22).
Siwañ Wa'aki, 'Chief Great-house'	A'an Med, '[Long-] feather Running'; Vi:g Med, '[Down-] feather Running'	Casa Grande National Monument		Casa Grande Ruin, headed by two brothers, Long-feather Running and Down-feather Running (story 23).

LIKELY PLACE-NAME	LIKELY CHIEF NAME	NEAREST PRESENT-DAY LOCATION	THIN LEATHER DATA	SMITH-ALLISON DATA
Siwañ Wa'aki, 'Chief Great-house'	Si'al Ce:hedag Siwañ, 'Morning Green Chief'	Casa Grande National Monument	Casa Grande, headed by Morning-Blue Sivan (Russell, 227); Casa Grande, headed by Stcheuadack Seeven (= 'Green Chief') (Lloyd, 154)	
O'odkam Wa'aki, 'Gravel Great-house'	Giadag Siwañ, 'Bow-string Chief'	Santan, Arizona	Sandy Ancient House, headed by Kia-atak, 'Handle' (really 'bow-string'). Russell, 24, 227) Awawtkum Vahahkkee, headed by Geeaduck Seeven (Lloyd, 115, 155)	
Unknown	Cew Ha'o Siwañ, 'Long Gourd Chief'	4 miles north of Santan, Arizona	Villages, headed by Tcuf Baowo Sivan (Russell, 24, 227) Place, headed by Cheofhahvo Seeven, 'Long Dipper Chief' (Lloyd, 156)	
Unknown	Da'a Siwañ, 'Flying Chief,' or Tas Siwañ, 'Sun Chief'	Sweetwater, Arizona	Sweetwater Pueblo, headed by Ta-a Sivan, 'Flying' (Russell, 24, 227) Place, headed by Dthas Seeven (Lloyd, 156)	
Unknown	Uam Wi:g Siwodagkam, 'Yellow Down [feather] Headfeather'	Just east of Casa Blanca, Arizona		Place, headed by Suan Veek Sil da kum, 'Yellow Soft-feather Plume' (story 24).

LIKELY PLACE-NAME	LIKELY CHIEF NAME	NEAREST PRESENT-DAY LOCATION	THIN LEATHER DATA	SMITH-ALLISON DATA
Cuk Tataikam Siwan Wa'aki, 'Black Sinew Chief Great-house'	Cuk Tataikam Siwañ, 'Black Sinew Chief'	Casa Blanca, Arizona	Place, headed by Tcotcuk Tatai Sivan, 'Black Sinew Chief' (Russell, 24, 228) Vahahkkees (wa:paki, 'Great-houses') headed by Tcheutchickadahtai Seeven (Lloyd, 156–157)	Vahki, headed by Sivan (story 25).
S-ko:ko'ig, 'Many Rattlesnakes'	Unknown	Snaketown, Arizona	Place, then called Odchee [Bahr cannot interpret], headed by a doctor (Lloyd, 158)	Place, with fugitives from battle at Casa Blanca Siwañ Wa'aki (story 26).
Unknown	Ñu:wi, 'Buzzard'	6 miles west of Casa Blanca, Arizona	Pueblo, headed by Vulture (Russell, 228–229)	
Kokodki Oidag, 'Sea-shell Field'	Jenasat Siwañ, 'Lizard Chief'	Near Gila Crossing, Arizona	Place, headed by Tcunarsat Sivan (Russell, 229); Ko-awt-kee Oy-yee-duck, 'Shell Field,' headed by Tcheunasset Seeven (Lloyd, 158–159)	
Unknown	Unknown	Possibly near Higley, Arizona		Place with house with ocotillo cactus foundation, headed by a medicine man (story 27).

LIKELY PLACE-NAME	LIKELY CHIEF NAME	NEAREST PRESENT-DAY LOCATION	THIN LEATHER DATA	SMITH-ALLISON DATA
Nu:wi Wa'aki, 'Buzzard Great-house,' or We:gaj(≥), 'Behind-it(≥)'	Ñu:wi, 'Buzzard,' Uam Ñu:wi, 'Yellow Buzzard'	South of South Mountain (south boundary of Phoenix, Ariz.) according to Lloyd's Thin Leather (127); Pueblo Grande Ruin (north of South Mountain) according to Smith-Allison (story 28)	Place, where Noo-ee, 'Buzzard,' lived (Lloyd, 127, 159; Russell, 225)	Place, where Huam a Nui, 'Yellow Buzzard,' lived (stories 19, 28).
Siwañ Wa'aki, or Cuk Tataikam Siwañ Wa'aki	Siwañ or Cuk Tataikam Siwañ	Casa Blanca, Arizona		Great-house, headed by Siivan (stories 25, 30).
Unknown	Unknown	North of Salt River, near Camelback Mountain (Cheof S:e-vick, in this text; better spelled "Cew S-weg," 'Long Red'	Place, where a chief and his brother lived (Lloyd, 159)	
O'odkam Wa'aki, 'Gravel Great-house'	A-an Hi:tpagi Siwañ, 'Feather Braids Chief'	Mesa, Arizona (Russell, 229); near Fort McDowell, Arizona (therefore on Verde River) (Lloyd, 133, 160); at Wukkakotk, a mountain (Weg Gakodk, 'Red Hill'), therefore near Verde River at north boundary of today's Salt River Indian Reservation (Fewkes, 51)	Pueblo, headed by A-an Hitupaki ('Feather Breathing') Sivan (Russell, 24, 229; Russell's translation notes must have said "braided" instead of "breathing," and he must have misread his writing); a place, Awawtkumva-hahkee, headed by a seeven (Lloyd, 160); a place, where Feather-plaited Doctor lived (Fewkes, 51)	

LIKELY PLACE-NAME	LIKELY CHIEF NAME	NEAREST PRESENT-DAY LOCATION	THIN LEATHER DATA	SMITH-ALLISON DATA
Unknown	Vi:g Iol Ma:kai Siwañ, 'Down-feather Turned-over Chief'; or S-toa Vi:g Siwañ, 'White Down-feather Chief'	Pueblo Grande Ruin, Phoenix, Arizona (Russell, 24); between Tempe and Phoenix (true of Pueblo Grande) (Fewkes: 51)	Place, headed by Vi-iki-ial Makai Sivan, 'Soft Feathers Rolling' (Russell, 24, 229); place, headed by Turavrik Civana, 'White Feather' (Fewkes: 51)	Two places, headed by chiefs (story 28). The second place was also the residence of Buzzard.
Unknown	Unknown	Unknown, probably west-central Arizona		Place, where defeated Hohokam had taken refuge and were spared further violence by the Pimas (story 31).
Unknown	Unknown	Unknown, western Arizona	Pueblos, defeated by the Pimas to complete their conquest of the Gila Valley (Russell, 229)	
Unknown	Towa Keli, 'Turkey Old-man'	Unknown, probably western Arizona		Place, inhabited by To va Kule (story 34).
Unknown	Unknown	West of the Colorado River (Lloyd); west of the Colorado river in very snowy country (Smith-Allison)	Place, where Choo-chawf Aw-aw-tam, 'Foxes,' lived in holes in the ground (probably Ce:co O'odham, 'Caves People') (Lloyd, 161)	Place, where people lived in snow-covered houses (story 35).
Unknown	Unknown	Yellowstone Park (or possibly hot springs in the Imperial Valley, California)		Place, inhabited by boiling, erupting water (story 35).

1. The native author N. Scott Momaday used essentially the same tripartite past in writing his books *The Way to Rainy Mountain* and *The Names*, especially the former. His terms for the three periods are "the mythical, the historical, and the immediate." His method was to form "triplet chapters," each chapter being composed of a short story from each time period, the three stories being unified by an overall concern or motif. H. David Brumble (1988) put this method into the perspective of Indian autobiography in general. For Brumble, the pre-Momaday native oral autobiographical tradition was confined to the immediate past (Vansina's period of personal accounts). This tradition classically consisted of recitations of fame-giving or fame-worthy events. Momaday's innovations on that tradition were, first, to expand the range and moods of remembered personal experience to conform to the range and moods of European autobiography and, second, to tribalize his personal accounts by juxtaposing them with pieces of group history and ancient myth. The result was a new form of autobiography, modern in its sense of self but invoking the full oral cultural time scale.

Smith and Allison do not do this. They stay in the realm of ancient time narrative. They certainly were more conservative and less formally schooled than Momaday, who was a good generation younger than them, and I would also say that they wanted to make a church scripture (see below), while Momaday wanted to make a more secular and modern kind of literature.

2. A people with the same culture, language, and myth tradition as the Pimas. The Pimas live along the Gila and Salt rivers in desert central Arizona. The Papagos live in the riverless desert to the south of them. I will refer to the two peoples jointly as the Pima-Papago.

3. I will make constant reference to Thin Leather's mythology. It was taken down independently three times, first by Frank Russell (published in condensed form in 1908), then by J. W. Lloyd (published in a more oral, more Indian English in 1911), and finally by J. W. Fewkes (excerpts published in 1912). The Lloyd version, which is quite close to Smith-Allison in content, completeness,

and style, was privately published and is now quite rare. The other two versions are also out of print. I will frequently supplement a Smith-Allison story with a Thin Leather version from one of these sources.

4. The latter transmissions are imperfect, I think, more due to problems of haste and in the reliability of translation than to problems of untranslatability. Granted, there are also problems of omission of materials that the narrator thought could make the tribe look silly or crude. One Papago summed these up as "the miracles and the dirty stuff." Finally, there are problems of misunderstanding and misapprehension on the part of the white collector. In general, these are not great because the collectors depended on and took few liberties with native translators, that is, people like Allison. The translators are the unsung heroes of myth collection. In the best texts, for example, the Smith-Allison text and Thin Leather's version published by the Lloyd Group, the native-language narrator was willing to speak and was not hurried, the translator had a keen sense of both languages, and the collector let the text write itself, off the translator's lips.

5. Note that such accounts can occur in any of Vansina's three temporal zones. There can be personal accounts of revelations and divine transports. I suppose that in Vansina's scheme these are disqualified as history because they lack independent sensory verification. We should also note that such eruptions of the divine into the present have the potential to change the sense of the ancient past. This occurs when the eruption is taken as informative about the past. Alfred Kroeber (1925: 754) felt that the Mojave Indians and other "Yuman" tribes near to the Pima-Papago believed that they received such information, hence they could update their mythologies. I know that the Pima-Papago say that they travel in dreams with the gods of their myths, but no one has told me that these travels actually changed their understanding of the past. Of course, it is likely that no Mojave told that to Kroeber, either. He probably surmised it.

6. I thank Todd Bostwick for pointing out in a letter of May 1993 that the Hohokam area contained several dozen settlements in which earth "platform mounds" were surrounded by "compound walls." Only a few of these—less than a dozen—had massive, multistory clay or adobe houses, that is, "great houses" in the strict sense.

7. Their names from bottom to top are Vahki, Estrella, Sweetwater, Snaketown, Gila Butte, Santa Cruz, Sacaton, Soho, and Civano. The first one and last two are from Pima-Papago mythology: Wa'aki, 'Great-house', S-e'ehe, 'Elder Brother', and Sivañ, 'Chief [of a great-house]'. The other names are of Pima villages, generally with Hohokam sites nearby, or of local geographic features.

Note that the period names, Pioneer, Colonial, Sedentary, and Classic, amount to a sketch history of the Hohokam, and it is a history that echoes that of Anglo-America. Of course, those terms have passionate meanings for America, and we do not know whether or how they registered in the minds of the Hohokam. On the basis of Smith-Allison, I suggest the following periods: Genesis, Flood (actually not a period but a hiatus), the Origin of Farming and Marriage, and the Killing of God.

8. Here is Hayden's opinion on the history of the Hohokam, as stated in a letter to me of January 23, 1993.

> To be simplistic, I imagine that the region was [very anciently] occupied by O'otam-Piman speakers who were hunters and gatherers. They had been part of a migration of such speakers at the end of the Altithermal period, 5000 [years] B.P. or so. Others of this migration went on to the vicinity of the Valley of Mexico where they learned canal irrigation and many other distinct traits [represented in the Colonial Hohokam period]. Around the time of Christ or before, some of these southern folk must have come back up to the Gila River, with which they must have been well acquainted, probably through Pima-speaking travelers in both directions. These returnees settled down very quickly at Snaketown, without any known developmental stages.
>
> These were the Hohokam, surrounded by the O'otam, whom they quickly influenced and taught the new ways that they had learned in the south. In time these Hohokam were joined by others with power, who became the big house builders and the constructors of the immense canal systems. These were the ones against whom the O'otam, the Emergents, arose, and whom the O'otam drove out as detailed in The Hohokam Chronicles, as you term the tales. Not many of us accept the concept of "Salado" per se, although influence from the Puebloans of the north is clear toward the last [of Hohokam history], and there was certainly trade between Hohokam and Pueblos. But I think it is safe to confine the history of Hohokam development to the southern influence and the immigrants from Mexico who were joining their congeners on the Gila.

9. Smith-Allison tend to deny this, but many other Pima-Papago mythologies claim it. See the introductory remarks to part 3.

10. It would be ideal if the text had been written in Pima, but Hayden was not trained in linguistics. More important, even if he or Allison were willing and able to tackle Pima prose (much more demanding than the writing of single key words), I doubt that

they could have obtained Smith's entire mythology through the painstaking, pain-giving method of face-to-face written dictation. In general, dictation is not used for texts as long and booklike as this one. (The Iroquois text mentioned below is an exception.) The method is best used for short texts and small series. Had Hayden or Allison attempted it, the result would probably not have been as long and lively as the text that was taken in English. And if I may say so on the basis of 30 years experience with Pima-Papago, Allison's translation is faithful but free.

In general, long native-language mythological texts such as Smith's have only been written by natives. The best-known examples are old, e.g., the Codex Chimalpopoca and the Popul Vuh from the early postconquest Aztecs and Quiche Mayas (see Bierhorst 1992 and Tedlock 1985 for recent editions of those works); a Tsimshian Raven cycle written by Henry Tate and published by Franz Boas (1916); and the Iroquois cosmology dictated in Onondaga and written and published by the Tuscarora J. N. B. Hewett (1928).

One would think that the era of tape recorders would be a boon to native mythological literature, and this is true. There have been some excellent tape recorder–based myth books in the early and middle 1970s, e.g., by Dennis Tedlock from the Zuni (published in 1972) and Gary Gossen and Robert Laughlin from Tzotzil Mayas (1974 and 1977). Of those, only Laughlin gives the native-language originals, but the original tapes are available. The pace of such publication quickened in the 1980s, especially for languages spoken in Alaska, Canada, and Mexico and due to the efforts, respectively, of the Alaska Native Language Center (University of Alaska, Fairbanks), the Mercury Series of the Canadian Ethnology Service, and the Summer Institute of Linguistics (especially for Mexico). Those publication programs are closely tied to particular native communities. In the United States, the Navajo Community College Press, for one, has done similar work. The programs are deliberately bilingual, being tied to school curricula.

To my knowledge those programs have not published many works like the Smith-Allison text, that is, texts formed by one author and covering the entire span of ancient, pre-European history. It is an open question how many such texts still exist in native communities. In the concluding section of this book, I speculate that the age of such mythologies may be past, but, of course, I would like to be proved wrong.

11. He is remembered as that today, rather than as Allison Smith.

12. I will sketch Bierhorst's reckoning because it is the most recent. In his study of Mexico and Central America, he distinguishes between pre-Columbian *motifs* and *tales*. A motif is a dominant episode or image, something that a whole story seems to

revolve upon, such as "Why the Earth Eats the Dead," "The Emergence of Ancestors," "The Man of Crops," "The Loss of the Ancients," and "The Seeds of Humanity." Those are in fact all of the major pre-Columbian motifs identified by Bierhorst in his book on the mythology of Mexico and Central America. Three of them (the second, third, and fourth) appear as stories—but with different titles—in the Smith-Allison text.

Tales are more specific and constraining than motifs. They are standard plots, made up of several or many incidents that recur from variant to variant (1990: 8). Of a total of 15 different pre-Columbian Mexican and Central American tale types that Bierhorst recognizes, only one appears as a story in the Smith-Allison text, namely, "The Flood Myth."

Those proportions are not unimpressive. One could say there are more than enough shared motifs to qualify our text as a Mexican or Central American mythology, although not enough shared tale types. These latter are quite specific, and they tend to come in alternative sets, e.g., five alternative myths about the sun. No people would have a perfect score on them, but nonetheless it appears true that Smith-Allison have too few of them, e.g., none of the sun myths as recognized by Bierhorst.

Turning briefly to the North American side, Bierhorst gives three basic myths for the Southwest portion of the pre-Columbian continent: "The Emergence" [from the underworld—a motif in the Mexico-Central America calculation], "[Boy] Heroes and Their Grandmothers," and "The Dying [Man-] God." The Smith-Allison text has the first and last but lacks the second, more than enough to establish their text's continuity with pre-Columbian North American peoples, not just in the Southwest but beyond. Bierhorst does not give a continentwide inventory, and I will not venture one.

The Pimas are about equally distant (1,200 mi.) from Mexico City and Chicago, so we should expect their stories to show relations both to the south and to the north.

13. The god Siuuhu is an exception in Smith-Allison. He has human morality constantly on his mind. His moral interest is more pronounced in Smith-Allison than in any other Pima-Papago mythology known to me, which is to say that their mythology comes closer than any other to violating this aspect of the First Commandment.

14. One may say that simply to credit gods with a formative role is to worship them, but I take worship to mean something more specific, namely, to accept a lasting covenant with gods, to seek personal and collective salvation through them, and to hope for joy in eventual eternal union with them. Such worship is urged and required in the Bible and the Book of Mormon, compatibly so in the eyes of the Mormons. It is not required in Smith-Allison or

any other Pima-Papago mythology, nor is it expressed in any traditional, non-Christian Pima-Papago ceremony known to me. It is expressed relative to God in Pima-Papago "established" and folk Christianity (see below for that distinction).

15. The recent African-centered world histories surely do Africanize Europe, and they do so similarly to the Mormons' Israelization of America. The African-centrists and Mormons do not dispute the race of the current Europeans and Indians, respectively, but they detect influence from their own kind of people on the land and customs of ancient Europe and America.

16. Other sources that I consulted on the Book of Mormon are Hugh Nibley's *Since Cumorah* (1967) and essays by Adele McCullum, Steven Sondrup, Bruce Jorgensen, Richard Rust, and George Tate in *Literature of Belief* (1981), edited by Neal Lambert. These works show that the scholarship on the Book of Mormon is confident and sophisticated. I hope I have done it justice.

17. For simplicity and due to my lack of knowledge, I limit this discussion to tribes, mythologies, governments, and churches within the United States.

18. The most churchlike native formation known to me, because it has a full mythology, is a complex that developed among Iroquois peoples at the turn of the nineteenth century and that still exists to day. The political aspect of this complex is the League or Confederacy of the Iroquois, a governmental structure that took shape well before 1800 and in fact before the first European contact. The ritual, liturgical, sacramental aspect is the Longhouse religion, which took its present form around 1800 under the impetus of the Seneca prophet Handsome Lake. The mythological aspect has three layers of texts: a creation story analogous to Smith-Allison, an account of the origin of the political league, and an account of prophetic impetus for the reform of the Longhouse religion. As I understand it, no Iroquois sovereignty within or outside the league has formally established this complex as *the* Iroquois religion, and yet its various components comprise a virtual, full church in the sense used in this essay. I thank John Bierhorst and William Fenton for personal discussions on aspects of this religion. I also consulted the writings of Elizabeth Tooker (1978*a*, 1978*b*), Anthony Wallace (1978), and Edmund Wilson (1960) in writing this note.

19. There is no use to lament that the songs were not written in Pima and translated literally. That would have been a very specialized activity. Perhaps many of them are still out there, and in any case, thousands of more or less similar ones, not necessarily used for creation myth-telling, are still there.

PART 0: PRELUDE, THE FONT TEXT

1. It is a nice thought that the -*ki* element of the word could be related to *ki:*, 'house', but I cannot defend this. It does seem likely that the *wa'a*- element has to do etymologically with moisture or water. Sometimes these places are poetically called "rainhouses" in English, for which the above analysis is a justification.

2. There was earlier Spanish contact with Pimas hundreds of miles to the south of these people. The southerners were called "Lower Pimas," while these to the north (including the Papagos) were called "Upper Pimas." Thus, Manje would be the first person to write Upper Pima.

3. It is important to note that the present status term *siwañ* (chief) is not used with a contemporary reference. It refers exclusively to mythical Hohokam "chiefs." My argument, then, is that a term that is already of narrow application, namely, "[Hohokam] chief," is based on something even narrower, that is, the name of a single such chief.

Two additional comments. First, Ruth Underhill has implied in her excellent Papago ethnography that "Siwañ" was a Papago status term ("The rain shaman is called Sivanyi" [1939: 46]). This is not so. The shamans or medicine men who divine for rain at "wine ceremonies" (see story 7) are not called by this term. But the term is used by people who give speeches prior to serving wine at the ceremonies. The speeches (discussed in connection with story 7 and illustrated with a text from Thin Leather given in part 3) tell of journeys to mythical siwañs to obtain rain. They are delivered during wine ceremonies to individuals who sit before baskets of wine, which they are about to serve. One could say that the wine servers impersonate siwañs, but they are not shamans, at least not during the ceremony. The shamans are others, and they are not called "siwañ."

Second, Underhill and others have noted that the Pima-Papago word "siwañ" is similar to a Zuni word spelled, for instance, as *shiwanni*. The Zuni word designates rain priests or priesthoods. (Here I am following the spelling and summary given in Teague and Deaver [1989]: 161, 165.) Thus, the Pima-Papago may have borrowed the Zuni word or vice versa. I have just proposed that the Pima-Papago word comes from their word for "bitter," but this could be a false or partial etymology. We need an etymology of the Zuni word *shiwanni*, but I do not know if one is available.

4. One can understand this. The rains were unpredictable, and perhaps the rivers were not; and as some anthropologists have supposed, people tend to ceremonialize more that which is unpredictable. I do not wish to dispute that idea, but I do suspect that peoples who were truly dependent on river irrigation—for ex-

ample, the ancient Egyptians and Sumerians, the Harappans (India) and Mochica (Peru)—may have had more river lore, ceremony, and magic than the Pimas.

5. We need evidence of ideology from the great-houses, from architecture or pottery decoration or pictographs or whatever. We cannot know their spoken myths, but we may be able to read ideologically coded physical artifacts, and we may find discontinuities with the present Pima-Papago encoded in them. The Hohokam "ball courts" are one such possibility, but I know of no substantive readings of what the ball court details meant to the Hohokam. There are only interesting speculations on what ball games could have meant to Hohokam trade politics (Wilcox 1991: 101–125). Wilcox believes that ball games enabled trade and gift giving (and betting, I would add) between "home" groups and visitors. The ball game–like betting game discussed in note 7, part 3, below, also served those purposes.

6. The full roster of variant names for this character is the following: S-e'ehe (and variants: Siuuhu, Soho, and many others), 'Elder-brother' (actually elder-brother-sister-or-cousin, as the word does not limit itself to sex or even full siblingship); Si:s Ma:kai, 'Elder-brother Medicine-man', or 'Elder-brother Shaman'; I'itoi, 'Drink-it-all-up'; and Mondisuma, 'Montezuma'. These four variants are mixed through Pima and Papago mythologies. For example, the Pima Thin Leather uses both names for this character and implies that the god was called I'itoi up to a certain point in the story and then took on the name S-e'ehe (Russell 1908: 209). The text is not explicit, and the Pima language is lacking, so one cannot see exactly where that change happened. Logically, it would have been when this god and two others met after surviving a flood. At that point there was a dispute over seniority (i.e., who had come to ground first), and the other gods averred to I'itoi's/S-e'ehe's insistence that he had been first.

I confess that no Pima-Papago has told me that I'itoi means "Drink-it-all-up." I have told this to them, and they have agreed, but they seem to think that the god's name merely sounds like it means "Drink-it-all-up" in their language—exactly like that, I believe. The reason for their reticence may be that there is nothing obvious in the story of I'itoi/S-e'ehe to earn him that name. He has no penchant for drinking anything in particular.

On the strength of the Font text, I think the reason for his name is his solar properties (discussed below). By drying things out, he seems to drink them up. Thus, his involvement with the mythical flood is a false lead into his name "Drinker." He does not drink the flood but takes refuge from it. Finally, I suspect that the Drinker name links him to the Aztec sun who "drank" human blood.

The sun, the earth, the moon, and the gods of vegetation and animal life all need annual rejuvenation by draughts of human blood. Without human sacrifices the earth's fruits wither and men perish, so that the continuation of the universe depends on the payment of a blood debt. (Kubler 1984: 92)

There is no human sacrifice in known Pima-Papago religion or mythology (except Jesus), but the "Drinker" name ties them to the system of thought that supported human sacrifice in pre-Columbian central and northern Mexico.

7. Beyond the friendly Opas, I assume the governor knew of unfriendly Yumas, Mojaves, and so on.

PART 1: GENESIS

1. This person is not the sun, the origin of which is narrated later in the text along with the origin of the moon and stars. "Light" is *tonlig* in Pima-Papago, "sun" is *taṣ*, "moon" is *maṣad*, and "star" is *hu'u*. This text's mention of a pure light (tonlig) preceding the other, separately named heavenly bodies is unique in Pima-Papago mythology.

2. Versions of what appear to be the very same song are in Russell (1908: 272), from Thin Leather, and Saxton and Saxton (1973: 3), from a Papago singer recorded by Dolores. It is an important song, being the first in the mythologies in which it occurs and therefore supposedly the first song that was sung in the universe. That so many narrators have it in the same form gives the illusion, if not the proof, that this oldest of all songs has been successfully preserved by generations of singers since pre-Hohokam times.

Both Thin Leather and the Dolores singer attribute the song's words to Earth Doctor, not to Jeoss as in the Smith text. In fact, there is no mention of the Christian God ("Jeoss") in the Thin Leather and Dolores versions. The Smith text has God *address* the song to Earth Doctor. That is, God calls the latter by name. The other versions state Earth Doctor's name at the beginning, as if he were being addressed, but the texts do not indicate that anyone else was on the scene. Strangely, these songs do imply that there was someone else present. They end with an imperative statement addressed to an unknown audience: roughly 'come and see what is happening' ("*miakuka nyuita hasitco-onyi*" in Russell and "*Miake ng neina k has juhni*" in Saxton). I would reconstruct the sung syllables in both versions as "*mi ya ke ko ñei na ke ha si ju u ñi*" and would transpose that sung language into Pima-Papago prose as "*miako ñeidk has i juñ.*"

The Smith song as translated by Allison into English says something different, "You make the earth now and started it going." We understand that God said this to Earth Doctor. Granted that we cannot know whether Smith actually sang that in Pima, we can say that the scene it conjures is actually less mysterious than the scene in the Thin Leather and Dolores versions. We really do not know who called Earth Doctor's name in those texts, nor do we know who called the attention of whom.

3. This process of turning back to repeat just the last part of a song is called the "turning" (noḍag), that is, the song or singer turns on something so as to repeat the song in an incomplete manner, with the very first line or lines missing. That is one interpretation of the notion of 'turning' as applied to songs. Another interpretation, touched on by Allison, is that it is not the song or the singing that turns but rather the *dancers* who do so: at the point where the incomplete repetition occurs, they reverse the direction of their dancing. If they have been moving counterclockwise, they commence to move clockwise. I think that the word refers to all of those things. It is a multimeaning theoretical term.

4. There is a star-making song in Russell, from Thin Leather (273). The Dolores text does not have one. The Thin Leather song, like this one, comes early in the mythology, and like this one it centers on Earth Doctor. Moreover and most interesting, both songs proceed through the same sequence of narrated acts: (1) someone makes stars, (2) the maker puts them in the sky, and (3) the earth shines, or is lit. There are differences, however. Here is the Russell Thin Leather version as interpreted into Pima-Papago prose and translated by me:

> Vanyingi Yo-ohowa nato
> Wañ huhu'u na:to
> I STARS MAKE
>
> vanyingi Y-ohoowa nato
> Wañ huhu'u na:to
> I STARS MAKE
>
> tamai nañgita
> Da:m dagito
> ABOVE THROW
>
> tcuwutu mamasi-i
> Jewed ma:si
> EARTH SHOWS
>
> (Alternate last line:
> tcuwutu tonoli-i
> Jewed tonlid
> EARTH SHINES ON).

More freely translated:

> *I make stars.*
> *I make stars,*
> *Toss above:*
> *Earth shows.*
>
> *I make stars.*
> *I make stars,*
> *Toss above:*
> *Shine on earth.*

This free translation is true to Thin Leather's Pima. I suspect that Juan Smith's song was very nearly the same because the sequence of acts is the same. Another reason to believe the songs are the same is that, in general, the songs about the very earliest things in creation tend to be uniform across Pima-Papago narrators. This was my impression in the 1970s and 1980s. At this time, narrators were proud of this uniformity, for it meant agreement on the most basic, earliest things. If singers differed, the differences tended to be in the myriad songs that come later in the narrative of world history.

Assuming that the Thin Leather and Smith songs are the same and that the different translations are simply more or less accurate, then the principal difference that I would point out, in criticism of Allison, is that his translation is too wordy. What Smith sang quite concisely, Allison translated quite wordily. This is a matter of style, which is important in my opinion; and the indications are that the Allison translations are generally too wordy.

There are slight differences of substance between the two translations. Thin Leather ascribes the making and putting of stars to a single person, Earth Doctor (rendered as "I"); and to judge from the translation, Smith ascribes the making and putting to a trinity, Jeoss, Earth Doctor, and Siuuhu (rendered as "we"). We will never know if the Pima text used "we" rather than "I." If it did, I suspect this was an innovation on J. Smith's part. That is, I suspect that far more singers of his era used "I" rather than "we" in their versions of this song.

5. Other versions of the mythology put this episode after a flood that comes later.

6. The word for "light," *tonlig*, is different from "sun," *taṣ*. Obviously more things than the sun give light. Recall that in the Smith-Allison text, pure light was created by God, and the sun and the various other celestial light sources were created later by Earth Doctor.

7. These *hihih*'s might be forms of the verb "to go," (*hi:hi* in the plural, *hihhi* in the "repetitive"), but Dolores must have felt that

they were more mysterious than "go" or that they were placed in the song for the sake of their sound and therefore are meaningless.

8. This story is widely told, especially among Maricopas and other Yuman language-speaking tribes. Except for this version, I have not heard of a place named from the story. I have not asked if anyone knows this place.

9. The Papago text actually says "Earth Doctor," not "First Born." This was a translator's liberty. The earlier Papago prose segments in this text do say "First Born" consistently, so that must have been this narrator's preference. When he sang the song, however, he used the more standard name.

PART 2: THE FLOOD

1. But note this difference. In the Thin Leather text, the abnormalities alarmed Earth Doctor, who caused the sky to fall on the people. Thus, the abnormalities caused god-sent destructions. In the present text, the destruction issues from the abnormality itself. I argue later that the abnormality is also a godly act of creation but a perverse one. Thin Leather has a version of this episode, too. It is simply that he led up to it with Earth Doctor's destructions.

2. The difference between God in the Bible and Earth Doctor in this respect is that God did not create the earth. The earth gathered itself, on God's command. Earth Doctor did create the earth, from his own extruded substance. Once the earth was formed, both God and Earth Doctor crafted the various life forms, Earth Doctor rather more physically and explicitly than God.

3. According to Thin Leather, quoted in the last part, this man was Buzzard. Note from that text that Earth Doctor had high hopes for Buzzard, who at that time was a man, perhaps a perfect man, not an ugly carrion-eating bird. Later in the mythology, Buzzard is the means used by the Hohokam to kill Siuuhu. Only he had the power, the sun magic or privileges, to do so. He is a sun god and not a rain god like Siba and the *sisiwañ* (see the discussion of the Font text). But he is an extra sun god in all Pima-Papago mythologies. Siuuhu is the main one. Buzzard is the Hohokam's friendly sun god; Siuuhu is their "unfriendly" one.

4. If the long-haired young man was the old man's son, which he was not, then *wosmaḍ* would be the proper term. In fact, the old man and his daughter were not kin at all to the baby since the baby came directly from the long-haired young man. Russell's version of Thin Leather tells how this happened.

> Her father told her to fetch some of the topmost thorns of the cholla cactus [very thorny, called "jumping cactus" in

English]. When she obeyed him he placed the thorns
upon her [it is commonly said that he put them in her
crotch], telling her not to be afraid of the young man. . . .
When he came . . . after exchanging good wishes for
health and happiness, they went to the dwelling prepared
for them. Soon the screams of a child aroused old South
Doctor [the girl's father] and his wife, who came running
desirous of seeing their grandchild. (209–210)

The Papago version of this story in Saxton and Saxton (1973:
45–55), recorded by Juan Dolores, has a normal marriage and
birth, not a series of weddings leading to a child born from the
groom. The child's tears cause a flood in this version, as in Thin
Leather and Smith, but in this Papago version the root cause of the
flood was the mother's refusal to move with the father and child
to the father's home village. The father and child went alone, the
shamed father left the child outside his home village, and the child
cried a flood of tears.

5. Most versions say the house is an olla, or jar, made from
creosote bush gum. Note that in the Thin Leather text recorded
at the end of the previous part, this bush is the first living thing
that Earth Doctor creates. Ants, the god's second creation, slowly
eat, digest, and apparently excrete the gum of this bush to produce
the present mass of the earth. Thus, the gum plus the ants are an
earth plasma.

6. In the sky. Most versions have him enter his cane and float
through the flood.

7. Near Apache Junction, Ariz.

8. Most versions say that the people turned to stone the instant
the dog spoke and that they can still be found and seen petrified
on top of the mountain. There are many songs, dreamed by medicine men, about visits to these petrified people. Recall that the
Font text (part 1) had the Drinker (Siuuhu in this story) take refuge
there without turning to stone. The Font story therefore lacks the
rebirth leveling and seniority contesting of this flood myth, which
is the myth that goes with the conquest mythology.

9. There is a song about this "house" in Russell (1908: 275).
The song begins, *Tcukoi vavahaki*, which is translated as 'Black
house'. The first word is *cuk*, 'black', in ordinary language, and the
second word is *va'aki*, our 'great-house' word. The element *Chok*
in the Smith transcription is probably the same 'black'. Perhaps
the element *-weecum* is the word *vi'ikam*, 'survivor', 'remainder'.
The house, therefore, would be 'Black remainder'.
Of course, it is interesting to find a lifesaving, floating pot called
a "great-house." Here is my writing of the Thin Leather song into

Pima ordinary (versus song) language, and below it is my literal translation:

Cuk wa'aki
Cuk wa'aki
Eḍa ñ-ulin
Eḍa ñ-ulin
We:maj a'ai ñ-himcud.

Black floating-house
Black floating-house
Inside I stay
Inside I stay
With it back-and-forth make-me-go.

10. This belongs to the same family of words as *vakolif*, words about waterborne debris, washing, swimming, oozing, rotting, and rusting.

PART 3: NEW CREATION AND CORN

1. The Dolores texts can be read as positing no connection between the people of the first creation and conquering emergents. The problem is that these texts are from a variety of narrators, and we cannot tell what any of these narrators' entire mythology would have been like. Moreover, not only is the Dolores collection a composite but Saxton and Saxton add additional narrators to those recorded by Dolores. Saxton and Saxton's book, therefore, is an organized anthology of Papago mythology. It is not, like the texts of Thin Leather and Smith, the comprehensive, organized, well-considered telling of one person. It is analogous to an American history composed of chapters taken from the works of different historians.

While not ideal, such anthologizing is not necessarily evil. The truth is, we do not know whether it is so or not, because the study of whole, single-narrator mythologies is a new field. Really, Thin Leather's is the only such work published from the Pima-Papago (happily, in three versions). Smith-Allison is the second. I should say that these are the only long works. The Pima narrator Anna Moore Shaw wrote a relatively short English-language book of Pima mythology. She meant it for the instruction of children on the virtues of the old life, and so it tends to avoid tales of conflict. To complete this survey, the native-language typescript of another Papago mythology exists. It was spoken by the narrator Frank Lopez for Bernard Fontana in the 1960s. This work has not yet been given a written English translation. Finally, Harold Bell Wright, a best-selling writer of inspirational fiction in the 1920s, edited and published a Papago mythology that, like Saxton and Saxton/Dolores, seems to have come from several narrators.

2. Songs about the circularity of the earth are in Russell (1908: 272) and Saxton and Saxton (1973: 3); but these songs are attributed to Earth Doctor at the time of the earth's creation. They do not refer to spinning or circular movement (*sikol him*), as in the Smith songs, but to the circular form of the newly made earth (*si-kolim na:to*, 'circularly made'). I imagine that Smith sang *sikol him*, not *sikol na:to*, and he took his phrasing as an expression, or even a product, of Siuuhu's dizzy change of heart regarding the second creation. In short, according to Smith, the world spins because Si-uuhu changed his mind.

3. Seems to be a hitherto unrecorded word for the collectivity of "Yuman" (by anthropological classification) language speakers. Note, however, that the Font text uses the term "Oba" to refer to a tribe or nation of Yuman-speakers. And "O'obab" is the Pima-Papago word now generally used to name the Maricopa tribe, the members of which share reservations with the Pimas. Conceivably, Smith actually said one of those two words; conceivably, Font's Oba, today's O'obab, and Smith's Obniu are the selfsame word and people.

4. This is the only Pima-Papago song I know of on the origin, as opposed to the recovery, of a farm crop. It is also the only song I know of on cotton, and it is the only instance of a singing seed. See note 6, below, on crop songs in general.

5. An allusion to a 1930s cartoon or magazine ad?

6. Some comments are in order on how such songs are reported elsewhere in the literature on Pima-Papago. In fact, a rich and consistent record is available, and it is time for someone to study it (no one has done so, so far).

Consistent with Smith's remarks, although he did not put the matter so firmly, there seem to be two categories of "farming" or "crop" songs. One category, let us call it Type A, goes with his story 5, "Corn Returns," *not* with the songs of his story 4, "Corn and Tobacco Leave." There are songs with that Corn and Tobacco story, as we have seen, but they do not have the distinctive linguistically unanalyzable "signature phrases" of the two categories of farming songs. The "Corn Returns" story is reported from throughout the Pima-Papago area. Thus, Underhill makes reference to it in *Papago Indian Religion* (1946: 80; she tries to distinguish it, misleadingly I think, from a "myth of the corn woman" that she discusses on 78); and Saxton and Saxton give an excellent bilingual version from Dolores in their *Legends and Lore* (1973: 27–44).

These Type A songs, uniformly in Pima-Papago country, have a distinctive, ending "signature" or "call" phrase, "*hi lu, ya a na.*" The phrase has no obvious meaning in the Pima-Papago language. Different writers write it differently (Hayden wrote Smith's rendition as *Hai lo Hya'an*). The above is simply my version, which I believe, however, to be phonetically correct for more singers than the ones I have personally heard.

Finally, the Type A songs, at least many of them, seem to be the thoughts or statements of the principal characters of "Corn Returns," or Corn Woman (better called Corn Man) myth, a story in which the key male character is Corn and the key female character is a human (not corn) woman. Most commonly, perhaps, the "I's" of the song texts refer to, or are taken to be the words of, Corn Man.

Type A songs are published by G. Herzog (1936: 335), 2 songs; F. Russell (1908: 333–334), 8 songs; D. Saxton and L. Saxton (1973: 29–30, 43–44), 4 songs; R. Underhill (1946: 78–81), 18 songs.

Type B songs seem to have no myth associated with them. They tend to be about rain, thundering, and crops—nature and water poetry. They are sometimes called Rain Songs (e.g., by Russell and Herzog) and can be taken as part of a crop-related rain ceremonialism that is distinct from the more famous and salient "wine drinks" or "cactus wine" ceremony (the subject of Smith's story 7). The wine ceremony songs do not have the distinctive signature phrase, and the wine ceremony is distinct from the ceremonies in which Type B songs are used.

Type B songs are sung to the accompaniment of a stick scraped over another, notched stick, with the latter pressed onto a basket resonator, thus "scraping stick songs" (Smith called them "basket rubbing," the same idea). It is not known whether Type A songs were sometimes or normally acompanied in the same manner, or whether, on the contrary, they were normally accompanied by shaking a gourd rattle, the more common, or "unmarked" form of Pima-Papago song accompaniment. (Gourd rattles are used for wine ceremony songs, for example.)

Type B songs have a distinct call or signature both at the beginning and at the end, and this signature, also not interpretable into Pima-Papago, is different from that of the Type A songs. At the beginning, it is something like *he eyanayo* (as Herzog wrote it), and the end has *heceya hahena* (again, as Herzog wrote it). I have heard them sung, respectively, as *[ṣoiya ṣoiya ṣoiya] hi ya nai hu* (the bracketed part, a separate initial line, was in the two songs I heard) and *hi ci ya ya'i na*.

Type B songs are published by G. Herzog (1936: 336), 8 songs; F. Russell (1908: 331–332), 9 songs; and R. Underhill (1946: 72–76), 24 songs.

This makes a total for the two types of 73 songs. Herzog, Russell, and Saxton and Saxton give them in Pima-Papago as well as in English translation, and the Pima-Papago originals for the Underhill songs must exist in her notebooks. There are probably additional crop songs in print or in archives, although it seems that

Densmore's *Papago Music* (1929) lacks them. In 1991, perhaps a thousand such songs were in Pima-Papago singers' minds and memories, but probably no one who was not closely associated with the traditional agriculture knows such songs, and now all those farmers are old and retired. The songs as oral literature will probably die with the last old farmers. (I must note that the Type A and Type B songs, with their distinct signatures, are different from the cotton song given earlier in this myth. That song lacks a vocable signature and is about the origin of cotton raising.)

Herzog, in 1936, traced connections between the Pima-Papago song signatures and those of various Pueblo Indian corn or farming songs, but he only opened the door for such considerations; and I would add that comparisons of poetry, ceremony, and myth should also be made southward, starting with the Yaquis, especially with Yaqui deer songs (Evers and Molina 1987). It is not idle to compare deer songs with crop or corn songs because the Pima-Papago Type B songs, as "scraping stick songs," were used for deer hunting and obtaining ocean salt as well as for farming; and the "Beneath the East" of Pima-Papago Type A songs should be compared with the "Wilderness World" of Yaqui deer songs.

7. A stick dice game whose goal is to move a marker called *ṣoiga* ('pet', 'slave', or 'horse'—but *kawiyu*, from Spanish *caballo*, is the normal word for horse) around a large rectangle marked with lines incised on the ground. The game is not unlike a U.S. Monopoly-type board game, except it is played outdoors on a rectangular playing surface, 8 feet by 12 (Russell 1908: 175–176).

The terminology of this game, which includes "hip," "burning," "fire," and "house" as well as the above-mentioned "pet/slave/horse" (all given in Russell), seems clearly related to the terminology of the Mesoamerican ball game (discussed extensively by Scarborough and Wilcox [1991]). Therefore gins may have some relation to the ball courts of the prehistoric Hohokam. The relation need not be of gins as a reduced, mock, or simulated version of former live-player Hohokam ball games. For one thing, the Aztecs had both a version of the dice game, called *patolli*, and a live-player ball game. Moreover, Pima-Papago women played a large playing field stickball game, called *toka*; and the men had kickball races. There are many games, probably all related.

Mythical associations will be crucial to establishing the relations. Concerning the present stories, I can only say that gins is the means by which female (mostly) Tobacco and male Corn parted company. Tobacco is associated with rain calling or rain magic, and corn is associated with unnatural abundance on the condition of nonmarriage.

8. *Hai ya ha'ai ya*, a standard lamenting phrase in songs. This is not one of the crop song signatures. Those signatures and this

one practically exhaust the "vocable phrases" (standardized special "words" that lack meaning within ordinary spoken Pima-Papago).

9. Superstition Mountain is at the east end of Pima country, and Santa Cruz is at the west. Corn's home was somewhere beyond Superstition Mountain. (Ta:tkam, of the next note, is actually 40 miles south of Superstition Mountain.) The version of this story published by Saxton and Saxton (1973: 27–43) puts Corn's home at "Below the East" (*Si'alig Weco*), the location of the Pima-Papago land of the dead, or their paradise. The same place figures into the end of this story by Smith.

10. Bahr had thought that this could be Ta:tkam, the large mountain east of Eloy, Ariz., because Thin Leather gives that mountain as the home of a Corn Man, the subject of Type A crop songs (Russell 1908: 333–334; see n. 6, above, for crop song types and myths). *Ta:tkam* does not mean "hole," however. It seems to mean "feeler." The word *"vag"* does mean "hole"; and "Vagkam" would mean "Hole-place." Hayden confirmed this in a letter of Feb. 1993.

> Vatcum—a butte east of Florence [Ariz.] with a hole on each opposing side, giving the appearance of passing all the way through. In 1930 George Boundy, custodian of Tumacacori [National Monument, Ariz.], took my father, Dr. Van Bergen and Art Woodward to it, claiming that the apparent passage forced a draft through the mountain which made for the efficient cremation of bodies, hence the Hohokam use of it as a crematory and the "smoked" walls and roof of the "tube." Not so, the holes are not connected and didn't go through.

11. In a letter of Feb. 1993, Hayden stated that this means "White Thin." If so, I would spell the Pima phrase S-toa Komalk. Hayden understood the phrase to be the name of a long east-west mountain range near Blackwater, Ariz. I think this range is normally called Ko:magi, 'Grey'. Thus, I think the last element is really the word for "grey," not the word for "thin" (or "flat"—another translation of "Komalk").

12. Except for the letter "d," which could be a typing error, this phrase is close to Hayden's rendition of the Type A crop song signature phrase as discussed in note 6, above.

13. Note that this episode says that the proper use of tobacco is in groups whose members know and state their kinship with each other. To know those relations, people must know their parenthood. In Pima-Papago and I suppose in all societies, the institution of marriage serves to make parenthood clear. Thus, this episode on the proper use of tobacco underlines what I take to be

the theme of this part, that with the new food crops came the regularization of marriage. Tobacco's father insists on it. No doubt he knew that he was Tobacco's father, but he insisted that all people know such things. They cannot smoke without testifying to that knowledge.

PART 4: THE WHORE

1. See the last story in this mythology, story 36, for more on the Apaches.

2. The place where this mythology was recorded.

3. This breath-sending seems to align Cadigum with a scented plant like tobacco. We may speculate that the cadigum scent is as far-reaching as tobacco smoke, but the cadigum plant does not need to be burned to be sensed at such a distance. Cadigum is a no-smoke, no-fire tobacco "substitute."

4. Note the resemblance between the first and third lines of this song and the American song, "Old McDonald." While I believe that there was a Pima song beneath this translation, and that the resemblance to "Old McDonald" is largely coincidental, I also suspect that some Smith songs, including this one and the mother's lament in story 10, depart from traditional Pima-Papago poetic practice in that they openly voice a complaint against another live, usually family, person. Thus, although the parallelism between "Old McDonald" and this song may be coincidental, the emergence in Smith of "protest song poetry" may reflect an American cultural influence.

5. These could be biblical references, to Sodom and some other biblical place (probably not Gomorrah, as that seems a little too remote from the rendering of this word).

6. This must be the synopsis, not the translation, of the song.

PART 5: ORIGIN OF WINE AND IRRIGATION

1. Examples of "wine drinks" speeches are published by Russell (1908: 347–352) from the Pima and by Saxton and Saxton (1973: 335–336, 338–339) and Underhill et al. (1979: 17–35) from the Papago. The Thin Leather corn myth speeches are different from the rain text published by Russell, and Russell's collection lacks those corn myth speeches.

2. It is quite likely that from Hohokam times on there was a local (Sonoran Desert-wide) distinction between River People, who tapped permanently flowing rivers for water, and Desert People, who could not and did not because they had no rivers to

tap. Thus, Smith and Allison may have felt that wine feasts are the only recourse of the Desert People, or of the rustics. True, but note the origin of wine feasts in the Pima Thin Leather's Tobacco and Corn myth. Now, one might take this as evidence that the Pimas were not fully acclimated to the rivers, that a people truly committed to river tapping would not have wine feasts or rain ceremonies at all, or that a truly river-acclimated people would not have the mythological "profile" on tobacco and rainfall that we observe for the Pima as well as the Papago. It is an interesting idea because it makes one wish to compare Pima-Papago mythology with the mythologies of other, perhaps more committed and centralized irrigation civilizations.

3. *Ogali*, the fathers of the *ogali* clan or sib. It is important to note that the first of these three sibs belongs to the Coyote moiety, the second belongs to the Buzzard moiety, and the third is considered to be "moietyless" (Underhill 1939: 30–34). Missing from this mythic wine ceremony is one additional sib name from each moiety, Apkigam from the Coyotes and Wawgam from the Buzzards. Later, in story 16, it will be said, somewhat ambiguously, that all or an important part of the Pima-Papago army was comprised of Coyote sib members. Had Smith identified the people of this myth as being entirely and exclusively Buzzards (comprised exclusively of *vav* and *ma;m* sih members), then the case could be made that an army comprised of "Coyotes" defeated and incorporated the Hohokam, who were all "Buzzards." Such an idea may have been at the back of Smith's mind, and Hayden (1970) considered it a novel and plausible solution to the long-standing archaeological riddle of what became of the prehistoric Hohokam people or culture, but I cannot say that Smith actually said that.

4. This does not resound with other Pima-Papago mythologies. There is a well-known myth about a threatened eruption of seawater from a hole near Santa Rosa, Ariz. (Saxton and Saxton [1973: 341–347] give a good bilingual version), but that is obviously not what this myth says. Smith and Allison use this episode of saltwater depletion to set the stage for the origin of irrigation: if Siuuhu could dig a hole to collect the ocean, humans could at least dig canals.

5. See the Appendix. The location would either be the site called Los Muertos or the one called Pueblo Grande. If the former, the canal had its tap into the Salt River near Granite Reef Dam, as Smith-Allison say. If the latter, the river tap was considerably downstream near today's Tempe.

6. Towa Kuadam Oks, 'White Eater Old-woman'. As Fewkes points out, there is little doubt that this is the Pima-Papago name for the same woman-god that Navajos and Hopis, for example,

call variously "White Shell Woman," "Woman of Hard Substance," and "Changing Woman." The Pimas locate her in the west. I am not sure about the other mythologies. But the Pimas, unlike those other peoples, do not really have myths about her. To them she is a true and important character of *other* peoples' mythologies, and she merely has a cameo walk-on role in their own. It is the same with another woman-god whom they call "Green Girl" (S-cehedagi Cehia): She figures prominently in Yuman (Maricopa, Yuman, Mojave, Cocopa) mythology, as a young woman who, as a frog, ate her father's feces after he almost tried to make love with her. Pima-Papago tell his story, but they tell it as a foreign, in that case Maricopa, myth. They tell the prose in Pima-Papago and sing the songs in Maricopa. I consider that these two women characters are different and are focal characters in two different but coordinate mythologies. Generally, a people who have one of the women do not have the other. And the Pima-Papago, as I said, have neither; they know about both but accept neither as pertaining directly to *their* history. They do have an equivalent for these women, however. She is the girl of the next story, of the next part, who gives birth to a witch.

7. See previous note.

8. This squares with the locational analysis in the introduction to this part. It implies that the engineering problems for the Hohokam canal system serving sites in today's Mesa and south Tempe area were greater than those for the canals serving today's central Phoenix. Clearly, the Mesa system originates upstream of the Phoenix system. It may in fact be the longer, more complex, and therefore politically more coordinated system.

PART 6: MORNING GREEN CHIEF AND THE WITCH

1. I think this is typical of North American and perhaps of all tribal, or simply of all human, mythologies. These are stories that treat of creations and origins in long-ago times. They are sacred and tell of miracles. As a rule, or at least as a strong tendency, these stories lack normal human procreation. One may say that they lack it precisely because a good deal of their sacred and miraculous creation is, as Freud would say, sublimated ("made sublime") sexual procreation. Such creation is instead of sexual procreation. It is achieved by retaining one member of the normal procreating pair, man or woman, and by keeping that person away from normal coitus with the opposite sex. This person normally manipulates or comes into contact with a sublimated form of the opposite sex (molds feminine earth, eats masculine worm, etc.). Finally and perhaps a sensitive issue to feminism, generally only man-gods, not woman-gods, create humans external to their bodies (e.g., the

god sits and molds mud). Perhaps this is not strictly true, and insofar as it is true it may not be abhorrent to feminists. I am not aware that this topic has been surveyed and judged relative to North American myth or tribal myth in general.

2. I consider this to be like procreation. It represents a woman-enacted counterpart to the molding of people from scratch by Si-uuhu, etc. It is a woman's "creation" of a character outside her body. As such, it contradicts or qualifies the rule on external creation as stated in the previous note.

3. This may be quibbling, but parrots are not people. The old woman does not equal the creator man-gods.

4. Another instance of this is a green hawk that is formed from the smoke from the baking witch. I take it that this hawk is solar, and yet its color is explicitly green (Saxton and Saxton 1973: 295–304).

5. As noted about the Wind and Cloud myths, however, this tendency is not absolute. There is a loss of Wind and Cloud myth in which the friends retreat to the east.

6. Uam Nu:wi, 'Yellow Buzzard'.
The Thin Leather version of this story has the two families, the mother's and the "father's," living respectively at Casa Grande Ruin and a place about 20 miles to the southeast, near a mountain called Ta:tkam in Pima-Papago, which is the large mountain just to the east of Eloy, Ariz. Thin Leather and Smith-Allison agree that the father's side is associated with the sun ("Sun Meeter" in Thin Leather, "Yellow Buzzard" in Smith-Allison). Thin Leather explicitly associates the mother's side with water ("Morning Green Chief," turquoises, etc.); and Smith-Allison do so implicitly, if I am correct that the direction west connotes wetness.

Smith's identifying the mother as a Mojave and his attaching the "father's" family to Yellow Buzzard aligns his version of this story to a myth called the Flute Lure. This myth is known by Pima-Papago, and it appears in several collections (e.g., Densmore 1929: 54–77), but they generally consider it to be a Maricopa or Mojave narrative. It is similar to the "ho'ok" myth in that it treats the career of a person born of a human woman. In the ho'ok story, this person is fathered miraculously by a kickball, while in the Flute Lure story, the person (actually twin boys) is fathered miraculously from underground and through water by a gopher.

Smith's mythology lacks a version of the Flute Lure story, except that he uses the Flute Lure geography, so to speak, to open his version of the ho'ok.

7. Russell's Thin Leather gives five songs that are said to have been sung on this occasion (278–279). Saxton and Saxton's two

versions of the story lack songs; and, so far as I know, the "Ho'ok killing" songs in Russell are the only ones that have been recorded so far. Those five contain many passages that Russell and his helpers could not understand. I cannot understand them either.

8. Muhadag. Most versions of this story put the location of the dance near the present Papago village of Poso Verde, Sonora, Mexico; and Smith himself stated earlier in the story that the girl grew up (and presumably met her end) in Papago country. This does not preclude that Siuuhu might have been summoned from his residence at a mountain in Pima country, near today's Phoenix, but it would have made it a long trip. (Some Papago versions of the story, I believe, place his residence at this time near Baboquivari Mountain in Papago country.)

9. The most prominent mountain on today's Papago or Tohono O'odham reservation.

10. Papago or Tohono O'odham village just south of the U.S./ Mexico border, 30 miles south of Baboquivari mountain.

11. I speculate that Fewkes put this term in quotations because the other settlement in question may not have been referred to as a "great-house" (wa'aki). In the most restrictive sense, it seems that the term was reserved for Casa Grande Ruin and for various distant, cosmic places such as the "Shining Great-house" named in the ceremonial speech by Corn in the Thin Leather version of the Corn and Tobacco myth. Thus, places such as the settlement in this myth are great-houses by extension or by courtesy.

12. Fewkes had Thin Leather staying with him at Casa Grande Ruin, hence the detail in this narrative.

13. The first two syllables add up to *taṣ*, 'sun'. The remaining three syllables cannot possibly yield the rest of that line, but they are probably the first line of the song. Fewkes should have written down *all* the syllables, start to finish, then one might use his English sketch to piece the song back together.

PART 7: FEATHER BRAIDED CHIEF AND THE GAMBLER

1. But for once, not Thin Leather. He says that warrior purification did originate through the killing of the eagle, but he does not say that Elder Brother the eagle killer passed through it. Nor, therefore, does he mention an old woman as officiant or purifier.

2. The Pima-Papago language does not have gender-specific personal pronouns (e.g., "he" and "she" vs. "it"). Instead, it has unisex pronouns equivalent to "it" (or "that one," "this one," etc.). Thus, unless it is made clear with a noun (e.g., "that *girl*"), one

cannot tell the sex of the person referred to in a sentence. This makes it inconvenient to translate Pima-Papago into English, because English requires that personal pronouns be genderized; and to use the genderless "it" in English translation implies that the thing being referred to is not human, or not even animate. Here we see Allison shifting between "it" and "he" at a point when the story has not yet openly stated that the baby is a boy.

3. This song is remote from any Pima-Papago song known to me. I have not heard any song as chiding and complaining, or one might say, as tattling, as this one; and I do not know any Pima-Papago expressions precisely equivalent to "naughty" and "scold." This is not to say that something very like this song was not sung, but I wish I had heard it.

4. *Gins*, a stick dice game.

5. I have heard this place called Waw S-do'ig, 'Rock Raw'. The latter word refers to the smell of raw meat, blood, fish, and female genitals. "Rotten" is a different word (*s-jew*). The implication of using "raw" for this place is that the corpses did not rot but remained rankly fresh. The place is said to be east of Pima-Papago country, perhaps in today's Apache country. Smith-Allison affirm the "Rock Raw" name in the next story, which says that Siuuhu told the people to call the eagle killing place, "Cliff that smells like blood."

6. Therefore, although not mentioned in the flood story, he must have found a way to save himself equivalent to the ways found by Earth Doctor, Siuuhu, and Coyote. In fact, no known Pima-Papago flood story involves a Nawicu character. It is as if the Nawicu character is an "extra" to that strand of world history.

7. Such a song is in Russell (228), under the title, "Song sung by Eagle's wife to put him to sleep." The word *yakahai* occurs but is left untranslated (very rare in Russell), while a later word, *sikosiimo*, is (properly) translated as "sleep." I conclude from this that Smith probably knew the same song that Russell recorded from Thin Leather and that the *yakahai* probably belongs to the untranslatable, or not understood, portion of the song. Certainly I know no Pima-Papago way to say "sleep" that sounds like *yakahai*.

8. Russell gives the entire song as:

> *Haya yakahai yahai mo,*
> *Haya yakahi mo,*
> *hovanyto sikosiimo,*
> *hovanyto sikosiimo—*

two lines, each repeated verbatim or nearly so. The second or "last" of the paired lines is translated as "I sleep." It seems that Smith was here quoting the first paired line.

9. Alluded to in the previous song.

10. No doubt *Siw Hewel*, 'Bitter Wind'. Densmore's translator probably pronounced the English word "bitter" in a manner that made Densmore think he had said "beater." Indeed, Papagos do pronounce the word "bitter" in this way, with a Mexican accent, so to speak. Densmore's other problem was that she could imagine a wind that "beats" but not one that is named for a taste or attitude. Such, however, is the case with this wind. Recall that Bitter Wind figured into the Origin of Irrigation story as the means used by White Eater Old-woman to deepen the canal and the principal great-house chief was named "Bitter" (Siba).

11. Like the Bitter Wind of the irrigation story.

12. Undoubtedly the same Pima-Papago name as Hayden and others translate "Yellow Buzzard." Their name is Uam Nu:wi, Yellow [or 'brown' or 'yellow-brown'] Buzzard.

13. Therefore, this house is the opposite of a Hohokam wa'aki (great-house) and the opposite of the cosmic wa:paki referred to in speeches such as Thin Leather gave in connection with the Corn Returns story. Those houses are always said to be full of rain, mist clouds, and lightning.

14. Thus would Buzzard have acquired or recharged the solar power that he would use to kill Siuuhu. (This killing is the topic of the next story of Smith and Allison.)

15. In my opinion the answer is, "No, you are not an eagle. You are destined to become a scalped buzzard bird, and at this moment you are acquiring solar power." Eagles are sometimes associated with rain and moistness in opposition to buzzards, which are associated with hot light. Thus, eagle feathers are said to drip moisture, and medicine men use them to fan and thereby to moisten and cool dehydrated and feverish patients.

16. Or, on the pattern of other speeches and ceremonials enacted for directional progressions, the third throw is to the south and the fourth to the west. See the speech for I'itoi's resurrection, given in three versions by Bahr (1975) for this directional progression in which the thrown object was I'itoi (or Siuuhu) rather than the boy "Feather Braided."

17. Conceivably, Garcia could have given this speech but chose not to. In any case, the sequence of tossings is surely in the speech, which Garcia was telling in "prose" rather than in the more measured, chanted mode of "oratory." See the discussion of modes or levels of memorization in the section on Pima-Papago

literature in the introduction. It is certain that the actual speech would have been more difficult to give than this prose precis. The question is whether Garcia could have given the speech if he was asked to do so for a cure or some other ceremony and if he had time in which to call it to mind.

18. *Komtan* and *ku:p*, both used for sicknesses pertaining to warfare and war purification.

19. *Gohimeli* and *hiwculida*, the first for the two nights of dancing that precede the wine drinks, the second being the Type B crop songs, discussed earlier. I do not consider this to be a proper myth of origin of those songs, since the songs are mentioned as acquired as a block, along with three other blocks of songs. A proper origin myth, I think, would have the songs appear one by one, on some actor's lips, like arias in an opera, as the Creation and various other kinds of songs originate in the Smith-Allison text.

20. But not as powerful as the songs actually used by medicine men to diagnose sicknesses, the so-called *duajida* songs. In this passage Garcia is mainly responding to Densmore's large interest in songs. She came to the tribe to write a book on their music.

21. This is the first mention of the old woman in the text. Densmore does not comment on that fact. Apparently this woman is neither the grandmother of the literalist boy nor the wife of the eagle. She is just an old woman.

22. This is probably just an English paraphrase of the song. Since the Papago text is not given, it is not safe to ponder the English words and meanings.

PART 8: SIUUHU'S DEATH AND RESURRECTION

1. The loss of the paradisiacal relation with Corn-man, etc., is also Edenic, but no great human sin is involved. Those are stories of humanity's lost innocence when no one quite knew what was happening. Smith-Allison's Siuuhu chimes into them after the fact with his sexual morality, but this seems different from God's pre- and postexpulsion relation to Adam and Eve. Such a relation is now at stake between Siuuhu and the Hohokam.

2. *Wuaga* in Pima-Papago. These are described enthographically in Underhill (1946:253–260); and autobiographically in Underhill (1938). Along with wine feasts and celebrations for war victories, the puberty ceremonies were the great festive and convivial occasions of nineteenth-century Pima-Papago life.

3. "On this view [Niebuhr's], the evil we find in history is not ... an accidental or transient thing; it is located in the permanent

human condition of 'original sin,' symbolized by the 'Fall.' In simplest terms, what this doctrine asserts is 'the obvious fact that all men are persistently inclined to regard themselves more highly and are more assiduously concerned with their own interests than any objective view of their importance would warrant.' . . . Sin is the tendency to rebel against God" (Dray 1964: 100, quoting R. Niebuhr, *The Irony of American History*, 1952).

4. See story 5. A baby was born from a girl who ate a worm from the corn-man's hair. Siuuhu caused the mother to drop the baby, which killed it.

5. Here begins the prose telling of what is also told in war oratory. Bahr (1975) compares three versions of the oration that goes with this episode, one from Thin Leather, one from another Pima named Thomas Vanyiko, and one from the Papago Juan Gregorio.

6. The version published by Russell (on 226), from Thin Leather, states that these underworld people had not been created there, as Smith says here, but were created by Earth Doctor on the earth's surface prior to the great flood. Earth Doctor saved them from drowning by enabling them to pass through a hole in the earth into the underworld. He made the hole for them with his powerful magic cane. Although I have heard Papagos say the same thing, the summary fo Papago mythology published by Underhill (1946: 11) leaves this point moot. While it explains the present people as emergents from the underworld, it neither claims nor denies that this people had any prior upperworldly experience.

Smith implies the same thing in his story 1, where he says that the Primas "came" from a man created on the earth's surface by Earth Doctor and Siuuhu. It is fair to say that Smith is ambiguous on this issue, unlike Thin Leather (in Russell); and, of course, Smith's mythology lacks the episode, present in Russell (211), in which Earth Doctor made a hole in the earth for the ancestral Pima-Papago to pass down through.

7. Note how this makes Ee-ee-toy/Siuuhu a sun god. His rays wither things.

8. All the texts in Saxton and Saxton are given both in Pima-Papago and English. Thus, one can check on the original wording. The word translated as "chief" is *ge'ejig*, 'one-made-big'. This is a standard word for chief. Significantly, the word *siwañ* was not used. In this text, *siwañ* serves as the personal name of the man who killed I'itoi. We know that there are other texts in which the word is used as a status term ("chief") rather than as an individual's name; and we can imagine texts about the Hohokam era in which some chiefs are called *siwan* and others are called *ge'ejig*, the *sisiwañ* being the great-house heads, the *ge'ejig* being lesser chiefs or, as in this text, chiefs of a region outside great-house control.

9. This "below" seems to mean the underworld, as if the above-ground south chief controls the communication to the underworld. The passage translated as "people below" is *t-weco hemajkam*, 'us-below people', or more freely, 'people below us'.

PART 9: THE CONQUEST UNTIL BUZZARD

1. More texts on the conquest are greatly desired. I may say that I have heard narrators from the Santa Rosa area of the Papagos name all of the places mentioned by Thin Leather, so a long Gila and Salt River valley conquest is a Papago as well as a Pima idea. But I have heard narrators from Gunsight and Charco 27 villages, in the west of Papago country, say that there was only one Siwañ, who lived at Casa Grande National Monument. These narrators speak of a battle against Buzzard near today's Gila Bend, Ariz. Gila Bend is 100 miles to the west-southwest of Snaketown and is beyond the scope of the Smith-Allison and Thin Leather battle narratives.

2. Smith's story 19 has Buzzard captured and scalped at an unidentified location, but his story 28 identifies Pueblo Grande Ruin, in Phoenix, as Buzzard's "house." Buzzard is not mentioned in the latter episode, presumably because he has already been subdued. Thin Leather assigns another chief to the great-house at Pueblo Grande, and so does Smith in his narrative of this later battle. Smith must have thought of the latter chief as Buzzard's assistant. I am surprised to see Buzzard so closely associated with a town and chief. To me, the Thin Leather version of Buzzard as a sun god and a loner, a counterpart to Siuuhu, makes more sense, but I do not dispute Smith's locating Buzzard at a recognized great-house.

3. Lynne Teague and William Deaver have made such a registry and have studied the conquest myths. They concluded that "all of the settlements definitely located by the Pima are, in fact, Classic period platform mound sites archaeologically known to have been surmounted by houses probably inhabited by religious and political leaders" (1989: 158). Of course, this does not prove that the conquest occurred. The Pimas would have been unobservant had they not noticed the mounds, but noticing them does not prove that their ancestors conquered them. The problem remains that other mythologies play down the conquest, and still others locate and figure it differently from Smith-Allison and Thin Leather. See note 1 for remarks on some of these different mythologies.

4. As the Appendix and the texts show, the battle at this place is climactic, that is, the hardest fought and most protracted. (It has

a final phase in which the defeated Siwañ is hunted down as a fugitive.) There are battles later at other Hohokam great-houses, to the north and west of Casa Blanca. Why was this place made critical? Apart from the possibility that it actually was so in ca. 1400, which cannot be proven, it seems significant that Casa Blanca was approximately in the center of the territory held by the Pimas in the eighteenth and nineteenth centuries. If it was at the middle of their land, which was strongly pressed by Apaches, it makes sense that the Pimas would consider Casa Blanca the center of ancient Hohokam resistance, the Rome, so to speak, of the Hohokam.

5. As we will see, the Pima-Papago emerge first in Europe.

6. Nasia, a woman character, a goddess, whose name does not seem to be of Pima-Papago origin. She is mentioned in a Pima war speech or oration published by Russell (358) but is not a major character in any Pima myth known to me. In Thin Leather's myth on the theft of Chief Morning Green's wives, a woman called Natci is said to be Morning Green's daughter. This woman married Tcernatsing, the thief or winner of Morning Green's wife. That is the only concrete reference to a Nasia in any Pima-Papago myth that I know. See the myth at the end of part 6.

7. *Tua kuadam oks*, literally, "White eater old lady," the name of a female character for which there is a well-defined and widely told myth, generally called the Flute Lure story. A long and good version is in Densmore (1929: 55–77). Although told in Pima-Papago, the story is generally considered to be of Mojave or Maricopa origin, and its songs are sung in a language understood to be Maricopa. There is no version of the Flute Lure Story in Juan Smith's mythology, and this is Smith's only reference to its principal female character. Most people who know the story do not equate this character with the mysterious Nasia. The same woman character appears in Lloyd's version of the origin of irrigation (part 5).

8. If I understand Smith correctly here, he thinks that *to quaidum ox*, although said in Pima, is in fact the Pima translation of a Maricopa name (I agree with this); that Nassya is an ancient Pima word (I doubt this on the basis of how it sounds but cannot explain why); and that the two words or names designate the same mythic person (I consider them distinct as explained in the previous note).

9. This reference to an ocean crossing prior to the main narrative of conquest is unique to Smith-Allison.

10. Apparently in Europe.

11. This pair of songs corresponds to a larger song composition from Thin Leather, in Russell, called "On Emergence from the

Netherworld" (280). Where Smith gives a pair of two-line songs (total of four lines), Russell gives such a pair, followed by another pair of three-line songs (total of ten lines). Simply, the first lines of Smith's pair (The land is getting closer / the mountains are getting closer) correspond to the first lines of Russell's Thin Leather's second, three-line pair (Kusi tohai tuctcuwuta(r) tamai ticitciviaka nyuhunatci / Kusi tcokwe totovaku tamait a-ahuka nyuhunatci; literally, White land upon arriving singing / Black mountains upon reaching singing). In this instance (and, of course, there are additional lines in the Thin Leather songs), Smith opposes "land" and "mountain," while Thin Leather opposes those plus "white" and "black" and "arriving" and "reaching" (distinct words in Pima). Thin Leather outdoes Smith in these particular songs.

12. Thin Leather has the same episode but with the equivalent of Smith-Allison's Sivain living near the present Casa Blanca village. He is called Black Sinew Chief. He sends his son to inquire of Morning Green Chief at Casa Grande (now) Ruin. Actually, Smith-Allison end up with their Siwañ fighting his last battle at Casa Blanca. The present reference to a place near today's Glendale, 40 miles northwest of Casa Blanca, could be an error that Smith later corrected.

13. Apkigam and Apapgam, two "clan" or "sib" names, both included in a higher "moiety" grouping called the **Ban** Wo:mgul, 'Coyote [as] Helper'. Distinct from them are the Ma:mgam and Vavgam clans or sibs, which belong to the Ñu:wi We:mgal, 'Buzzard [as] Helper'. Also existing but lacking a "Helper" (either not classed at all or not so readily classed as to "moiety") is the Ogali clan or sib. Underhill (1939: 31–34) gives a good discussion of this system among the Papagos, but what she says also holds for the Pimas.

14. Who were not the whole of what became today's system or inventory of clans and moieties. Specifically, the "Buzzard" portion is lacking; and as Hayden believes (1970) and Juan Smith says (story 18), that portion was incorporated by conquest. To them, the Buzzards descend from the conquered Hohokam, in part at least. Actually, as stated in n. 112, Hayden is more firm on this point than Smith.

15. And therefore the content of Sivian's song was dreamed by a man near the ocean.

16. An attribution of wet power to the Hohokam but not to a person called Siwañ, 'Chief'. Conceivably, this woman might have that status, but the text does not say so. Nor would Smith-Allison say so, since they consider that there is only one Siwañ.

17. This statement can be interpreted two ways: either that the advancing emergents made their homes where the destroyed

Jackrabbit Eaters had lived or that the Jackrabbit Eaters, fleeing into Mexico, made homes on land that they gained there by conquest: the ones who fled became conquerers.

18. Probably Ko:lo'ogam, 'Whippoorwill' (e.g., Saxton, Saxton, and Enos 1983: 33), a bird very like the local nighthawk (Peterson 1961: 151, 165).

Note that here the emergents, people quite like today's Indians, are making an animal (bird) species, an act that one would not have thought possible, given Smith-Allison's accounts of earlier struggles between humans and gods over the power of creation.

Note also that Hayden's spelling of this probable whippoorwill word is not so different from the word spelled as "Cadigum" in story 4. Smith-Allison thought that the word meant a bird, but on the strength of a similar word in Lloyd's Thin Leather, I consider it to be a plant name. Since I imagine that Hayden would have heard the "l" if it had been part of the first name, I consider these to be two different words, so I will stay with the idea that "cadigum" is a plant name.

19. This is a medicine man in the process of divining or "seeing." As mentioned in note j, part 1, I take this to be the essential activity of medicine men/*mamakai*. Here the object of the divination is an enemy, Buzzard. Papago medicine men did the same sort of seeing in their warfare against Apaches. Underhill (1946, 1979) discusses it.

20. Here is another essential medicine man/*mama:kai* activity, the use of animals or spirit helpers to learn about and to affect (e.g., disable) enemies, game animals, etc. Owls are often used for this purpose. They are understood to be spirits of the dead. People are said to turn into owls after dying.

21. Probably *ṣel ñe'i*, 'straight song', a term meant to designate the kind of dance step or choreography that goes along with the singing. Thus, there are "circle" and "straight" dances. In the first, people join hands and move counterclockwise in a large circle, and in the second, they form straight lines and advance and retreat, often facing people in an opposing straight line.

The most important kind of straight dancing, the one relevant here, is for girls' adolescence or puberty ceremonies, called *wuaga*. (The songs used for these could equally be called "straight songs" or "wuaga songs"). These ceremonies, that were celebrated over many days and nights, and other but not all ceremonies as well were occasions for lovemaking.

Many versions of the mythology, including Thin Leather's, attribute these songs to Siuuhu, and these mythologies also state that Siuuhu was killed because he pestered or stole the girls at the dances. Smith gives a different reason for Siuuhu's murder, and in the present story he attaches the ceremonies to Buzzard rather than Siuuhu.

22. This could be a reference to Snaketown, the site of the excavations. The text (from a Papago, via Dolores) gives Ko'oi Ki:, 'Rattlesnake House', as the name of the place, while the more usual Pima name for Snaketown is S-ko:ko'owik, Many Rattlesnakes'.

23. Mount Lemon, near Tucson, is generally called Frog Mountain, but the usual reason given by Pima-Papago is that the Maricopas and Yumas have a story in which a girl frog ("Green Woman," see n. 6, part 4) eats her father's feces. The father dies from this, and the girl flees eastward, eventually reaching and staying thereafter at Frog Mountain. If that mountain is meant in this story, the implication is that the place of emergence is somewhere rather far to the south of Tucson, e.g., in Mexico. But this text seems most fragmentary, and it is likely that Densmore either received or rendered it garbled.

24. Note that both of these skin cuttings echo what Smith-Allison's and Thin Leather's warriors do to Buzzard. Hendricks has that episode as well, in the next textual supplement.

PART 10: THE CONQUEST UNTIL SIWAÑ WA'AKI

1. 'Bad Willow-place' [I think]. "Willow-place" is the name of a Papago village north of Santa Rosa. As I understand it, this story belongs particularly to that people, and they take their place-name from a willowy place where they formerly lived, some say around the location of the present-day town of Queen Creek, Ariz., between the Gila and Salt rivers, 20 or 30 miles northeast of Snaketown (Snaketown is located where that creek joins the Gila River).

2. "Mescal" probably means the agave cactus (*Agave americana*), which is sometimes called mescal cactus.

3. This is the exact wording of the manuscript. I cannot envision the scene clearly.

4. This "mind" could be a mistyping of "wind." There are many songs that say "green wind," but this would be the first known to me that says "green mind." Note that the pair of songs seem to grant solar ("shining") and wet ("green" and presumably cloud-having) powers to the Hohokam.

5. Probably the former.

6. Probably the former.

7. Like the mention of seawater as discussed in connection with story 8, this mention of a whale connects to an important

Papago myth, namely, an account of Siuuhu's (there called I'itoi, or Montezuma) killing a menacing whale or sea monster (*ñe:big* in Pima-Papago). Interestingly, both the seawater/children's shrine myth (connected to story 8) and the Papago whale-killing myth are closely associated with wi:gita ceremonies, which were large, famous, and highly sacred affairs. Wi:gitas were performed (so far as is known, from the nineteenth century to the present) at just two locations, both in Papago country, one near Santa Rosa, Ariz., and the other at Quitovac, Sonora, Mexico. The Arizona ceremony venerated the children's shrine myth, and the Sonora one venerated the myth of the killing of the whale; which is to say that those myths justified and were the charters of those two wi:gitas.

Pimas knew about the ceremonies, including the ceremonies' origin myths, but Pimas did not have a wi:gita of their own. Had they had one, it seems that they would also have needed a localized origin of myth for it, equivalent to the children's shrine or whale-killing myth. Now, in effect, Smith passes (as in card playing) on this matter. I assume that he knew the established, localized Papago wi:gita myths. He does not tell them outright but tells localized (set in Pima country) refractions of them. He does not use those refractions to justify a wi:gita in Pima country, which he could not do because there *was* no wi:gita in Pima country. Rather, he passes, mentioning the appropriate ancient things (seawater in a hole, a whale) but not advocating a Pima wi:gita. I may mention that these Smith-Allison whale songs do not refer to salt water, as do the wi:gita origin myths, but to wind and clouds, typical Hohokam/siwañ properties. See Hayden (1987), Galinier (1991), and Bahr (1991), on the mythology and performance of the wi:gita.

8. This was part of the method used by I'itoi to kill the whale in one of the wi:gita foundation myths (Saxton and Saxton 1973: 305–316).

9. This is almost the only reference to death among the invaders. Part 11, on the aftermath of the conquest, has the proper, individualized origin of death among them.

10. This corresponds closely with a song in Russell (281). Russell's narrator, Thin Leather, assigned the song to the point at which the Wooshkam (Russell did not record that word, but it is certainly correct, although better spelled as "wu:ṣkam") approached Sacaton. Here is how I would edit (correct, slightly modify) Russell's song language transcription and literal translation.

> *Pipinu havavaki   kutda hamo-olina.*
> *Mud   their-house inside their-[they]-stay.*
>
> *Kutda   maka hitcu,*
> *Inside [the house] become-medicine-men,*

Kotdena sinyu-upuiitoka,
Inside   very-frighten me,

Kutda ahamo-olina,
Inside there-[I? they?]-stay,

Pipinu havavahaki kutda maka hitcu.
Mud   their-house inside become-medicine-men.

11. This pair roughly corresponds with a single song in Russell (281), designated "As they approached the village below Santan":

Amuko   vu-uhonyui-ita,
You-[imperative]-go-and truly see-it,

Amuko   vu-uhonyuita-a,
You-[imperative]-go-and truly see-it,

Hamonyui-i-i.
will-see-some.

Kuhiyu hukiva mu-ulihoku rso-onuka   puva-aki   nyui-i.
Just-the old   ocotillo   based   the-rainhouse see.

12. Archaeological ruin in Phoenix, Arix.

13. Archaeological ruin in Phoenix, Ariz.
    In a letter of June 1993 Hayden wrote,

> After the detailed descriptions of the arduous conquest of the Big Houses of the Gila Valley, this brief mention of the taking of the Guadalupe and Pueblo Grande (Hua-manui-ki) Big Houses is almost in passing. This is curious, for the Salt River Valley contained the largest and densest population in the Hohokam region. Its many Big Houses with their attendant villages oversaw a vast system of canals with their intakes, their distribution ditches, and their broad irrigated fields of the monocrop, corn, the apparent basis of Hohokam life there. Why was the conquest of this valley given so little attention?
>
> An answer to this is now known: in all likelihood, the valley of the Salt was deserted when Emergents entered, and they faced little or no opposition. A flood of a 2,000-year magnitude from the Verde and Salt rivers had inundated the valley in 1358–59, destroying the canals, the fields, and ditches, and, in short, the food supplies of the people. This was followed by a very severe 20-year drought, and three more consecutive years of flood completed the destruction of the once prosperous valley. Recent excavations of some 500 or more burials of the time revealed very high infant and young mortality, and skeletal pathologies associated with starvation and malnutrition, osteoporosis even in the very young, arthritis,

hypoplasia, etc. Accompanying this was evidence of a rapid decrease of corn pollen in the village soils and a marked increase in pollens of wild native food plants, marking a surely desperate and futile attempt to replace corn with gathering. Deliberate abandonment of the valley ensued, for the undamaged pithouse floors of the terminal occupation had been swept clean of artifacts. By 1400 or at the latest 1425, the Salt River Valley was empty. Several lines of evidence indicate that some of the people moved north to join the Hopi and perhaps the Zuni communities; certain clans of both claim descent from the immigrants. The Emergents, then, swept through a deserted Salt River region, meeting perhaps stragglers and last-ditch folk. (Teague and Deaver 1989: 145–167, and C. Breternitz, personal communication)

15. He probably means the two sibs of the Coyote moiety. See note 13, part 9, and note 15, above.

PART 11: AFTER THE CONQUEST

1. There are two mentions of death among the invaders during the conquest. These are in stories 24 and 25. The first is a single sentence, not an individualized death story such as this one. The second is longer but still not individualized. It relates to the battle for Siwañ Wa'aki, near Casa Blanca, the invaders' biggest fight.

2. Those are the manucsript's exact, ambiguous words.

3. Yellowstone Park?

4. See story 14 and notes 6 and 7, part 9. Here it seems that Nassya and White Eater are taken to be the same thing, or rather, White Eater is a variety of Nassya.

5. The place of emergence, according to Hendricks. There is an Ashes Hill near the village of Santa Rosa. It is the "trash mound" of a Hohokam site, where the Hohokam living nearby dumped their ashes and trash. I have not heard of this hill as a point of emergence. Perhaps Hendricks had a different ashes hill in mind.

REFERENCES

Bahr, D.

1971   Who Were the Hohokam? The Evidence from Pima-Papago Myth. *Ethnohistory* 18(3): 145–166.

1975   *Pima-Papago Ritual Oratory: A Study of Three Texts.* San Francisco: Indian Historian Press.

1988*a*   Pima-Papago Christianity. *Journal of the Southwest* 30(2): 238–240.

1988*b*   La Modernisation du Chamanisme pima-papago. *Recherches Amerindiennes au Quebec* 18(2–3): 69–81.

1991   Papago Ocean Songs and Wi:gita. *Journal of the Southwest* 33(4): 539–556.

Bahr, D., J. Gregorio, D. Lopez, and A. Alvarez

1974   *Piman Shamanism and Staying Sickness.* Tucson: University of Arizona Press.

Bahr, D., and J. Haefer

1978   Song in Piman Curing. *Ethnomusicology* 22(1): 89–122.

Bierhorst, J.

1985   *The Mythology of North America.* New York: William Morrow.

1988   *The Mythology of South America.* New York: William Morrow.

1990   *The Mythology of Mexico and Central America.* New York: William Morrow.

1992   *History and Mythology of the Aztecs: The Codex Chimalpopoca.* Tucson: University of Arizona Press.

Boas, F.

1916   Tsimshian Mythology. *Bureau of American Ethnology Annual Report 31:* 29–1037. Washington, D.C.

Brumble, H. D.

1990   *American Indian Autobiography*. Berkeley, Los Angeles, and Oxford: University of California Press.

Densmore, F.

1929   Papago Music. *Bureau of American Ethnology Bulletin 90*. Washington, D.C.: Smithsonian Institution.

Di Peso, C.

1979   Prehistory: O'otam. In A. Ortiz, ed., *Handbook of North American Indians* 9: 91–99. Washington, D.C.: Smithsonian Institution.

1979   Prehistory: Southern Periphery. In A. Ortiz, ed., *Handbook of North American Indians* 9: 152–161. Washington, D.C.: Smithsonian Institution.

Dray, W.

1964   *Philosophy of History*. Englewood Cliffs, N.J.: Prentice-Hall.

Evers, L., and F. Molina

1987   *Yaqui Deer Songs*. Tucson: University of Arizona Press.

Ezell, P.

1983   History of the Pima. In A. Ortiz, ed., *Handbook of North American Indians* 9: 149–160. Washington, D.C.: Smithsonian Institution.

Fewkes, J.

1912   Casa Grande, Arizona. *28th Annual Report of the Bureau of American Ethnology*. Pp. 25–179. Washington, D.C.

Galinier, J.

1991   From Montezuma to San Francisco: The Wi:gita Ritual in Papago (Tohono O'odham) Religion. *Journal of the Southwest* 33(4): 486–538.

Gladwin, H., E. Haury, N. Sayles, and N. Gladwin

1937   Excavations at Snaketown. I: Material Culture. *Gila Pueblo, Medallion Paper 25*. Globe, Ariz. Reprinted by Arizona State Museum, Tucson, 1965.

Gossen, G.

1974   *Chamulas in the World of the Sun: Time and Space in a Mayan Oral Tradition*. Cambridge: Harvard University Press.

Gummerman, G., and E. Haury

1979 Prehistory: Hohokam. In A. Ortiz, ed., *Handbook of North American Indians* 9: 75–90. Washington, D.C.: Smithsonian Institution.

Haury, E.

1945 The Excavation of Los Muertos and Neighboring Ruins in the Salt River Valley, Southern Arizona. *Papers of the Peabody Museum of American Archaeology and Ethnology, Harvard University* 24(1). Cambridge, Mass.

1976 *The Hohokam, Desert Farmers and Craftsmen: Excavations at Snaketown, 1964–1965.* Tucson: University of Arizona Press.

Hayden, J.

1970 Of Hohokam Origins and Other Matters. *American Antiquity* 35(1): 87–93.

1987 The Vikita Ceremony of the Papago. *Journal of the Southwest* 29(3): 173–324.

Herzog, G.

1936 A Comparison of Pueblo and Pima Musical Styles. *Journal of American Folklore* 49: 284–417.

Hewett, J.

1928 Iroquoian Cosmology, pt. 2. *Bureau of American Ethnology Annual Report* 43: 449–819. Washington, D.C.

Jackson, K.

1985 Latter-Day Saints: A Dynamic Scriptural Process. In F. Denny and R. Taylor, eds., *The Holy Book in Comparative Perspective.* Columbia: University of South Carolina Press, 63–83.

Jaeger, E.

1941 *Desert Wildflowers.* Stanford: Stanford University Press.

Kroeber, A.

1925 Handbook of the Indians of California. *Bureau of American Ethnology Bulletin 78.* Washington, D.C.

Kubler, G.

1984 *The Art and Architecture of Ancient America.* New York: Penguin.

Lambert, N.

    1981   *Literature of Belief*. Provo, Utah: Religious Studies Center, Brigham Young University.

Laughlin, R.

    1977   Of Cabbages and Kings: Tales From Zinacantan. *Smithsonian Contributions to Anthropology 25*. Washington, D.C.

Lloyd, J.

    1911   *Aw-aw-tam Indian Nights: Being Myths and Legends of the Pimas of Arizona*. Westfield, N.J.: The Lloyd Group.

Marty, M.

    1970   *Righteous Empire*. New York: Dial.

Mathiot, M.

    N.d.   A Dictionary of Papago Usage. *Language Science Monographs* 9(1,2). Bloomington: Indiana University.

Mattina, A., and M. DeSautel

    1985   *The Golden Woman: The Colville Narrative of Peter Seymour*. Tucson: University of Arizona Press.

Momaday, N. S.

    1969   *The Way to Rainy Mountain*. New York: Ballantine.

    1976   *The Names*. New York: Harper and Row.

Nibley, H.

    1967   *Since Cumorah*. Salt Lake City: Deseret Books.

Parker, K.

    1972   *An Illustrated Guide to Arizona Weeds*. Tucson: University of Arizona Press.

Peterson, R.

    1961   *A Field Guide to Western Birds*. Boston: Houghton Mifflin.

Russell, F.

    1908   The Pima Indians. *26th Annual Report of the Bureau of American Ethnology*. Pp. 3–389. Washington, D.C. Reprinted by University of Arizona Press, Tucson, 1975.

Saxton, D., and L. Saxton

1969   *Dictionary: Papago and Pima to English, English to Papago and Pima.* Tucson: University of Arizona Press.

1973   *O'odham ho'ok a'agitha: Legends and Lore of the Papago and Pima Indians.* Tucson: University of Arizona Press.

Saxton, D., L. Saxton, and S. Enos

1983   *Dictionary: Papago/Pima–English, English–Papago/Pima.* Tucson: University of Arizona Press.

Scarborough, V., and D. Wilcox, eds.

1991   *The Mesoamerican Ballgame.* Tucson: University of Arizona Press.

Shaw, A.

1968   *Pima Indian Legends.* Tucson: University of Arizona Press.

Spier, L.

1933   *Yuman Tribes of the Gila River.* Chicago: University of Chicago Press.

Stewart, O.

1987   *The Peyote Religion, A History.* Norman: University of Oklahoma Press.

Teague, L., and W. Deaver

1989   The 1982–1984 Excavations at Las Colinas: Syntheses and Conclusions. *Cultural Resource Management Division, Arizona State Museum, University of Arizona, Archaeological Series 162*, vol. 6. Tucson: University of Arizona.

Tedlock, D.

1972   *Finding the Center: Narrative Poetry of the Zuni Indians.* New York: Dial.

1985   *The Popul Vuh: The Mayan Book of the Dawn of Life.* New York: Simon and Schuster.

Thompson, S.

1946   *The Folktale.* New York: Holt, Rinehart, and Winston.

Tooker, E.

1978a   The League of the Iroquois: Its History, Politics, and Ritual. In B. Trigger, ed., *Handbook of North American*

Indians 15. Washington, D.C.: Smithsonian Institution.

1978*b*   Iroquois Since 1820. In B. Trigger, ed., *Handbook of North American Indians* 15. Washington, D.C.: Smithsonian Institution.

Underhill, R.

1936   The Autobiography of a Papago Woman. *Memoirs of the American Anthropological Association*, no. 46. Menasha, Wisc.

1939   Social Organization of the Papago Indians. *Columbia University Contributions to Anthropology*, vol. 30. New York: Columbia University Press.

1946   *Papago Indian Religion.* New York: Columbia University Press.

Underhill, R., D. Bahr, B. Lopez, J. Pancho, and D. Lopez

1979   Rainhouse and Ocean: Speeches for the Papago Year (*American Tribal Religions 4*). Flagstaff: Museum of Northern Arizona.

Vansina, J.

1985   *Oral Tradition as History.* Madison: University of Wisconsin Press.

Wallace, A.

1978   Origins of the Longhouse Religion. In B. Trigger, ed., *Handbook of North American Indians*, vol. 15. Washington, D.C.: Smithsonian Institution.

Wilcox, D.

1991   The Mesoamerican Ballgame in the American Southwest. In V. Scarborough and D. Wilcox, eds., *The Mesoamerican Ballgame*, Tucson: University of Arizona Press, 101–125.

Wilson, E.

1960   *Apologies to the Iroquois, with A Study of the Mohawks in High Steel, by Joseph Mitchell.* New York: Farrar, Strauss, and Cudahy.

Wright, H.

1929   *Long Ago Told (Huk-kew Ah-kah).* New York: Appleton.

Zepeda, O.

1983   *A Grammar of Papago.* Tucson: University of Arizona Press.

Designer: Seventeenth Street Studios
Compositor: Wilsted & Taylor
Text: Stempel Schneidler
Display: Copperplate
Printer: Haddon Craftsmen, Inc.
Binder: Haddon Craftsmen, Inc.